THE EMPEROR *and* SHAH OF SHAHS

Ryszard Kapuściński was born in eastern Poland in 1932. After studying Polish history at Warsaw University, he began work as a domestic reporter. Later, as a foreign correspondent for the Polish Press Agency (until 1981), he gained critical and popular praise for his coverage of civil wars, revolutions and social conditions in the Third World. In Latin America, Africa and the Middle East, he ventured into the 'bush' – the word that has become his trademark – to search out hidden stories. In addition to his books on the Third World, Kapuściński has written about the Polish provinces and the Asian and Caucasian republics of the Soviet Union. He lives in Warsaw.

RYSZARD KAPUŚCIŃSKI

THE EMPEROR

AND

SHAH OF SHAHS

TRANSLATED FROM THE POLISH BY
WILLIAM R. BRAND
AND
KATARZYNA MROCZKOWSKA-BRAND

PICADOR

The Emperor first published in Great Britain 1983 by Quartet Books Ltd
First published in Picador 1984 by Pan Books Limited

Shah of Shahs first published in Great Britain 1985 by Quartet Books Ltd
First published in Picador 1986 by Pan Books Limited

This combined edition published 1994 by Picador
a division of Pan Macmillan Publishers Limited
Cavaye Place London SW10 9PG
and Basingstoke

Associated companies throughout the world

ISBN 0 330 33185 X

1 3 5 7 9 8 6 4 2

A CIP catalogue record for this book is available from
the British Library

Typeset by Intype, London
Printed by Cox & Wyman Ltd, Reading, Berkshire

THE EMPEROR

CONTENTS

THE THRONE

Forget about me—
The candle's been snuffed.
(*Gypsy tango*)

Negus, our Negus,
Only you can save us
Our lines in the south
Have been caught in a rout
And to the north of Makale
All our tactics are folly.
Negus, our Negus,
Give me shot, give me powder.
(*prewar Warsaw song*)

Observing the behavior of individual fowl in a henhouse, we note that birds lower in rank are pecked by, and give way to, birds of higher rank. In an ideal case, there exists a linear order of rank with a top hen who pecks all the others. Those in the middle ranks peck those below them but respect all the hens above them. At the bottom there is a drudge who has to take it from everyone.
(Adolf Remane, *Vertebrates and Their Ways*)

Man will get used to anything, if only he reaches an appropriate degree of submission.
(C. G. Jung)

The DOLPHIN, desiring to sleep, floats atop the water; having fallen asleep, he sinks slowly to the floor of the sea; being awakened by striking the bottom, he rises again to the surface. Having thus risen, he falls asleep again, descends once more to the bottom, and revives himself anew in the same fashion. He thus enjoys his rest in motion.
(Benedykt Chmielowski, *The New Athens, or, An Academy Replete with All the Sciences*)

In the evenings I listened to those who had known the Emperor's court. Once they had been people of the Palace or had enjoyed the right of admission there. Not many of them remained. Some had perished, shot by the firing squad. Some had escaped the country; others had been locked in the dungeons beneath the Palace, cast down from the chambers to the cellars. Some were hiding in the mountains or living disguised as monks in cloisters. Everyone was trying to survive in his own way, according to the possibilities open to him. Only a handful remained in Addis Ababa, where, apparently, it was easiest to outwit the authorities' vigilance.

I visited them after dark. I had to change cars and disguises. The Ethiopians are deeply distrustful and found it hard to believe in the sincerity of my intentions: I wanted to recapture the world that had been wiped away by the machine-guns of the Fourth Division. Those machine-guns are mounted next to the drivers' seats on American-made jeeps. They are manned by gunners whose profession is killing. In the back sits a soldier taking orders by radio. The jeeps are open, so the drivers, gunners, and radiomen wear dark motorcycle goggles under the brims of their helmets to protect themselves from the dust. You can't see their eyes, and their bristled ebony faces have no expression. These three-man crews know death so well that the drivers race their vehicles around suicidally, making abrupt high-speed turns, driving against the flow on one-way streets. Everything scatters when they come careening along. It's best to stay out of their range. Shouts and nervous screams blare amid crackles and squeals from the radio on the knees of the one in the back. You never can tell if one of the hoarse screams is an order to open fire. It's better to disappear. Better to duck into a side street and wait it out.

I penetrated the muddy alleys, making my way into houses that from the outside looked empty and abandoned. I was afraid. The houses were watched, and I was afraid of getting caught along with their inhabitants. Such a thing was possible, since they often made a sweep through a neighborhood or even a whole quarter of the town in search of weapons, subversive leaflets, or people from the old regime. All the houses were watching each other, spying on each other, sniffing each other out. This is civil war; this is what it's like. I sit down by the window, and immediately they say, "Somewhere else, sir, please. You're visible from the street. It would be easy to pick you off." A car passes, then stops. The sound of gunfire. Who was it? These? Those? And who, today, are "these", and who are the "those" who are against "these" just because they are "these"? The car drives off, accompanied by the barking of dogs. They bark all night. Addis Ababa is a dog city, full of pedigreed dogs running wild, vermin-eaten, with malaria and tangled hair.

They caution me again, needlessly: no addresses, no names, don't say that he's tall, that he's short, that he's skinny, that his forehead this or his hands that. Or that his eyes, or that his legs, or that his knees . . . There's nobody left to get down on your knees for.

F.:

It was a small dog, a Japanese breed. His name was Lulu. He was allowed to sleep in the Emperor's great bed. During various ceremonies, he would run away from the Emperor's lap and pee on dignitaries' shoes. The august gentlemen were not allowed to flinch or make the slightest gesture when they felt their feet getting wet. I had to walk among the dignitaries and wipe the urine from their shoes with a satin cloth. This was my job for ten years.

L. C.:

The Emperor slept in a roomy bed made of light walnut. He was so slight and frail that you couldn't see him — he was lost among the sheets. In old age, he became even smaller. He weighed fifty kilograms. He ate less and less, and he never drank alcohol. His knees stiffened up, and when he was alone he dragged his feet, swaying from side to side as if on stilts. But when he knew that someone was watching him, he forced a certain elasticity into his muscles, with great effort, so that he moved with dignity and his imperial silhouette remained ramrod-straight. Each step was a struggle between shuffling and dignity, between leaning and the vertical line. His Majesty never forgot about this infirmity of his old age, which he did not want to reveal lest it weaken the prestige and solemnity of the King of Kings. But we servants of the royal bedchamber, who saw his unguarded moments, knew how much the effort cost him.

He had the habit of sleeping little and rising early, when it was still dark outside. He treated sleep as a dire necessity that purposelessly robbed him of time he would rather have spent ruling or at Imperial functions. Sleep was a private, intimate interval in a life meant to be passed amid decorations and lights. That's why he woke up seeming discontented with having slept, impatient with the very fact of sleep. Only the subsequent activities of the day restored his inner balance. Let me add, however, that the Emperor never showed the slightest sign of irritation, nervousness, anger, rage, or frustration. It seemed that he never knew such states, that his nerves were cold and dead like steel, or that he had no nerves at all. It was an inborn characteristic that His Highness knew how to develop and perfect, following the principle that in politics nervousness signifies a weakness that encourages opponents and emboldens subordinates to make secret jokes. His Majesty knew that a joke is a dangerous form of opposition, and he kept his psyche in perfect order. He got up at four or five and, when going abroad on a visit, at three in the morning. Later, when things grew worse in our country, he traveled more often. Then, the only business of the Palace was to prepare the Emperor for new journeys. Upon waking, he rang the buzzer on his nightstand — the vigilant servants were waiting for the sound. The lights were turned on in the Palace. It was a signal to the Empire that His Supreme Majesty had begun a new day.

Y. M.:

The Emperor began his day by listening to informers' reports. The night breeds dangerous conspiracies, and Haile Selassie knew that what happens at night is more important than what happens during the day. During the day he kept his eye on everyone; at night that was impossible. For that reason, he attached great importance to the morning reports. And here I would like to make one thing clear: His Venerable Majesty was no reader. For him, neither the written nor the printed word existed; everything had to be relayed by word of mouth. His Majesty had had no schooling. His sole teacher — and that only during his childhood — was a French Jesuit, Monsignor Jerome, later Bishop of Harar and a friend of the poet Arthur Rimbaud. This cleric had no chance to inculcate the habit of reading in the Emperor, a task made all the more difficult, by the way, because Haile Selassie occupied responsible administrative positions from his boyhood and had no time for regular reading.

But I think there was more to it than a lack of time and habit. The custom of relating things by word of mouth had this advantage: if need be, the Emperor could say that a given dignitary had told him something quite different from what had really been said, and the latter could not defend himself, having no written proof. Thus the Emperor heard from his subordinates not what they told him, but what he thought should be said. His Venerable Highness had his ideas, and he would adjust to them all the signals that came from his surroundings. It was the same with writing, for our monarch not only never used his ability to read, but he also never wrote anything and never signed anything in his own hand. Though he ruled for half a century, not even those closest to him knew what his signature looked like.

During the Emperor's hours of official functions, the Minister of the Pen always stood at hand and took down all the Emperor's orders and instructions. Let me say that during working audiences His Majesty spoke very softly, barely moving his lips. The Minister of the Pen, standing half a step from the throne, had to bend his ear close to the Imperial lips in order to hear and write down the Imperial decisions. Furthermore, the Emperor's words were usually unclear and ambiguous, especially when he did not want to take a definite stand on a matter that required his opinion. One had to admire the Emperor's dexterity. When asked by a dignitary for the Imperial decision, he would not answer straight out, but would rather speak in a voice so quiet that it reached only the Minister of the Pen, who moved his ear as close as a microphone. The minister transcribed his ruler's scant and foggy mutterings. All the rest was interpretation, and that was a matter for the minister, who passed down the decision in writing.

The Minister of the Pen was the Emperor's closest confidant and enjoyed enormous power. From the secret cabala of the monarch's words he could construct any decision that he wished. If a move by the Emperor dazzled everyone with its accuracy and wisdom, it was one more proof that God's Chosen One was infallible. On the other hand, if from some corner the breeze carried rumors of discontent to the monarch's ear, he could blame it all on the minister's stupidity. And so the minister was the most hated personality in the court. Public opinion, convinced of His Venerable Highness's wisdom and goodness, blamed the minister for any thoughtless or malicious decisions, of which there were many. True, the servants whispered about why Haile Selassie didn't replace the minister, but in the Palace questions were always asked from top to bottom, and never vice versa. When the first question was asked in a direction opposite to the customary one, it was a signal that the revolution had begun.

But I'm getting ahead of myself and must go back to the moment when the Emperor appears on the Palace steps in the morning and sets out for his early walk. He enters the park. This is when Solomon Kedir, the head of the Palace spies, approaches and gives his report. The Emperor walks along the avenue and Kedir stays a step behind him, talking all the while. Who met whom, where, and what they talked about. Against whom they are forming alliances. Whether or not one could call it a conspiracy. Kedir also reports on the work of the military cryptography department. This department, part of Kedir's office, decodes the communications that pass among the divisions — it's good to be sure that no subversive thoughts are hatching there. His Distinguished Highness asks no questions, makes no comments. He walks and listens. Sometimes he stops before the lions' cage to throw them a leg of veal that a servant has handed to him. He watches the lions' rapacity and smiles. Then he approaches the leopards, which are chained, and gives them ribs of beef. His Majesty has to be careful as he approaches the unpredictable beasts of prey. Finally he moves on, with Kedir behind continuing his report. At a certain moment His Highness bows his head, which is a signal for Kedir to move away. He bows and disappears down the avenue, never turning his back on the Emperor.

At this moment the waiting Minister of Industry and Commerce, Makonen Habte-Wald, emerges from behind a tree. He falls in, a step behind the Emperor, and delivers his report. Makonen Habte-Wald keeps his own network of informers, both to satisfy a consuming passion for intrigue and to ingratiate himself with His Venerable Highness. On the basis of his information, he now briefs the Emperor on what happened last night. Again, His Majesty walks on, listening without questions or comments, keeping his hands behind his back. He approaches a flock of flamingos, but the shy birds scatter when he comes near. The Emperor smiles at the sight of creatures that refuse to obey him. At last, still walking, he nods his head; Habte-Wald falls silent and retreats backward, disappearing down the avenue.

Next, as if springing up from the ground, rises the hunched silhouette of the devoted confidant Asha Walde-Mikael. This dignitary supervises the government political police. He competes with Solomon Kedir's Palace intelligence service and battles fiercely against private informer networks like the one that Makonen Habte-Wald has at his disposal.

The occupation to which these people devoted themselves was hard and dangerous. They lived in fear of not reporting something in time and falling into disgrace, or of a competitor's reporting it better so that the Emperor would think, "Why did Solomon give me a feast today and Makonen only bring me leftovers? Did he say nothing because he didn't know, or did he hold his tongue because he belongs to the conspiracy?" Hadn't His Distinguished Highness often experienced, at cost to himself, betrayal by his most trusted allies? That's why the Emperor punished silence. On the other hand, incoherent streams of words tired and irritated the Imperial ear, so nervous loquaciousness was also a poor solution. Even the way these people looked told of the threat under which they lived. Tired, looking as if they hadn't slept, they acted under feverish stress, pursuing their victims in the stale air of hatred and fear that surrounded them all. They had no shield but the Emperor, and the Emperor could undo them with one wave of his hand. No, His Benevolent Majesty did not make their lives easy.

As I've mentioned, Haile Selassie never commented on or questioned the reports he received, during his morning walks, about the state of conspiracy in the Empire. But he knew what he was doing, as I shall show you. His Highness wanted to receive the reports in a pure state, because if he asked questions or expressed opinions the informant would obligingly adjust his report to meet the Emperor's expectations. Then the whole system of informing would collapse into subjectivity and fall prey to anyone's willfulness. The monarch would not know what was going on in the country and the Palace.

Finishing his walk, the Emperor listens to what was reported last night by Asha's people. He feeds the dogs and the black panther, and then he admires the anteater that he recently received as a gift from the president of Uganda. He nods his head and Asha walks away, bent over, wondering whether he said more or less than what was reported by his most fervent enemies — Solomon, the enemy of Makonen and Asha; and Makonen, the enemy of Asha and Solomon.

Haile Selassie finishes his walk alone. It grows light in the park; the fog thins out, and reflected sunlight glimmers on the lawns. The Emperor ponders. Now is the time to lay out strategies and tactics, to solve the puzzles of personality, to plan his next move on the chessboard of power. He thinks deeply about what was contained in the informants' reports. Little of importance; they usually report on each other. His Majesty has made mental notes of everything. His mind is a computer that retains every detail; even the smallest datum will be remembered. There was no personnel office in the Palace, no dossiers full of personal information. All this the Emperor carried in his mind, all the most important files about the elite. I see him now as he walks, stops, walks again, lifts his head upward as though absorbed in prayer. O God, save me from those who, crawling on their knees, hide a knife that they would like to sink into my back. But how can God help? All the people surrounding the Emperor are just like that — on their knees, and with knives. It's never comfortable on the summits. An icy wind always blows, and everyone crouches, watchful lest his neighbor hurl him down the precipice.

T. K.-B.:

Dear friend, of course I remember. Wasn't it just yesterday? Yesterday, but a century ago. In this city, but on a planet that is now far away. How all these things get confused: times, places, the world broken in pieces, not to be glued back together again. Only the memory — that's the only remnant of life.

I spent a lot of time around the Emperor as a clerk in the Ministry of the Pen. We began work at eight, so that everything would be ready when the monarch arrived at nine. His Majesty lived in the New Palace, across from Africa Hall, and he performed his official duties in the Old Palace of the Emperor Menelik, built on a hill nearby. Our office was in the Old Palace, where most of the Imperial institutions were located, since Haile Selassie wanted to have everything within easy reach. He was brought there in one of the twenty-seven automobiles that made up his private fleet. He liked automobiles. He prized the Rolls-Royces for their dignified lines, but for a change he would also use the Mercedes-Benzes and the Lincoln Continentals. I'll remind you that our Emperor brought the first cars into Ethiopia, and he was always well-disposed toward the exponents of technical progress, whom unfortunately our traditional nation always disliked. Didn't our Emperor almost lose his power, and his life, when he brought the first airplane from Europe in the twenties? The simple airplane struck people as an invention of Satan, and in the courts of magnates there sprung up conspiracies against the Emperor as if he were a cabalist or a necromancer. His Revered Highness had to control ever more carefully his inclinations to act the pioneer until, in that stage of life when novelty holds little interest for an aged man, he almost gave them up.

And so at nine o'clock he would arrive at the Old Palace. Before the gate a crowd of subjects waited to try to hand petitions to the Emperor. This was theoretically the simplest way of seeking justice and charity in the Empire. Because our nation is illiterate, and justice is usually sought by the poor, people would go into debt for years to pay a clerk to write down their complaints and demands. There was also a problem of protocol, since custom required the humblest ones to kneel before the Emperor with their faces to the ground. How can anyone hand an envelope to a passing limousine from that posture? The problem was solved in the following manner. The vehicle would slow, the benevolent face of the monarch would appear behind the glass, and the security people from the next car would take some of the envelopes from the extended hands of the populace. Only some, for there was a whole thicket of these hands. If the mob crawled too close to the oncoming cars, the guards had to push back and shoo away the soliciting multitude, since security and the solemnity of majesty required that the procession be smooth and free of unexpected delays.

Now the vehicles drove up the ascending avenue and stopped in the Palace courtyard. Here, too, a crowd awaited the Emperor, but a different one from the rabble that had been furiously driven away by the select members of the Imperial Bodyguard. Those waiting in the courtyard to greet the Emperor were from the monarch's own circles. We all gathered early so as not to miss the Emperor's arrival, because that moment had a special significance for us. Everyone wanted very badly to be noticed by the Emperor. No, one didn't dream of special notice, with the Revered Emperor catching sight of you, coming up, and starting a conversation. No, nothing like that, I assure you. One wanted only the smallest, second-rate sort of attention, nothing that burdened the Emperor with any obligations. A passing notice, a fraction of a second, yet the sort of notice that later would make one tremble inside and overwhelm one with the triumphal thought "I have been noticed." What strength it gave afterward! What unlimited possibilities it created! Let's say that the Imperial gaze just grazes your face — just grazes! You could say that it was really nothing, but on the other hand, how could it really be nothing, when it did graze you? Immediately you feel the temperature of your face rise, and the blood rush to your head, and your heart beat harder. These are the best proofs that the eye of the Protector has touched you, but so what? These proofs are of no importance at the moment. More important is the process that might have taken place in His Majesty's memory. You see, it was known that His Majesty, not using his powers of reading and writing, had a phenomenally developed visual memory. On this gift of nature the owner of the face over which the Imperial gaze had passed could build his hopes. Because he could already count on some passing trace, even an indistinct trace, having imprinted itself in His Highness's memory.

Now, you had to maneuver in the crowd with such perseverance and determination, so squeeze yourself and worm through, so push, so jostle, so position your face, dispose and manipulate it in such a way, that the Emperor's glance, unwillingly and unknowingly, would notice, notice, notice. Then you waited for the moment to come when the Emperor would think, "Just a minute. I know that face, but I don't know the name." And let's say he would ask for the name. Only the name, but that's enough! Now the face and the name are joined, and a person comes into being, a ready candidate for nomination. Because the face alone — that's anonymous. The name alone — an abstraction. You have to materialize yourself, take on shape and form, gain distinctness.

Oh, that was the good fortune most longed for, but how difficult it was to realize! Because in the courtyard where the Emperor's retinue awaited him, there were tens, no, I say it without exaggeration, hundreds eager to push their faces forward. Face rubbed against face, the taller ones squelching down the shorter ones, the darker ones over-shadowing the lighter ones. Face despised face, the older ones moving in front of the younger ones, the weaker ones giving way to the stronger ones. Face hated face, the common ones clashing with the noble ones, the grasping ones against the weaklings. Face crushed face, but even the humiliated ones, the ones pushed away, the third-raters and the defeated ones, even those — from a certain distance imposed by the law of hierarchy, it's true — still moved toward the front, showing here and there from behind the first-rate, titled ones, if only as fragments: an ear, a piece of temple, a cheek or a jaw . . . just to be close to the Emperor's eye! If His Benevolent Majesty wanted to capture with his glance the whole scene that opened before him when he stepped from his car, he would perceive that not only was a hundred-faced magma, at once humble and frenetic, rolling toward him, but also that, aside from the central, highly titled group, to the right and to the left, in front of him and behind him, far and even farther away, in the doors and the windows and on the paths, whole multitudes of lackeys, kitchen servants, janitors, gardeners, and policemen were pushing their faces forward to be noticed.

And His Majesty takes it all in. Does it surprise or amaze him? I doubt it. His Majesty himself was once a part of the hundred-faced magma. Didn't he have to push his face forward in order to become the heir to the throne at the age of only twenty-four? And he had a hell of a lot of competition! A whole squadron of experienced notables was striving for the crown. But they were in a hurry, one cutting in front of the other, at each other's throats, trembling, impatient. Quickly, quickly, to the throne! His Peerless Majesty knew how to wait. And that is an all-important ability. Without that ability to wait, to realize humbly that the chance may come only after years of waiting, there is no politician. His Distinguished Majesty waited for ten years to become the heir to the throne, and then fourteen more years to become Emperor. In all, close to a quarter of a century of cautious but energetic striving for the crown. I say "cautious" because it was characteristic of His Majesty to be secretive, discreet, and silent. He knew the Palace. He knew that every wall had ears and that from behind every arras gazed eyes attentively scrutinizing him. So he had to be cunning and shrewd. First of all, one can't unmask oneself too early, showing the rapacity for power, because that galvanizes competitors, making them rise to combat. They will strike and destroy the one who has moved to the fore. No, one should walk in step for years, making sure not to spring ahead, waiting attentively for the right moment. In 1930 this game brought His Majesty the crown, which he kept for forty-four years.

When I showed a colleague what I was writing about Haile Selassie, or rather about the court and its fall as described by the people who had frequented the chambers, offices, and corridors of the Palace, he asked me whether I had gone alone to visit the ones in hiding. Alone? That would hardly have been possible. A white man, a foreigner — none of them would have let you get a foot in the door without powerful recommendations. And in any case, none of them would want to confide in you (in general, it's hard to get the Ethiopians to open up; they can be as silent as the Chinese). How would you know where to look for them, where they are, who they were, what they could tell you?

No, I was not alone. I had a guide.

Now that he is no longer alive, I can say his name: Teferra Gebrewold. I came to Addis Ababa in the middle of May 1963. In a couple of days the presidents of independent Africa were to meet there, and the Emperor was preparing the city for the meeting. Addis Ababa was then a large village of a few hundred thousand inhabitants, situated on hills, amid eucalyptus groves. Goats and cows grazed on the lawns along the main street, Churchill Road, and cars had to stop when nomads drove their herds of frightened camels across the street. It was raining, and in the side streets vehicles spun their wheels in the gluey brown mud, digging themselves in deeper until there were columns of nearly submerged, immobilized automobiles.

The Emperor realized that the capital of Africa must look more presentable, so he ordered the construction of several modern buildings and the cleaning up of the more important streets. Unfortunately, the construction dragged on endlessly, and when I saw the wooden scaffoldings scattered about the city with workers on them, I remembered the scene described by Evelyn Waugh (in They Were Still Dancing*) when he came to Addis Ababa to see the Emperor's coronation in 1930:*

> The whole town seemed still in a rudimentary stage of construction. At every corner were half-finished buildings;

some had been already abandoned; on others, gangs of ragged Guraghi were at work. One afternoon I watched a number of them, twenty or thirty in all, under the surveillance of an Armenian contractor, at work clearing away the heaps of rubble and stone which encumbered the courtyard before the main door of the palace. The stuff had to be packed into wooden boxes swung between two poles, and emptied on a pile fifty yards away. Two men carried each load, which must have weighed very little more than an ordinary hod of bricks. A foreman circulated among them, carrying a long cane. When he was engaged elsewhere the work stopped altogether. The men did not sit down, chat, or relax in any way; they simply stood stock-still where they were, motionless as cows in a field, sometimes arrested with one small stone in their hands. When the foreman turned his attention towards them they began to move again, very deliberately, like figures in a slow-motion film; when he beat them they did not look round or remonstrate, but quickened their movements just perceptibly; when the blows ceased they lapsed into their original pace until, the foreman's back being turned, they again stopped completely.

This time, great activity reigned on the main streets. Huge bulldozers rolled along the edges of the thoroughfares, destroying the first row of mud huts that had been abandoned the day before, when the police chased their occupants out of town. Next, brigades of masons built high walls to screen the remaining hovels from view. Other groups painted national designs on the wall. The city smelled of fresh concrete, paint, cooling asphalt, and the palm leaves with which the entry gates had been decorated.

The Emperor threw an imposing reception for the meeting of the presidents. Wine and caviar were flown in from Europe specially for the occasion. At a cost of twenty-five thousand dollars, Miriam Makeba was brought from Hollywood to serenade the leaders with

Zulu songs after the feast. All told, more than three thousand people, divided hierarchically into upper and lower categories, were invited. Each category received invitations of a different color and chose from a different menu.

The reception took place in the Emperor's Old Palace. The guests passed long ranks of soldiers from the Imperial Guard, armed with sabers and halberds. From atop towers, spotlit trumpeters played the Emperor's fanfare. In the galleries, theatrical troupes performed scenes from the lives of past Emperors. From the balconies, girls in folk costumes showered the guests with flowers. The sky exploded in plumes of fireworks.

When the guests had been seated at tables in the great hall, fanfares rang out and the Emperor walked in with President Nasser of Egypt at his right hand. They formed an extraordinary pair: Nasser a tall, stocky, imperious man, his head thrust forward with his wide jaws set into a smile, and next to him the diminutive silhouette — frail, one could almost say — of Haile Selassie, worn by the years, with his thin, expressive face, his glistening, penetrating eyes. Behind them the remaining leaders entered in pairs. The audience rose; everyone was applauding. Ovations sounded for unity and the Emperor. Then the feast began. There was one dark-skinned waiter for every four guests. Out of excitement and nervousness, things were falling from the waiters' hands. The table setting was silver, in the old Harar style. Several tons of priceless antique silver lay on those tables. Some people slipped pieces of silverware into their pockets. One sneaked a fork, the next one a spoon.

Mountains of meat, fruit, fish, and cheese rose on the tables. Many-layered cakes dripped with sweet, colored icing. Distinguished wines spread reflected colors and invigorating aromas. The music played on, and costumed clowns did somersaults to the delight of the carefree revelers. Time passed in conversation, laughter, consumption.

It was a splendid affair.

During these proceedings I needed to find a quiet place, but I didn't know where to look. I left the Great Chamber by a side door that led outside. It was a dark night, with a fine rain falling. A May rain, but a chilly one. A gentle slope led down from the door, and some distance below stood a poorly lit building without walls. A row of waiters stood in a line from the door to this building, passing dishes with leftovers from the banquet table. On those dishes a stream of bones, nibbled scraps, mashed vegetables, fish heads, and cut-away bits of meat flowed. I walked toward the building without walls, slipping on the mud and scattered bits of food.

I noticed that something on the other side was moving, shifting, murmuring, squishing, sighing, and smacking its lips. I turned the corner to have a closer look.

In the thick night, a crowd of barefoot beggars stood huddled together. The dishwashers working in the building threw leftovers to them. I watched the crowd devour the scraps, bones, and fish heads with laborious concentration. In the meticulous absorption of this eating there was an almost violent biological abandon — the satisfaction of hunger in anxiety and ecstasy.

From time to time the waiters would get held up, and the flow of dishes would stop. Then the crowd of beggars would relax as though someone had given them the order to stand at ease. People wiped their lips and straightened their muddy and food-stained rags. But soon the stream of dishes would start flowing again — because up there the great hogging, with smacking of lips and slurping, was going on, too — and the crowd would fall again to its blessed and eager labor of feeding.

I was getting soaked, so I returned to the Great Chamber, to the Imperial party. I looked at the silver and gold on the scarlet velvet, at President Kasavuba, at my neighbor, a certain Aye Mamlaye. I breathed in the scent of roses and incense, I listened to the suggestive Zulu song that Miriam Makeba was singing, I bowed to the Emperor (an absolute requirement of protocol), and I went home.

After the departure of the presidents (a hurried departure, since too long a stay abroad could lead to the loss of one's position), the Emperor invited us — the contingent of foreign correspondents assembled here on the occasion of the first conference of the leaders of African states — for breakfast. The news was brought to us at Africa Hall, where we spent days and nights in the hopeless and nerve-racking expectation of establishing contact with our capitals, by our local guardian, a section head from the Ministry of Information: none other than Teferra Gebrewold, a tall, handsome, usually silent and reserved Amhara. Now, however, he was excited. The striking thing was that every time he said the name of Haile Selassie, he bowed his head ceremoniously.

"This is wonderful news!" cried the Greco-Turko-Cypriot-Maltese Ivo Svarzini, who supposedly worked for the non-existent MIB Press Agency but really served as a spy for the Italian oil company ENI. "We'll be able to complain to the guy about how they've organized our communications here." I must add that the company of foreign correspondents at the farther corners of the globe consists of hardened, cynical men who have seen everything and lived through everything, and who are used to fighting a thousand obstacles that most people could never imagine, just to do their jobs. So nothing can excite them, and when they are exhausted and angry they are likely to gripe even to an emperor about the lack of assistance they've received from local authorities. Yet even such people stop and think about their actions from time to time. Such a moment occurred now, when we noticed that at Svarzini's words Teferra had become pale and nervous, drooped forward, and begun muttering something of which we could understand only the conclusion: if we made such a report, the Emperor would have his head cut off. He repeated it over and over again. Our group split. I agitated for letting it ride and not having a man's life on our consciences. The majority felt the same way, and finally we decided to avoid the subject in our conversation with the Emperor. Teferra was listening to the discussion, and he should have been relieved at its outcome, but like all Amharas he was suspicious and distrustful, especially of foreigners. Depressed and downcast, he left us.

The next day, we were leaving the Emperor's presence, having received gifts of silver medallions bearing his arms. The master of ceremonies was leading us through a long corridor toward the front entrance. And there stood Teferra, against the wall in the posture of the accused before sentencing, with sweat covering his face. "Teferra!" shouted the amused Svarzini. "We praised you to the skies!" (as indeed we had). "You are going to be promoted," he added, and clapped Teferra on his trembling shoulders.

Afterward, for as long as he lived, I visited Teferra every time I was in Addis Ababa. Following the Emperor's deposition, he was active for some time. Fortunately for him, he had been kicked out of the Palace in the last few months of Haile Selassie's reign. But he knew all the people from the Emperor's circle, and he was related to some of them by blood. As is characteristic of the Amharas, who are very conscious of their honor, he knew how to show gratitude. He always remembered that we had saved his neck. Soon after the Emperor was deposed, I met with Teferra in my room in the Hotel Ras. The town was swept up in the euphoria of the first months after the revolution. Noisy demonstrators flowed through the streets, some supporting the military government and others calling for its resignation; there were marches for agricultural reform, for bringing the old regime to justice, for distributing the Emperor's property among the poor. The feverish crowd filled the streets from early morning; fights broke out, and in the melee rocks were thrown. There in the room I told Teferra that I would like to find the Emperor's people. He was surprised, but he agreed to take it on himself. Our surreptitious expeditions began. We were a couple of collectors out to recover pictures doomed to destruction: we wanted to make an exhibition of the old art of governing.

At about that time the madness of the fetasha, *which later grew to unprecedented proportions, broke out. We all fell victim to it — everyone, without regard to color, age, sex, or social status.* Fetasha *is the Amharic word for search. Suddenly, everyone started searching everyone else. From dawn to dusk, and around the clock, unceasingly, not stopping for breath. The revolution had divided people into camps, and the fighting began. There were no trenches or barricades, no clear lines of demarcation, and therefore anyone could be an enemy. The threatening atmosphere fed on the Amharas' pathological suspicion. To them, no man could be trusted, not even another Amhara. No one's word can be trusted, no one can be relied upon, because people's intentions are wicked and perverse; people are conspirators. Because the Amharic philosophy is pessimistic and sad, their eyes are sad but at the same time watchful and searing, their faces solemn, their features tense, and they can rarely bring themselves to smile.*

All of them have weapons; they are in love with them. The wealthy had whole arsenals in their courts, and maintained private armies. In officer's apartments there were arsenals, too. Machine-guns, pistols, boxes of grenades. A couple of years ago, you could buy guns in the stores like any other merchandise. It sufficed to pay for them; nobody asked any questions. The arms of the plebeians were inferior and often quite old: flintlocks, breechloaders, muskets, shotguns, a whole museum to carry on one's back. Most of these antiques are useless because nobody produces ammunition for them any more. Thus, on the street market the bullet is often worth more than the gun. Bullets are the most valuable currency in that market, more in demand than dollars. After all, what is a dollar but paper? A bullet can save your life. Bullets make your weapons more significant, and that makes you more significant.

A man's life — what is that worth? Another man exists only to the degree that he stands in your way. Life doesn't mean much, but it's better to take it from the enemy before he has time to deliver a blow. All night (and also during the day) there is the sound of shooting, and later the dead lying in the streets. "Negus," I say to the driver, "they're shooting too much. It's not good." He remains silent, not answering. I don't know what he thinks. They have learned to draw their guns for any old reason and shoot.

To kill.

And perhaps it could be otherwise. Perhaps none of this is necessary. But they think differently. Their thoughts run not toward life but toward death. At first they talk quietly, then a quarrel breaks out, and the dispute ends in gunfire. Where do so much stubbornness, aggression, and hatred come from? All this without a moment's thought, without brakes, rolling over the edge of a cliff.

To get things under control, to disarm the opposition, the authorities order a complete fetasha, *covering everyone. We are searched incessantly. On the street, in the car, in front of the house, in the house, in the street, in front of the post office, in front of an office building, going into the editor's office, the movie theater, the church, in front of the bank, in front of the restaurant, in the marketplace, in the park. Anyone can search us, because we don't know who has the right and who hasn't, and asking only makes things worse. It's better to give in. Somebody's always searching us. Guys in rags with sticks, who don't say anything, but only stop us and hold out their arms, which is the signal for us to do the same: get ready to be searched. They take everything out of our briefcases and pockets, look at it, act surprised, screw up their faces, nod their heads, whisper advice to each other. They frisk us: back, stomach, legs, shoes. And then what? Nothing, we can go on, until the next spreading of arms, until the next* fetasha. *The next one might be only a few steps on, and the whole thing starts all over again. The searchers never give you an acquittal, a general clearance, absolution. Every few minutes, every few steps, we have to clear ourselves again.*

The most tiring searchers are the ones we meet on the road when traveling by bus. It happens scores of times. Everybody gets out, and the luggage is torn open and tossed around until it's in pieces. Every screw gets taken out and everything is spread out on the ground, and then it all gets browsed through slowly and thoroughly. We're searched, frisked, squeezed. Then the luggage, which has expanded like rising dough, all has to be stuffed back into the bus. At the next fetasha *it all gets tossed out again, and clothes, tomatoes, and pots and pans get strewn and kicked around until the scene resembles an impromptu roadside bazaar. The searchers make the trip so miserable that halfway to anywhere you just want to stop the bus and get off, but what do you do then, in the middle of some field high up in the mountains that are full of bandits?*

Sometimes the searchers work over a whole quarter of the city. That's trouble. Then it's the army that does the fetasha *looking for ammunition dumps, underground printing presses, and anarchists. During these operations you hear shots and see bodies. If anybody, no matter how innocent, gets in the way, he'll live through some difficult hours. He'll walk between the gun barrels with his hands over his head, waiting for his sentence. Usually, however, you have to deal with amateur searchers, and after a while you learn to put up with them. These lonesome searchers hold their own frisks, outside the general plan, lone wolves that they are. We're walking down the street when a stranger stops us and stretches out his arms. No way out of it; we have to spread ours and get ready. He'll give us a good feel, pluck around a little bit, give us a squeeze, and tell us we're free to go on. For a while he must have suspected us; now we're left in peace. We can forget him and go on. One of the guards in my hotel really enjoyed searching me. Sometimes when I was in a hurry and sprinted straight through the lobby and up the stairs to my room, he'd give chase. Before I could get through the door and lock him out, he'd get a foot in, wriggle in, and do a* fetasha. *I had* fetasha *dreams. A multitude of dark, dirty, eager, creeping, dancing, searching hands covered me, squeezing, plucking, tickling, threatening to throttle me, until I awoke in sweat. I couldn't get back to sleep until morning.*

Despite these difficulties, I continued to go into the houses that were opened to me by Teferra. I listened to stories of the Emperor, stories that already seemed to come from another world.

A. M.-M.:

As the keeper of the third door, I was the most important footman in the Audience Hall. The Hall had three sets of doors, and three footmen to open and close them, but I held the highest rank because the Emperor passed through my door. When His Most Exalted Majesty left the room, it was I who opened the door. It was an art to open the door at the right moment, the exact instant. To open the door too early would have been reprehensible, as if I were hurrying the Emperor out. If I opened it too late, on the other hand, His Sublime Highness would have to slow down, or perhaps even stop, which would detract from his lordly dignity, a dignity that meant getting around without collisions or obstacles.

G. S.-D.:

His Majesty spent the hour between nine and ten in the morning handing out assignments in the Audience Hall, and thus this time was called the Hour of Assignments. The Emperor would enter the Hall, where a row of waiting dignitaries, nominated for assignment, bowed humbly. His Majesty would take his place on the throne, and when he had seated himself I would slide a pillow under his feet. This had to be done like lightning so as not to leave Our Distinguished Monarch's legs hanging in the air for even a moment. We all know that His Highness was of small stature. At the same time, the dignity of the Imperial Office required that he be elevated above his subjects, even in a strictly physical sense. Thus the Imperial thrones had long legs and high seats, especially those left by Emperor Menelik, an exceptionally tall man. Therefore a contradiction arose between the necessity of a high throne and the figure of His Venerable Majesty, a contradiction most sensitive and troublesome precisely in the region of the legs, since it is difficult to imagine that an appropriate dignity can be maintained by a person whose legs are dangling in the air like those of a small child. The pillow solved this delicate and all-important conundrum.

I was His Most Virtuous Highness's pillow bearer for twenty-six years. I accompanied His Majesty on travels all around the world, and to tell the truth — I say it with pride — His

Majesty could not go anywhere without me, since his dignity required that he always take his place on a throne, and he could not sit on a throne without a pillow, and I was the pillow bearer. I had mastered the special protocol of this speciality, and even possessed an extremely useful, expert knowledge: the height of various thrones. This allowed me quickly to choose a pillow of just the right size, so that a shocking ill fit, allowing a gap to appear between the pillow and the Emperor's shoes, would not occur. In my storeroom I had fifty-two pillows of various sizes, thicknesses, materials, and colors. I personally monitored their storage, constantly, so that fleas — the plague of our country — would not breed there, since the consequences of any such oversight could lead to a very unpleasant scandal.

T. L.:

My dear brother, the Hour of Assignments set the whole Palace trembling! For some, it was the trembling of joy, and a deeply sensuous delight; for others, well, it was the trembling of fear and catastrophe, since in that hour His Distinguished Majesty not only handed out prizes and distributed nominations and plums, but also punished, removed from office, and demoted. No, I've got it wrong. Really there was no division into happy and frightened ones: joy and fear simultaneously filled the heart of everyone summoned to the Audience Hall, since no one knew what awaited him there.

This uncertainty and obscurity with regard to our monarch's intentions caused the Palace to gossip incessantly and lose itself in supposition. The Palace divided itself into factions and coteries that fought incessant wars, weakening and destroying each other. That is exactly what His Benevolent Majesty wanted. Such a balance assured his blessed peace. If one of the coteries gained the upper hand, His Highness would quickly bestow favors on its opponents, restoring the balance that paralyzed usurpers. His Majesty played the keys — a black one and then a white one — and brought from the piano a harmonious melody soothing to his ears. Everyone gave in to such manipulation because the only reason for their existence was the Emperor's approbation, and if he withdrew it they would disappear from the Palace within the day, without a trace. No, they weren't anything on their own. They were visible to others only as long as the glamorous light of the Imperial crown shone upon them.

Haile Selassie was a constitutional Chosen One of God, and he could not associate himself with any faction (although he used one or another more than others), but if any one of the favored coteries went too far in its eagerness, the Emperor would scold or even formally condemn it. This was especially so for the extreme factions that our Emperor used to establish order. The Emperor's speeches were remarkably kindly, gentle, and comforting to the people, who had never heard his mouth form a harsh or angry word. And yet you cannot rule an Empire with kindness. Someone has to check opposing interests and protect the superior causes of Emperor, Palace, and State. That is what the extreme factions, the hard factions, were doing, but because they did not understand the Emperor's subtle intentions, they slipped into error — specifically the error of overdoing it. Desirous of His Majesty's approbation, they tried to introduce absolute order, whereas His Supreme Majesty wanted basic order with a margin of disorder on which his monarchical gentleness could exert itself. For this reason, the extremists' coterie encountered the ruler's scornful gaze when they tried to cross into that margin.

The three principal factions in the Palace were the aristocrats, the bureaucrats, and the so-called "personal people." The aristocrats, made up of great landowners and conservative in the extreme, grouped themselves mostly in the Crown

Council, and their leader was Prince Kassa, who has since been executed. The bureaucrats, most enlightened and most progressive since some of them had a higher education, filled the ministries and the Imperial offices. The faction of "personal people" was a peculiarity of our regime, created by the Emperor himself. His Supreme Majesty, a partisan of a strong state and centralized power, had to lead a cunning and skillful fight against the aristocratic faction, which wanted to rule in the provinces and have a weak, pliable Emperor. But he could not fight the aristocracy with his own hands, so he always promoted into his circle, as representatives of the people, bright young men from the lowest orders, chosen from the lowest ranks of the plebeians, picked often on little more than a hunch from the mobs that surrounded His Majesty whenever he went among the people. These "personal people" of the Emperor, dragged straight from our desperate and miserable provinces into the salons of the highest courtiers — where they met the undisguised hatred of the long-established aristocrats — served the Emperor with an almost indescribable eagerness, indeed a passion, for they had quickly tasted the splendors of the Palace and the evident charms of power, and they knew that they had arrived there, come within reach of the highest state dignities, only through the will of His Highness. It was to them that the Emperor would entrust the positions requiring greatest confidence: the Ministry of the Pen, the Emperor's political police, and the superintendency of the Palace were manned by such people. They were the ones who would uncover intrigues and battle the mean, haughty opposition.

Listen here, Mr. Journalist, not only did the Emperor decide on all promotions, but he also communicated each one personally. He alone. He filled the posts at the summit of the hierarchy, and also its lower and middle levels. He appointed the postmasters, headmasters of schools, police constables, all the most ordinary office employees, estate managers, brewery directors, managers of hospitals and hotels — and, let me say it again, he chose them personally. They would be summoned to the Audience Hall for the Hour of Assignments and lined up there in an unending line, because it was a multitude, a multitude of people awaiting the Emperor's arrival. Each one approached the throne in turn, emotionally stirred, bowing submissively, listening to the Emperor's decision. Each would kiss the hand of his benefactor and retreat from the presence without turning his back, bowing all the time. The Emperor supervised even the lowliest assignment, because the source of power was not the state or any institution, but most personally His Benevolent Highness. How important a rule that was! A special human bond, constrained by the rules of hierarchy, but a bond nevertheless, was born from this moment spent with the Emperor, when he announced the assignment and gave his blessing, from which bond came the single principle by which His Majesty guided himself when raising people or casting them down: the principle of loyalty.

My friend, you could fill a library with the informants' reports that flowed into the Emperor's ears against the person closest to him, Walde Giyorgis, the Minister of the Pen. His was the most perverse, corrupt, repulsive personality ever to have been supported by the floors of our Palace. The very act of submitting a report against that man threatened one with the grimmest consequences. You can imagine how bad things must have been if, in spite of that, reports kept coming in. But His Highness's ear was always closed. Walde Giyorgis could do what he wanted, and his cruel self-indulgence knew no limits. And yet, blinded by his own arrogance and impunity, he once took part in the meeting of a conspiratorial faction about which the Palace security service informed His Sublime Majesty. His Majesty waited for Walde Giyorgis to inform him about this misdeed on his own, but Walde never so much as mentioned it — in other words, he violated the principle of loyalty. The next day His Majesty began the Hour of

Assignments by dealing with his own Minister of the Pen, a man who almost shared power with His Exalted Majesty. From the second position in the state, Walde Giyorgis fell to the post of a minor functionary in a backward southern province. When he was informed of the assignment — just imagine the surprise and horror he must have been suppressing at that moment — he kissed the hand of his benefactor according to custom, withdrew backward, and left the Palace forever.

Or take a personality like Prince Imru. He was perhaps the most outstanding individual among the elite, a man deserving of the highest honors and positions. (But what of it, since, as I have already mentioned, His Majesty never made appointments on the basis of a person's talent, but always and exclusively on the basis of loyalty.) Nobody knows why or under what circumstances, but suddenly Prince Imru began to smell of reform, and without asking the Emperor's permission he gave some of his lands to the peasants. Thus, having kept something secret from the Emperor and acted by his own lights, in an irritating and even provocative way he violated the principle of loyalty. His Benevolent Highness, who had been preparing a supremely honorable office for the prince, had to exile him from the country for twenty years.

Here let me mention that His Majesty did not oppose reform. He always sympathized with progress and improvement. But he could not stand it when someone undertook reform on his own, first because that created a threat of anarchy and free choice, and second because it might create the impression of there being other charitable ones in the Empire besides His Magnanimous Highness. So, if a clever and astute minister wanted to carry out even the smallest reform in his own backyard, he would have to direct the case in such a way and so present it to His Majesty that it would irrefutably, in the commonly accepted fashion, seem that the gracious, concerned innovator and advocate of the reform was His Imperial Highness himself, even if in reality the Emperor did not quite understand what the reform was all about. But not all ministers have brains, do they? It sometimes happened that young people unacquainted with Palace tradition or those who, guided by their own ambition and also seeking popular esteem — as if the Emperor's esteem weren't the only one worth seeking! — tried independently to reform some little matter or other. As if they didn't know that by doing so they violated the principle of loyalty and buried not only themselves but also their reform, which without the Emperor's authorship didn't have a chance to see the light of day.

I'll come right out and say it: the King of Kings preferred bad ministers. And the King of Kings preferred them because he liked to appear in a favorable light by contrast. How could he show himself favorably if he were surrounded by good ministers? The people would be disoriented. Where would they look for help? On whose wisdom and kindness would they depend? Everyone would have been good and wise. What disorder would have broken out in the Empire then! Instead of one sun, fifty would be shining, and everyone would pay homage to a privately chosen planet. No, my dear friend, you cannot expose the people to such disastrous freedom. There can be only one sun. Such is the order of nature, and anything else is a heresy. But you can be sure that His Majesty shined by contrast. How imposingly and kindly he shone, so that our people had no doubts about who was the sun and who the shadow.

Z. T.:

At the moment of granting the assignment, His Majesty saw before him the bowed head of the one he was calling to an exalted position. But even the far-reaching gaze of His Most Unrivaled Majesty could not foresee what would happen afterward to that head. The head, which had been bobbing up and down in the Hall of Audiences, lifted itself high and stiffened into a strong, decisive shape as soon as it passed through the door. Yes, sir, the power of the Emperor's assignment was amazing. An ordinary head, which had moved in a nimble and unrestrained way, ready to turn, bow, and twist, became strangely limited as soon as it was anointed with the assignment. Now it could move in only two directions: down to the ground, in the presence of His Highness, and upward, in the presence of everyone else. Set on that vertical track, the head could no longer move freely. If you approached from the back and suddenly called, "Hey, sir," he wouldn't be able to turn his head in your direction, but instead would have to make a dignified stop and turn his whole body to face your voice.

Working as a protocol official in the Hall of Audiences, I noticed that, in general, assignment caused very basic physical changes in a man. This so fascinated me that I started to watch more closely. First, the whole figure of a man changes. What had been slender and trim-waisted now starts to become a square silhouette. It is a massive and solemn square: a symbol of the solemnity and weight of power. We can already see that this is not just anybody's silhouette, but that of visible dignity and responsibility. A slowing down of movements accompanies this change in the figure. A man who has been singled out by His Distinguished Majesty will not jump, run, frolic, or cut a caper. No. His step is solemn: he sets his feet firmly on the ground, bending his body slightly forward to show his determination to push through adversity, ordering precisely the movement of his hands so as to avoid nervous disorganized gesticulation. Furthermore, the facial features become solemn, almost stiffened, more worried and closed, but still capable of a momentary change to optimism or approval. All in all, however, they are set so as to create no possibility of psychological contact. One cannot relax, rest, or catch one's breath next to such a face. The gaze changes, too: its length and angle are altered. The gaze is trained on a completely unattainable point. In accordance with the laws of optics, an appointee cannot perceive us when we talk to him, since his focal point is well beyond us. We cannot be perceived because he looks obliquely, and, by a strange periscopic principle, even the shortest appointees look over our heads toward an unfathomable distance or in the direction of some particular, private thought. In any case, we feel that even though his thoughts may not be more profound, they are certainly more responsible. We realize that an attempt to convey our own thoughts would be senseless and petty. Therefore we fall silent. Nor is the Emperor's favorite eager to talk, since a change in speech is another postassignment symptom. Multiple monosyllables, grunts, clearings of the throat, meaningful pauses and changes of intonation, misty words, and a general air of having known everything better and for a longer time replace simple, full sentences. We therefore feel superfluous and leave. His head moves upward on its vertical track in a gesture of farewell.

As it happened, however, not only did His Benevolent Majesty advance people; unfortunately, upon perceiving disloyalty, he demoted people as well. If you will excuse my vulgar words, he kicked them into the street. Then one could observe an interesting phenomenon: upon contact with the street, the effects of promotion disappear. The physical changes reverse themselves, and the one who has hit the street returns to normal. He even manifests a certain exaggerated proclivity to fraternize, as if he wanted to sweep the whole affair under the rug, to wave it away and say, "Let's forget all that," as if it had been some illness not worth mentioning.

M.:

You ask me, friend, why, in the last days of the Emperor's reign, the plebeian Aklilu, a man with no official functions, exercised more power than the distinguished Prince Makonen, head of the government? Because the degree of power wielded by those in the Palace corresponded not to the hierarchy of positions, but rather to the frequency of access to His Worthy Majesty. That was our situation in the Palace. It was said that one was more important if one had the Emperor's ear more often. More often, and for longer. For that ear the lobbies fought their fiercest battles; the ear was the highest prize in the game. It was enough, though it was not easy, to get close to the all-powerful ear and whisper. Whisper, that's all. Get it in, let it stay there if only as a floating impression, a tiny seed. The time will come when the impression solidifies, the seed grows. Then we will gather the harvest. These were subtle maneuvers, demanding tact, because His Majesty, despite amazingly indefatigable energy and perseverance, was a human being with an ear that one could not overload and stuff up without causing irritation and an angry reaction. That's why access was limited, and the fight for a piece of the Emperor's ear never stopped.

The course of this fight was one of the liveliest topics of the gossiping Palace, and it echoed around the rabid town. For instance, Abeje Debalk, a low official in the Ministry of Information, enjoyed access four times a week and his boss only twice. People whom the Emperor trusted were scattered even among the lowest ranks, and yet because of their access they enjoyed powers that their ministers and the Crown Councillors couldn't dream of. Fascinating struggles were going on. The worthy general Abiye Abebe had access three times a week, and his adversary Kebede Gebre (both since shot) only once. But Gebre's lobby so managed things and so undermined Abebe's decrepit lobby that Abebe fell to two, and finally to only one, while Gebre, who had valuable international connections and had done well in the Congo, jumped to four times a week. In my best period, my friend, I could count on access once a month, even though others thought it was more. But even that was something, a significant position, because below those with access stood another whole hierarchy of those with no access at all, who had to go through one, two, or three others to reach the Emperor's ear. Even there you could see the claws: struggles, maneuvers, subterfuge. Oh, how everyone would bow to someone with a lot of access, even if he wasn't a minister. And one whose access was diminishing knew that His Majesty was pushing him down the slippery slope. I will add that, in relation to his modest size and pleasing form, His Supreme Majesty had ears of a large configuration.

I. B.:

I was the purse bearer to Aba Hanna Jema, the God-fearing confessor and treasurer to the Emperor. The two dignitaries were of the same age, of similar height, and they looked alike. To speak of a personal resemblance to His Distinguished Majesty, the Chosen One of God, sounds like a punishable impudence, but I am allowed such boldness in the case of Aba Hanna since the Emperor held him in the highest confidence. Aba Hanna's unlimited access to the throne proved the intimacy of this relationship. You could even call it continuous access. As keeper of the cashbox and confessor to our much-lamented monarch, Aba could look into the Imperial soul and the Imperial pocket — in other words, he could see the Imperial person in its dignified entirety. As his purse bearer, I always accompanied Aba in his fiscal activities, carrying behind him the bag of top-grade lambskin that those who destroyed everything later exhibited in the streets. I also took care of another bag, a large one that was filled with small coins on the eve of national holidays: the Emperor's birthday, the anniversary of his coronation, and the anniversary of his return from exile. On such occasions our august ruler went to the most crowded and lively quarter of Addis Ababa, Mercato, where on a specially constructed platform I would place the heavy, jingling bag from which His Benevolent Majesty would scoop the handfuls of coppers that he threw into the crowd of beggars and other such greedy riffraff. The rapacious mob would create such a hubbub, however, that this charitable action always had to end in a shower of police batons against the heads of the frenzied, pushy rabble. Saddened, His Highness would have to walk away from the platform. Often he was unable to empty even half the bag.

W. A.-N.:

. . . and so, having finished the Hour of Assignments, His Indefatigable Majesty would move on to the Golden Hall. Here began the Hour of the Cashbox. This hour came between ten and eleven in the morning. His Highness was accompanied by the saintly Aba Hanna, who in turn was assisted by his faithful bag bearer. Someone with good ears and a good nose could tell how the Palace rustled with money, smelled of it. But this called for special imagination and sensitivity, because money was not lying around the chambers, and His Merciful Highness had no inclination to spread packets of dollars among his favorites. No, His Highness cared little for that sort of thing.

Even though, dear friend, it might seem incomprehensible to you, not even Aba Hanna's little bag was a bottomless treasury. The masters of ceremony had to use all sorts of stratagems to prevent the Emperor from being embarrassed financially. I remember, for instance, how His Majesty paid the salaries of foreign engineers but showed no inclination to pay our own masons after the construction of the Imperial Palace called Genete Leul. These simple masons gathered in front of the Palace they had built and began asking for what was due them. The Supreme Master of Palace Ceremony appeared on the balcony and asked them to move to the rear of the Palace, where His Magnanimous Highness would shower them with money. The delighted crowd went around back to the indicated spot — which enabled His Supreme Majesty to leave unembarrassed through the front door and go to the Old Palace, where the court awaited him.

Wherever His Majesty went, the people showed their uncontrolled, insatiable greed. They asked now for bread, now for shoes, now for cattle, now for funds to build a road. His Majesty liked to visit the provinces, to give the plain people access to him, to learn of their troubles and console them with promises, to praise the humble and the hardworking and scold the lazy and the disobedient. But this predilection of His Majesty's drained the treasury, because the provinces had to be put in order first: swept, painted, the garbage buried, the flies thinned out, schools built, the children given uniforms, the municipal buildings remodeled, the flags sewn, and portraits of His Distinguished Highness painted. It wouldn't do if His Majesty appeared suddenly, unexpectedly, like some poor tax collector, or if he merely came into contact with life as it is. One can imagine the surprise and mortification of the local dignitaries. Their trembling! Their fear! Government can't work under threat, can it? Isn't government a convention, based on established rules?

Imagine His Worthy Highness's having the habit of arriving unannounced! Let's say our monarch is flying north, where everything has been prepared, the protocol spruced up, the ceremonies well rehearsed, the province gleaming like a mirror, and then suddenly in the airplane His Distinguished Highness beckons to the pilot and tells him, "Son, turn this plane around. Let's fly south." In the south, there is nothing! Nothing ready! The south is loafing around, a mess, in rags, black with flies. The governor is off in the capital, the dignitaries asleep, the police have slithered off to the villages to plunder the peasants. How badly His Benevolent Majesty would feel! What an affront to his dignity! And, not to mince words, how ridiculous! We have provinces where the people are depressingly savage, pagan, and naked; without instructions from the police they might do something that would offend His Highness's dignity. We have other provinces where the benighted peasantry would flee at the sight of the monarch. Just imagine it, friend. His Most Extraordinary Majesty steps off the airplane, and around him — nothing. Silent emptiness, deserted fields, and everywhere you look, not a living soul. No one to speak to, no one to console, no welcoming arch, not even a car. What can you do? How can you act? Set up the throne and roll out the carpet? That would only make it more ridiculous. The throne adds dignity only by contrast to the surrounding humility. This humility of the subjects creates the dignity of the throne and gives it meaning. Without the humility around it, the throne is only a decoration, an uncomfortable armchair with worn-out velvet and twisted springs. A throne in an empty desert — that would be disgraceful. Sit down on it? Wait for something to happen? Count on someone's showing up to render homage? What's more, there isn't even a car to get you to the nearest village to look for the viceroy. Our distinguished monarch knows who he is, but how to find him? So what remains for His Majesty to do? Look around the neighborhood, get back into the plane, and fly north after all, where everything waits in excitement and impatient readiness: the protocol, the ceremonies, the province like a mirror.

Is it surprising that in such circumstances His Benevolent

Majesty did not sneak up on people? Let's say that he would surprise first one, then another, here and there. Today he would surprise the province of Bale, in a week the province of Tigre. And he notes: "loafing around, filthy, black with flies." He summons the provincial dignitaries to Addis Ababa for the Hour of Assignments, scolds them, and removes them from office. News of this spreads throughout the Empire, and what is the result? The result is that dignitaries stop doing everything except looking at the sky to see whether His Distinguished Highness is coming. The people waste away, the province declines, but all that is nothing compared to the fear of His Majesty's anger. And what's worse, because they feel uncertain and threatened, not knowing the hour or the day, united by common inconvenience and fear, they start murmuring, grimacing, grumbling, gossiping about the health of His Supreme Highness, and finally they start conspiring, inciting others to rebel, loafing, undermining what seems to them an uncharitable throne — oh, what an impudent thought — a throne that won't let them live. Therefore, in order to avoid such unrest in the Empire and to avoid the paralysis of government, His Highness introduced a happy compromise that brought peace to him and to the dignitaries. Nowadays, all those who destroyed the monarchy point out that in each province His Most Worthy Majesty maintained a Palace always ready for his arrival. It is true that some excesses were committed. For instance, a great Palace was constructed in the heart of the Ogaden Desert and maintained for years, fully staffed with servants and its pantry kept full, and His Indefatigable Majesty spent only one day there. But what if His Distinguished Majesty's itinerary were such that at some point he had to spend a night in the heart of the Desert? Wouldn't the Palace then prove itself indispensable? Unfortunately, our unenlightened people will never understand the Higher Reason that governs the actions of monarchs.

E.:

The Golden Hall, Mr. Kapuchitsky, the Hour of the Cashbox. Next to the Emperor stand the venerable Aba Hanna and, behind him, his purse bearer. At the other end of the Hall people are crowding in, apparently without order, but everyone remembers his place in the line. I can call it a crowd, since His Gracious Majesty received an endless number of subjects every day. When he stayed in Addis Ababa the Palace overflowed. It pulsated with exuberant life — though, naturally, a hierarchy was to be found here as well — rows of cars flowed through the courtyard, delegations crowded the corridors, ambassadors chatted in the antechambers, masters of ceremony rushed around with feverish eyes, the guard changed, messengers ran in with piles of papers, ministers dropped by, simply and modestly, like ordinary people. Hundreds of subjects tried to finagle their petitions or denunciations into the hands of the dignitaries. One could see the general staff, members of the Crown Council, managers of Imperial estates, deputies — in other words, an excited and exhilarated crowd.

All this would disappear in an instant when His Distinguished Majesty would leave the capital on a visit abroad or to some province to lay a cornerstone, open a new road, or find out about the troubles of the people in order to encourage or console them. The Palace would immediately become empty and change into a replica of itself, a prop. The Palace servants did their laundry and strung their wash on clotheslines, the Palace children grazed their goats on the lawns, the masters of ceremony hung out in local bars, the guards would chain the gates shut and sleep under the trees. Then His Majesty would return, the fanfares would sound, and the Palace would come to life again.

In the Golden Hall there was always electricity in the air. One could feel the current flowing through the temples of those who had been summoned, making them quiver. Everyone knew the source of that current: the little bag of finest lambskin. People would approach His Benevolent Highness by turns, saying why they needed money. His Majesty would listen and ask questions. Here I must admit that His Highness was most meticulous about financial matters. Any expenditure, anywhere in the Empire, of more than ten dollars required his personal approval, and if a minister came to ask approval for spending only one dollar, he would be praised. To repair a minister's car — the Emperor's approval is needed. To replace a leaking pipe in the city — the Emperor's approval is needed. To buy sheets for a hotel — the Emperor must approve it.

How you should admire, my friend, the diligent thrift of His August Majesty, who spent most of his royal time checking accounts, listening to cost estimates, rejecting proposals, and brooding over human greed, cunning, and meddling. His lively curiosity, vigilance, and exemplary economy always attracted mention. He had a fiscal bent, and his Minister of Finance, Yelma Deresa, was counted among those with the most access to the Emperor. Yet to those in need, His Highness would stretch out a generous hand. Having listened as his questions were answered, His Charitable Majesty would inform the petitioner that his financial needs would be met. The delighted subject would make the deepest bow. His Magnanimous Highness would then turn his head in the direction of Aba Hanna and specify in a whisper the sum of money that the saintly nobleman was to take from the purse. Aba Hanna would plunge his hand into the bag, take out the money, put it into an envelope, and hand it to the lucky recipient. Bow after bow, backward, backward, shuffling his feet and stumbling, the fortunate one would leave.

And afterward, Mr. Kapuchitsky, one could unfortunately hear the cries of the wretched ingrate. Because in the envelope he would find only a fraction of the sum that — as the insatiable thieves always swore — had been promised to him by our generous Emperor. But what could he do? Go back? Hand in a petition? Accuse the dignitary closest to His Majesty's heart? No such thing was possible. What hatred therefore surrounded the God-fearing treasurer and confessor! Because, since general opinion dared not stain the dignity of His Highness, it reviled Aba Hanna as a miser and a cheat, who dipped so lightly into the bag and sifted so much with his thick fingers, who reached in with such disgust that the bag could have been full of poisonous reptiles, who knew the weight of money so well that he stuffed the envelope without looking and then gave the sign to shuffle away backward. That's why, when he was executed, I think no one but His Merciful Highness cried for him.

An empty envelope! Mr. Kapuchitsky, do you know what money means in a poor country? Money in a poor country and money in a rich country are two different things. In a rich country, money is a piece of paper with which you buy goods on the market. You are only a customer. Even a millionaire is only a customer. He may purchase more, but he remains a customer, nothing more. And in a poor country? In a poor country, money is a wonderful thick hedge, dazzling and always blooming, which separates you from everything else. Through that hedge you do not see creeping poverty, you do not smell the stench of misery, and you do not hear the voices of the human dregs. But at the same time you know that all of that exists, and you feel proud because of your hedge. You have money; that means you have wings. You are the bird of paradise that everyone admires.

Can you imagine, for instance, a crowd gathering in Holland to look at a rich Dutchman? Or in Sweden, or in Australia? But in our land — yes. In our land, if a prince or count appears, the people run to see him. They will run to see a millionaire, and afterward they will go around and say, "I saw a millionaire." Money transforms your own country into an exotic land. Everything will start to astonish you — the way people live, the things they worry about, and you will say, "No, that's impossible." Because you will already belong to a different civilization. And you must know this law of culture: two civilizations cannot really know and understand one another well. You will start going deaf and blind. You will be content in your civilization surrounded by the hedge, but signals from the other civilization will be as incomprehensible to you as if they had been sent by the inhabitants of Venus. If you feel like it, you can become an explorer in your own country. You can become Columbus, Magellan, Livingstone. But I doubt that you will have such a desire. Such expeditions are very dangerous, and you are no madman, are you? You are already a man of your own civilization, and you will defend it and fight for it. You will water your own hedge. You are exactly the kind of gardener that the Emperor needs. You don't want to lose your feathers, and the Emperor needs people who have a lot to lose. Our kindly monarch would throw coppers to the poor, but to the people of the Palace he would make gifts of great worth. He would give them estates, land, peasants from whom they could collect taxes; he gave gold, titles, and capital.

Though everyone — if he proved his loyalty — could count on a bountiful gift, there were still continuous quarrels between lobbies, constant struggles for privileges, incessant grabbing, and all because of the needs of that bird of paradise that fills every man. His Most Extraordinary Majesty liked to watch this elbowing. He liked the people of the court to multiply their belongings, he liked their accounts to grow and their purses to swell. I don't remember His Magnanimous Highness's ever demoting someone and pressing his head to the cobblestones because of corruption. Let him enjoy his corruption, as long as he shows his loyalty! Thanks to his unequaled memory and also to the constant reports, our monarch knew exactly who had how much. But as long as his subject behaved loyally, he kept this knowledge to himself and never made use of it. But if he sensed even the slightest shadow of disloyalty, he would immediately confiscate everything and take the bird of paradise away from the embezzler. Thanks to that system of accountability, the King of Kings had everyone in his hand, and everyone knew it.

One case, though, was different. An outstanding patriot and a leader of the partisans in the war against Mussolini, Tekele Wolda Hawariat by name, was ill disposed toward the Emperor. He refused to accept graciously tendered gifts, refused special privileges, never showed any inclination to corruption. His Charitable Majesty had him imprisoned for many years, and then cut his head off.

G. H.-M.:

Even though I was a high ceremonial official, behind my back they called me His Distinguished Majesty's cuckoo. That was because a Swiss clock, from which a cuckoo would jump out to announce each hour, hung in the Emperor's office. I had the honor to fulfill a similar duty during the hours that His Highness devoted to his Imperial duties. When the time came for the Emperor, in accordance with official protocol, to pass from one activity to another, I would stand before him and bow several times. It was a signal to His Perspicacious Majesty that one hour was ending and that the time had come to start another.

The scoffers, who in any Palace like to make fun of their inferiors, would say jokingly that bowing was my only profession and even my sole reason for existing. Indeed, I had no other duty than bowing before His Distinguished Highness at a given moment. But I could have answered them — had my rank entitled me to such boldness — that my bows were of a functional and efficacious character and that they served a purpose of state, which is to say a superior purpose, whereas the court was full of nobles bowing whenever the occasion presented itself. And it was no superior purpose that made their necks so flexible, but only their desire to flatter, their servility, and their hope for gifts and promotions. I had to be careful not to let my own formal and functional bow get lost among those of the crowd. And I had to place myself where those pushy flatterers would not jostle me to the rear. After all, if our kindly monarch did not receive the established signal in time, he could fall into confusion and prolong his current activity at the expense of another equally important duty.

But, unfortunately, earnestness in performing my duty had little effect when it was time to finish the House of the Cashbox and begin the Hour of the Ministers. The Hour of the Ministers was devoted to Imperial matters, but who cares about Imperial matters when the treasure chest is open and the favorites and chosen ones are swarming around it like ants! No one wants to go away empty-handed, without a gift, without an envelope, without a promotion, without having cashed in. Sometimes His Highness would answer such greediness with a kindly scolding, but he never became angry, since he knew that it was because of the open purse that they pressed around him and served him more humbly. Our Emperor knew that one who is satiated will defend his own contentedness, and where else could one be satiated but in the Palace? Even the Emperor himself partook of this plenty, about which the destroyers of the Empire are now making so much noise.

I'll tell you, friend, that it got worse later on. The more the foundations of the Empire were crumbling, the more the chosen ones pressed forward to the cashbox. The more impudently the destroyers raised their heads, the more greedily the favorites stuffed their purses. The closer it got to the end, the more horrible was the grabbing and the unrestrained snatching. Instead, my friend, of applying himself to the tiller or the sails as the boat started to sink, each one of our magnates stuffed his bag and looked around for a comfortable lifeboat. Such fever broke out in the Palace, such scrambling for the purse, that even those who were not particularly interested in enriching themselves were dragged in, egged on, and so pressed upon that in the end, for their own peace and for dignity's sake, they also put something into their pockets. Because, my friend, things somehow got so turned around that it was decency to take and dishonor not to take. Not taking was seen as a frailty, some sort of laziness, some sort of pathetic and pitiable impotence. On the other hand, the one who had taken would go around looking as though he wanted to show off his masculinity, as if he wanted to say, full of self-assurance, "Kneel, you wretches!" It was all so topsy-turvy that I couldn't be blamed for tardily bringing the Hour of the Cashbox to an end so that His Benevolent Majesty could get on with the Hour of the Ministers.

P. H.-T.:

The Hour of the Ministers began at eleven o'clock and ended at noon. It was no trouble to call the ministers, since by custom these dignitaries stayed in the Palace all morning; various ambassadors often complained of being unable to visit a given minister in his office to take care of problems because the secretary would invariably say, "The minister has been summoned to the Emperor." In point of fact, His Gracious Highness liked to keep an eye on everyone, he liked to keep everyone within reach. A minister who stayed away from the Palace appeared in a bad light and never lasted long. But the ministers, God knows, didn't try to stay away. No one ever reached such a position without knowing the monarch's likings and trying assiduously to comply with them. Whoever wanted to climb the steps of the Palace had first of all to master the negative knowledge: what was forbidden to him and his subalterns, what was not to be said or written, what should not be done, what should not be overlooked or neglected. Only from such negative knowledge could positive knowledge be born — but that positive knowledge always remained obscure and worrisome, because no matter how well they knew what *not* to do, the Emperor's favorites ventured only with extreme caution and uncertainty into the area of propositions and postulates. There they would immediately look to His Distinguished Majesty, waiting to hear what he would say. And since His Majesty had the habit of being silent, waiting, and postponing things, they, too, were silent, waited, and postponed things.

Life in the Palace, however lively and feverish, was actually full of silence, waiting, and postponement. Each minister chose the corridors in which he thought he would have the greatest chance of meeting the distinguished monarch and making a bow. A minister who got the word that he had been denounced for disloyalty would show the greatest eagerness in this selection of itineraries. He would spend whole days trying to create an occasion for an obsequious meeting with His Highness in the Palace, in order to prove the falsity and maliciousness of the denunciation by constant attendance and radiant alacrity. His Most Extraordinary Majesty was in the habit of receiving each minister separately because a dignitary would then denounce his colleagues more boldly, giving the monarch a better insight into the operation of the Imperial apparatus. It is true that the minister being received at an audience preferred to talk about the disorders reigning in other departments rather than about those in his own, but precisely for this reason His Imperial Majesty, by talking to all the dignitaries, could put together an overall view. Anyway, it didn't matter if a given dignitary measured up or not, as long as he showed unshakable loyalty.

His Benevolent Highness would show favor to those ministers who were not distinguished by quick wits or perspicacity. He treated them as a stabilizing element in the life of the Empire, while he himself, as everyone knows, was always the champion of reform and progress. Reach, my dear friend, for the autobiography dictated by the Emperor in his last years, and you will be convinced of how His Valiant Highness fought against the barbarity and obscurantism that reigned in our country. [*He goes into the other room and returns with the London edition, published by Ullendorff, of* My Life and Ethiopia's Progress, *leafs through it, and continues talking.*] Here, for example, His Majesty mentions that at the beginning of his reign he forbade the customary punishment of cutting off hands and legs for even minor offenses. Next, he writes that he forbade the custom that a man who had been accused of murder — and this was only an accusation by the common people, because there were no courts — would have to be publicly executed by disembowelment, with the execution performed by the closest member of his family, so that, for example, a son would execute his father and a mother her son. To replace that custom, His Majesty instituted the office of state executioner, designated specific sites and procedures for executions, and stipulated that execution be only by shooting. Next, he purchased out of his own funds (a point that he emphasizes) the first two printing presses and recommended that the first newspaper in the history of the country begin publication. Next, he opened the first bank. Next, he introduced electricity to Ethiopia, first in the Palaces and then in other buildings. Next, he abolished the custom of shackling prisoners in chains and iron stocks. From then on, prisoners were watched over by guards paid from the Imperial treasury. Next, he promulgated a decree condemning the slave trade. He decided to end that trade by 1950. Next, he abolished by decree a method that we call *lebasha*, for the discovery of thieves. Medicine men would give a secret herb to small boys, who, dizzy, stupefied, and directed by supernatural forces, would go into a house and point out the thief. The one who had been pointed out, in accordance with tradition, had his hands and legs cut off. Just try to imagine, my friend, life in a country where, even though you are completely innocent of crime, you can at any moment have your hands and legs cut off. Yes, you're walking down the street when a stupefied child grabs your trouser leg, and immediately the crowd starts chopping. You're sitting at home eating a meal when a drunken boy rushes in; they drag you outside and chop you up in the courtyard. Only when you imagine such a life can you understand the profundity of the breakthroughs that His Distinguished Highness made.

And he kept on reforming: he abolished forced labor, he imported the first cars, he created a postal service. He retained public flogging as a punishment, but he denounced the *afarsata* method. If an offense were committed somewhere, the forces of order would surround the village or little town where it had occurred and starve the population until the guilty one was denounced. But the inhabitants all watched one another so that there would be no denunciation, because everybody feared that he would be denounced. And so, guarding each other this way, they would all die of hunger. This was the *afarsata* method. Our Emperor condemned such practices.

Unfortunately, driven by the desire for progress, His August Majesty committed a certain imprudence. Because there used to be no public schools or universities in our country, the Emperor began sending young people abroad to study. At some point in the past His Majesty himself directed this effort, choosing youngsters from good, loyal families. But later — ah, these modern times make your head throb — such pressure came to be applied, such pushing to go abroad, that His Benevolent Majesty gradually lost control over this craze that possessed our youth. More and more of these youngsters ventured to Europe or America for their studies, and — how else could it have ended? — after a few years the trouble started. Because, like a wizard, His Majesty breathed life into the supernatural destructive force that comparison of our country with others proved to be. These people would return home full of devious ideas, disloyal views, damaging plans, and unreasonable and disorderly projects. They would look at the Empire, put their heads in their hands, and cry, "Good God, how can anything like this exist?"

Here you have, my friend, another proof of the ingratitude of youth. On the one hand so much care taken by His Majesty to give them access to knowledge, and on the other hand his reward in the form of shocking criticism, abusive sulking, undermining, and rejection. It's easy to imagine the bitterness with which these slanderers filled our monarch. The worst thing is that these tyros, filled with fads unknown to Ethiopia, brought into the Empire a certain unrest, an unnecessary mobility, disorder, a desire for action against authority, and it is here that the ministers who were not distinguished by quick wits or perspicacity came to His Distinguished Highness's aid. Well, it wasn't deliberate help, but spontaneous and unbidden, and yet how very important for keeping peace in the Empire. Because it was enough for one of those favorites of His Distinguished Highness to issue a thoughtless decree. These young smart alecks see it, and they immediately imagine some fatal result and come running to the rescue. They start trying to mend things, straighten things out, patch things up and untangle them. And so instead of using their energy to build their own vision of the future, instead of trying to put their irresponsible, destructive fantasies into action, our malcontents had to roll up their sleeves and start untangling what the ministers had knotted up. And there's always a lot of work to untangling! So they untangle and untangle, drenched in sweat, wearing their nerves to shreds, running around, patching things up here and there, and in all this rush and overwork, in this whirlwind, their fantasies slowly evaporate from their hot heads.

So now, my friend, let's look below the top levels. The

lower Imperial officials also cook up decrees, and the commoners stagger around, untangling. That is what the stabilizing role of His Majesty's favorites amounted to. These courtiers, once they had driven the cultured, educated dreamers and the stupid, uneducated common people to untangling, reduced all disloyal tendencies to zero — because where could you find the energy for aspiration if all your energy has been spent on untangling? Thus, my friend, was maintained the blessed and amiable balance in the Empire over which His Exalted Majesty ruled so wisely and so kindly.

The Hour of the Ministers, nevertheless, caused anxiety among the humble ministers, since no one knew exactly why he was being summoned, and if His Majesty did not like what the minister said, or detected in it some reticence or beating around the bush, he could be replaced the next day during the Hour of Assignments. And in any case His Majesty was in the habit of constantly shuffling and reshuffling the ministers so that they would not get too comfortable or surround themselves with friends and relations. His Gracious Majesty wanted to reserve control of promotions to himself, and for that reason he looked with a malignant eye on any dignitary who tried to promote someone on the side. Such arbitrariness — immediately punished — threatened to upset the balance that His Distinguished Majesty had established; a bothersome disproportion would creep in and His Highness would have to worry about restoring the balance, instead of occupying himself with more important affairs.

B. K.-S.:

At noon, in my function as cloakroom attendant in the Imperial Court, I used to put upon the shoulders of His Most Extraordinary Highness a black, floor-length robe in which the monarch opened the Hour of the Supreme Court of Final Appeal, which lasted until one o'clock and was known in our language as *chelot*. His Majesty enjoyed this hour of justice, and when he was in the capital he never neglected his duty as a judge, even at the expense of other important duties. In accordance with tradition, His Majesty spent this hour standing, listening to cases and pronouncing sentences.

Our Imperial court was once a camp that moved from place to place and province to province in response to reports by the Emperor's secret service, whose task it was to determine in what region the harvest looked promising and where a bountiful birth of cattle had been noted. In such blessed places the itinerant capital of the Empire would arrive and the Imperial court would set up its innumerable tents. Afterward, when the grain and meat were gone, the Imperial court, directed by the ubiquitous secret service, would strike camp and move along to the next province on which an abundant harvest had been bestowed. Our modern capital, Addis Ababa, was the last stopping place of the Emperor Menelik's court. That illustrious Emperor ordered the establishment of the town and built the first of the three Palaces that adorn the city.

During the itinerant period, one of the tents, a black one, was a prison in which those suspected of particularly dangerous offenses were kept. In those days the Emperor, enclosed in a covered cage because no one was allowed to see his radiant face, presided over the Hour of Justice in front of the black tent. His Majesty of our days performed the function of supreme judge in a specially constructed building next to the main Palace. Standing on a platform, His Highness would hear the case as it was presented by counsel, and then pronounce his verdict. This was according to a procedure established three thousand years ago by the Israelite King Solomon, of whom His Most Exalted Majesty was a direct descendant — as established by constitutional law. Verdicts announced on the spot by the Emperor were final, without appeal, and if he imposed the death penalty it was carried out immediately. That was the punishment that fell on the heads of conspirators who impiously and without fear of anathema reached for power. But His Majesty's judgment showed its benevolent side when by accident — whether it was because of the guard's negligence or because of some amazing cunning — some smallest of the small would manage to appear before the face of the highest judge, begging for justice and denouncing some nobleman who had victimized him. Then, His Benevolent Majesty would pronounce a sentence recommending the scolding of that dignitary, and the next day during the Hour of the Cashbox he would order Aba Hanna to pay a generous amount to the one who had been wronged.

M.:

At one o'clock His Distinguished Highness left the Old Palace and proceeded to the Anniversary Palace, his residence, for dinner. The Emperor was accompanied by members of his family and dignitaries invited for the occasion. The Old Palace quickly emptied, silence filled the corridors, and the guards fell into their midday slumber.

IT'S COMING, IT'S COMING

One often observes a fear of falling in people. Yet even the best of competitive figure skaters can fall. We also meet with falls in everyday life. One has to learn how to fall painlessly. Of what does a painless fall consist? It is a directed fall, which is to say that after losing balance we direct the body so that it lands on the side where the least damage will be done. As we fall, we relax our muscles and roll up, protecting the head. A fall that follows in accordance with these principles is not dangerous. On the other hand, trying desperately to avoid a fall often causes a painful spill at the last moment, when there is no chance to prepare for it.

(Z. Osiński, W. Starosta, *Speed- and Figure-Skating*)

Too many laws are made, and too few examples given.

(Saint-Just)

There are public figures about whom nothing is known except that one should not offend them.

(Karl Kraus, *Aphorisms*)

Courtiers of all ages feel one great need: to speak in such a way that they do not say anything.

(Stendhal, *Racine and Shakespeare*)

They . . . have walked after vanity, and are become vain.

(Jeremiah)

You have sat long enough unless you had done more good.

(Cromwell, to the members of the Long Parliament)

F. U.-H.:

Yes, that was '60. A woeful year, my friend. A venomous maggot began to infest the robust and succulent fruit of our Empire, and everything took such a morbid and irreparable course that instead of juice, alas, the fruit oozed blood. Let the flags fly at half-mast and our heads droop sorrowfully. Let us lay our hands upon our hearts. Today we know that it was already the beginning of the end and that what came next was irreversibly fated.

I was then serving His Most Sublime Majesty as an officer in the Ministry of Ceremonies, Department of Processions. In only five years of zealous and unblemished service, I bore so many tribulations that every hair on my head turned white! This happened because each time our monarch was to go abroad or leave Addis Ababa to honor some province with his presence, savage competition broke out in the Palace for places in the traveling Imperial party. There were two rounds in this struggle. During the first, all our notables contended to be part of the Imperial party. In the second round, those who had triumphed in the preliminary stage strove for high and honorable places in the party. We officers at the very head of the procession, its first ranks, weren't involved in the struggle, since His Benevolent Highness chose those ranks himself, and an Imperial assistant passed his decrees to us by way of the master of Palace ceremonies. At the top of the list stood members of the royal family, the Crown Council, and luminaries that His Ineffable Highness had decided to keep within his royal view because he suspected that in his absence they might foment a conspiracy in the capital. Nor had we any problems defining the servants in the party: bodyguards, cooks, pillow bearers, valets, purse bearers, gift bearers, dog-keepers, throne bearers, lackeys, and maids. But between the top and the bottom of the list yawned an emptiness into which the favorites and courtiers tried to insinuate themselves.

We ceremonial officers lived as if suspended between two great millstones, waiting for one of them to crush us. It was we who had to compile the list and send it on to our superiors. On us the crowd of favorites descended, attacking first with pleas and then with threats, first with laments and then with solemn vows of revenge; one asked for mercy while another proffered bribes, one promised heaps of gold while the next threatened to submit an informer's report about us. Patrons of the favorites dunned us constantly, and each recommended putting his chosen one on the list, backing up his words with threats. Yet who could blame these patrons? They themselves acted under pressure. All the while their underlings were making demands, and they themselves were jostling each other, for what a disgrace it would be for the patron who failed if another patron managed to place his favorite. Yes, the millstones began to turn and we ceremonial officers watched our hair turn white. Any one of these mighty patrons could crush us to a pulp, but was it our fault if the whole Empire could not fit into the traveling party?

And when everyone possible had been squeezed in and the list determined, pushing and undermining and elbowing began anew. Those who were lower were determined to rise. Number forty-three wanted to be twenty-sixth. Seventy-eight had an eye on thirty-two's place. Fifty-seven climbed to twenty-nine, sixty-seven went straight to thirty-four, forty-one pushed thirty out of the way, twenty-six was sure of being twenty-second, fifty-four gnawed at forty-six, sixty-three scratched his way to forty-nine, and always upward toward the top, without end. In the Palace there was agitation, obsession, running back and forth through the corridors. Coteries conferred, the court thought of nothing but the list until the word spread from office to salon to chamber that, yes, His Highness had heard the list, made wise and irrevocable corrections, and approved it. Now nothing could be changed and everyone knew his place. The chosen ones could be identified by their manner of walking and speaking, because on such an occasion a temporary hierarchy came into being alongside the hierarchy of access to the Emperor and the hierarchy of titles. Our Palace was a fabric of hierarchies and if you were slipping on one you could grab hold of another, and everyone found some satisfaction and reason to be proud of himself. Everyone spoke with admiration and jealousy of those who had made the list: "Look who's going!" Any dignitary distinguished several times in this way became a respected veteran.

All the machinations intensified greatly when His Highness was to visit a foreign country, from which one could return laden with presents and glorious decorations. In late 1960, our Emperor was preparing to visit Brazil. The court whispered that there would be abundant feasts, much buying, and the chance to stuff a bundle of cash into one's pockets. Thus a tournament for places began, and so fierce and grave was the jousting that no one noticed the malignant growth of a conspiracy in the very center of the Palace. But did no one catch the scent of it, my friend? Later it became evident that Makonen Habte-Wald had detected its stink early on, got hold of it, and reported it.

This Makonen, now deceased, was a strange personage. A minister, one of the select few, he had as much of a claim on the royal ear as he wanted, and yet he was a true favorite, a dignitary, who never thought of lining his own purse. His Majesty, even though he had little use for saints, pardoned his minister's bizarre weakness because he knew that Makonen forsook self-enrichment only to give his every thought to serving the Emperor. Makonen, my friend, was an ascetic of power, the Palace's great example of self-abnegation. He wore old suits, drove an old Volkswagen, and lived in an old house. His All-Dispensing Majesty liked Makonen's whole family, a humble clan who had climbed up from the dregs of society. He raised Makonen's brother Aklilu to the dignity of premier and made another brother, Akalu, a minister. Makonen himself was Minister of Industry and Commerce, but only rarely and unwillingly did he see to the duties of that station. He dedicated all his time and money to fostering his private network of informers. Makonen built a state within the state; he sowed his vassals in every institution, in offices, in the army, and in the police force. Day and night he reaped and winnowed his information, sleeping little, wearing himself out until he looked like a shadow. He was a penetrating man, but he penetrated quietly, like a mole, without theatricality, without rodomontade, gray, sour, hidden in the dusk, himself like the dusk. He tried to burrow deeply into the precincts of the competing spy networks, drawn by the scent of danger and treason, and — as we now know — rightly so. According to His Majesty's precept, if one sticks one's nose in deeply and well, it stinks everywhere. Yes . . .

He tells me that in Makonen's cabinet, the private files of this fantastic dirt-collector, the folder with Germamé Neway's name on it suddenly began to swell. The history of folders is strange, he says. Some linger for years on the shelf, thin and faded, like dried leaves. Closed, gathering dust, forgotten, they await the day when, untouched until that moment, they are finally torn up and thrown into the stove. These are the folders of loyal people who have led exemplary lives of devotion to the Emperor. Let's open the section marked "Activities": nothing negative. "Statements": not a single sheet of paper. And let's say there is one page, but on it, by order of the venerable Emperor, the minister has written fatina bere, *which means "a slip of the pen," "an inkblot." This means that the Emperor considered the report a mere dry run by a young employee of Makonen, who hadn't yet learned whom one can denounce with confidence, and when. So there is a page, but it is invalidated, like a canceled invoice.*

It can also happen that a folder which for years has remained thin and yellow comes to life at a certain moment, rises from the dead, starts getting fat. There is a well-known odor that comes from a place where an act of disloyalty has been committed. Makonen's nose is particularly sensitive to that odor. He begins to follow the scent, he watches, he increases his vigilance. Often the life of such a folder, which has begun to stir and gain weight, ends as abruptly as the life of its hero. They both disappear, he from the world and his folder from Makonen's cabinet.

There is a sort of inverse proportionality between the corpulence of folders and of people. He who wears himself out, loses weight, and wastes away in fighting against the Palace has a folder that grows fatter and fatter. On the other hand, he who plants himself with dignified loyalty at His Majesty's side grows fat with favors while his folder remains as thin as the membrane of a bladder. I mentioned that Makonen noticed the swelling of Germame Neway's folder. Germame came from a loyal and noble family, and when he finished school the benevolent monarch sent him on a scholarship to the United States, where he graduated from a university. He came back to the country at the age of thirty. He had six years to live.

A. W.:

Germame! Germame, Mr. Richard, was one of those disloyal people who, upon returning to the Empire, threw up their hands in exasperation. But they did that secretly. In public they displayed loyalty, and in the Palace they said what was expected of them. And His August Majesty — oh, how I reproach him for it today — let himself be taken in. When Germame stood before him, His Compassionate Majesty looked on him with a loving eye and made him governor of a region in the southern province of Sidamo. The good soil there yields rich coffee. Hearing of this appointment, everyone in the Palace said that Our Omnipotent Ruler was laying open the path to the highest honors for the young man.

Germame left with the Emperor's blessing, and at first things were quiet. The proper thing for him to have done was to wait patiently — patience is a cardinal virtue in the Palace — for His Benevolent Majesty to summon him and elevate him to the next grade. But forget that! After some time, dignitaries from the province of Sidamo began to appear. They came and loitered around the Palace, circumspectly inquiring of their cousins and friends about whether or not one could submit a denunciation of the governor. It is a slippery business, Mr. Richard, to denounce one's superiors. One cannot do it haphazardly, without first buckling on one's armor, because the governor might just have a mighty patron in the Palace. The patron could fly into a rage, look upon the dignitaries as backstabbers, and perhaps even rebuke them. So the dignitaries started their denunciations in monosyllables, hints, whispers, but then more and more boldly (even if still informally), delicately, dropping hints in conversational lulls — that Germame took bribes and used them to build schools.

Now just imagine how worried these dignitaries must have been. After all, it was understandable that a governor accepted tributes; all the dignitaries accepted tributes. Power begat wealth, as it had since the beginning of the world. But the abnormality of it was this, that a governor should use these tributes to build schools. And the example at the top was a command to subordinates, which meant that all the dignitaries should give money for schools. Now just for a moment let us admit a base thought. Let us say that a second Germame springs up in a second province and starts to give away his bribes. Immediately we would have a mutiny of the dignitaries, protesting against this principle of giving away bribes. The result: the end of the Empire. A fine prospect — at first a few pennies, and finally the fall of the monarchy. Oh, no! The whole Palace cried out, "Oh, no!"

Yet the strange thing, Mr. Richard, was that His Most Venerable Highness said nothing. He heard it all, but he did not say a word. He kept silent, which meant that he was still giving Germame a chance. But Germame could no longer return to the road of obedience. Eventually, the dignitaries from Sidamo reappeared. They bore a report that Germame had gone too far: he had begun turning uncultivated acreage over to landless peasants, he was seizing private property by force. Germame had turned out to be a communist. Oh, what a grave matter, my good sir! Today he gives away wasteland, tomorrow the property of landowners, and he will finish with the Imperial holdings! Now His Most Benevolent Majesty could hold his tongue no longer. Germame was summoned to the capital for the Hour of Assignments and sent down to be governor of Jijiga, where he couldn't give away land because the only inhabitants were nomads. During the ceremony, Germame committed an offense that should have awakened the utmost vigilance in His August Majesty: after hearing his appointment read, Germame failed to kiss the monarch's hand. Unfortunately . . .

It was then, he says, that Germame hatched his conspiracy. He hated Germame, and yet he also admired the man. There was something about him that drew people to him. Burning faith, a gift of persuasion, courage, decisiveness, keenness. Thanks to these characteristics he stood out against the gray, servile, fearful mass of yes-men and flatterers that filled the Palace. The first person Germame won over to his plan was his older brother, General Mengistu Neway, the chief of the Imperial Guard, an officer of fearless character and uncommon masculine good looks. Then the brothers gained the cooperation of the head of the Imperial Police, General Tsigue Dibou, the chief of Palace security, Colonel Workneh Gebayehu, and other members of the Emperor's inner circle. Working in strict secrecy, the conspirators set up a revolutionary council that numbered twenty-four people at the time of the coup. Officers of the Select Imperial Guard and the Palace security service made up the majority. Mengistu was the oldest at forty-four, but the younger Germame remained in command until the end.

The man who is telling me all this claims that Makonen started to suspect something and reported it to the Emperor. Then Haile Selassie summoned Colonel Workneh and asked him if it was true, but Workneh answered, "Not at all." Workneh was one of the Emperor's "personal people" — the monarch had lifted him straight up from the nether regions of society into the Palace chambers and had limitless confidence in him. He was probably the only man the Emperor really trusted. Suspicion of everyone is tiring; there has to be someone to trust, someone to feel at ease with. Furthermore, the Emperor discounted Makonen's reports because at the time he was directing his suspicions not at the Neway brothers, but at someone else: the dignitary Endelkachew, who lately seemed enervated, gloomy, anxious, drained of his usual spirit. Acting on his suspicions, the Emperor added Endelkachew to the traveling party so that he could keep an eye on him during the visit to Brazil.

My informant reminds me that the details of what happened next can be found in the testimony delivered by General Mengistu before the court martial. After the Emperor's departure, Mengistu handed out weapons to the officers of his Guard and instructed them to wait for further orders. It was Tuesday, the thirteenth of December. That evening, in the Empress Menen's residence, Haile Selassie's family and a group of high dignitaries gathered for supper. As they sat down at the table, Mengistu's messenger arrived with news that the Emperor had fallen ill during his trip, that he was dying, and that everyone should meet in the Palace to discuss the situation. When they had all assembled there, they were arrested. Meanwhile, officers of the Guard were arresting other dignitaries at their homes. But, as so often happens in a nervous situation, many dignitaries were forgotten. Several managed to escape from the city or to hide in friends' houses. Furthermore, the perpetrators of the coup were slow to cut off the telephones, and the Emperor's people had a chance to communicate and organize themselves. They were able to notify the Emperor that very night through the British Embassy. Haile Selassie broke off his visit and started for home, but without hurrying. He was giving the revolution time to collapse.

The following day, at noon, the Emperor's eldest son and the heir to the throne, Asfa Wossen, read a proclamation on the radio in the name of the rebels. Asfa Wossen was a weak, compliant man with no views of his own. There was animosity between him and his father, and it was whispered that the Emperor had doubts about whether Asfa was indeed his son. Something didn't quite fit in the dates of the Emperor's journeys and the time the Empress was blessed with her first child. Later, the forty-year-old son would try to justify himself to his father by saying that the rebels had forced him at gunpoint to read the proclamation. "In the last years," Asfa Wossen read from what Germame had written for him, "stagnancy has reigned in Ethiopia. An atmosphere of discontent and disappointment has spread among peasants, merchants, office workers, in the army and the police, among students, all through society. There is no progress being made anywhere, in any quarter. This results from the fact that a handful of dignitaries have locked themselves into a course of egoism and nepotism, instead of working for the good of the whole community. The people of Ethiopia have waited for the day when poverty and backwardness would cease to be, but nothing has been achieved after innumerable promises. No other nation has borne so much in patience. . . ." Asfa Wossen announced that a People's Government had been formed, and he declared himself its head. But very few people had radios in those days, and the words of the proclamation drowned without a ripple. The city was quiet. Business thrived, the normal bustle and disorder reigned in the streets. Few people had heard anything, and those who had did not know what to think about the whole affair. For them it was a Palace matter, and the Palace had always been inaccessible, unreachable, impenetrable, beyond understanding, on a different planet.

That very day Haile Selassie flew to Monrovia, Liberia, and made radio contact with his son-in-law General Abiye Abebe, the governor of Eritrea. In the meantime this son-in-law had been conducting talks with a group of generals who, from the bases surrounding the capital, were preparing an assault on the rebels. Generals Merid Mengesha, Assefa Ayena, and Kebede Gebre, all relatives of the Emperor, led this group. My informant tells me that the coup was staged by the Guard and that there was sharp antagonism between the Guard and the army. The Guard was enlightened and well paid, the army ignorant and poor. Now the generals take advantage of this antagonism to hurl the army against the Guard. They tell the soldiers, "The Guard wants power so it can exploit you." What they say is cynical, but it convinces the army. The soldiers shout, "Let us perish for our Emperor!" Zeal drives the battalions about to go to their death.

On Thursday, the third day of the coup, the regiments loyal to the generals enter the suburbs of the capital. Indecision in the rebel camp. Mengistu gives no orders for defense; he doesn't want blood to be spilled. The city remains peaceful, with normal traffic in the streets. An airplane circles overhead dropping leaflets. The leaflets contain the text of the anathema that the Patriarch Basilios, head of the Church and friend of the Emperor, has pronounced on the rebels. The Emperor has already flown from Monrovia to Fort Lamy, Chad. He receives a message from his son-in-law that he can fly on to

Asmara. In Asmara things are peaceful and everyone is waiting submissively. But his DC-6 loses an engine. He decides to proceed on three engines. At noon Mengistu comes to the university to meet the students. He shows them a piece of dry bread. "This," he says, "is what we fed to the dignitaries today, so that they will know what our people live on. You must help us." Shooting breaks out in the city. The battle for Addis Ababa begins. Hundreds meet death in the streets.

Friday, the sixteenth of December, is the last day of the coup. Fighting between army and Guard regiments has been going on since morning. The revolutionary council defends itself in the Palace. The assault on the Palace begins in the afternoon. A battalion of tanks, commanded by the Emperor's son-in-law Captain Dereji Haile-Mariam, leads the assault. "Surrender, you dogs!" cries the captain from the turret of his tank. He falls, cut down by a burst of machine-gun fire. Shells explode inside the Palace. Smoke, flames, and a terrible din fill the corridors and chambers. Further defense is impossible. The rebels burst into the Green Chamber, where the dignitaries from the Emperor's circle have been held prisoner since Tuesday. The rebels open fire. Eighteen of the people who had been closest to the Emperor die. Now the leaders of the conspiracy and scattered regiments of the Guard leave the Palace grounds and withdraw from the city toward the eucalyptus woods on the Entoto Hills. Evening draws near. The airplane carrying the Emperor lands in Asmara.

A. W.:

Oh, our loyal and humble people gave heartwarming proof of their devotion to His Most Praiseworthy Highness on that day of judgment, Mr. Richard. Because when the crushed infidels abandoned the Palace and fled to the neighboring woods, the populace, inspired by our Patriarch, set off in pursuit. Mind you, they had no tanks or cannon, so they grabbed whatever they could and joined the chase. Sticks, stones, pikes, daggers, everything went into action. The people of the streets, whom His Kindly Majesty used to shower with such generous alms, took furiously and hatefully to breaking the crazed heads of the calumniators and rebels who wanted to deprive them of God and prepare them for goodness knows what sort of life. If His Majesty were no longer there, who would give alms and fortifying words of comfort?

Following the bloody trail of the fugitives, the city dwellers drew village folk after them, so that you could see peasants with whatever weapons they could get their hands on — sticks, knives — cursing the slanderers. The peasants threw themselves into battle to avenge the affront to their generous ruler. Surrounded bands of the Guard defended themselves in the woods while their ammunition held out; later some gave themselves up, and others perished at the hands of the soldiers and the mob. Three thousand people, or perhaps as many as five thousand, ended up in prison, and twice that number died, to the joy of hyenas and jackals that came from far away to roam the woods in search of food. For a long time those woods laughed and howled all night long.

And those who had insulted His Unrivaled Majesty went straight to hell, my friend. General Dibou, for example, fell during the attack on the Palace and the mob hung his body in front of the gate of the First Division's base. Later it came out that after Colonel Workneh left the Palace, he was surrounded in the suburbs. They wanted to take him alive. But he didn't give in, Mr. Richard. He was shooting until the end. He even managed to kill a few soldiers. Then, when he was down to his last bullet, he put the barrel of the gun into his mouth, fired, and fell dead. They hung his body from a tree in front of Saint George's Cathedral. It may strain credulity, but His Highness could never bring himself to believe that Workneh had betrayed him. It was whispered afterward that even after many months the Emperor would summon servants to his bedroom late at night and ask them to call for the Colonel.

His Majesty flew into Addis Ababa on Saturday evening, when shooting could still be heard in the city and rebels were being executed in the squares. There was fatigue on our monarch's face, care and sorrow over the wrong that had been done him. He rode in his car, in the middle of a column of tanks and armored vehicles. All the citizens came out to pay humble and imploring homage. The whole city was kneeling on the ground, the people beating the sidewalks with their foreheads, and as I knelt in that crowd I heard moans, cries of woe, sighs, and wailing. No one dared look up into the face of our honorable monarch. At the gates of the Palace, Prince Kassa, who was hardly guilty, who had fought and had clean hands, kissed the Emperor's shoes. That same night His Unrivaled Highness ordered that his favorite lions be shot, because instead of defending the Palace they had admitted the traitors.

And now you ask about Germame. That evil spirit, together with his brother and a certain Captain Baye of the Imperial Guard, fled the city and remained in hiding for a week. They traveled only at night, for a price of five thousand dollars had immediately been put on their heads and everyone was looking for them, since that is a great deal of money. They tried to make their way south, probably intending to cross into Kenya. But after a week, as they sat hidden in the bushes — not having eaten for several days and fainting from thirst, afraid to show themselves in any village to get food and water — they were captured by peasants who had been beating the bush to find them. As Mengistu later testified, Germame decided to end it all right there. Germame, according to this survivor of the old regime, understood that he had gotten a step ahead of history, that he had walked more quickly than others, and he knew that someone who strides ahead of history with a gun in his hand is bound to perish. And he probably preferred that he and his fellow fugitives see to their own deaths. So when the peasants rushed forward to capture them, Germame shot Baye, then he shot his brother, and finally he shot himself.

The peasants thought they had lost their reward, because it was a reward for live capture, and they saw three corpses. However, only Germame and Baye were dead. Mengistu lay with his face covered with blood, but he was still alive. They rushed them to the capital and carried Mengistu into a hospital. His Majesty was informed of all this, and when he heard it he said that he wanted to see Germame's body. Accordingly, the corpse was brought to the Palace and thrown on the steps in front of the main entrance. His Majesty came out and stood for a long time, looking at the body that was lying there. He remained silent, gazing without saying a word. There were some others with him, and no one heard a sound. Then the Emperor turned, as if he had been startled, and went back into the main building, ordering his lackeys to close the door. Later I saw Germame's body hanging from a tree in front of Saint George's Cathedral. A crowd was standing around jeering at the traitors, hooting and raising vulgar cries. Mengistu was still alive. When he left the hospital, he faced a court martial. During the trial he behaved proudly and, contrary to Palace custom, showed neither any signs of humility nor any desire to obtain His Distinguished Majesty's pardon.

He said he wasn't afraid of death because when he decided to raise his head against injustice and attempt the coup, he expected to die. He said they had wanted to start a revolution, and since he would not live to see it he offered his blood so that the green tree of justice could sprout from it. They hanged him on the thirtieth of March, at dawn, in the main square. They hanged six other Guard officers along with him. He didn't look like himself at all. His brother's bullet had torn out his eye and shattered his whole face, which had grown a disheveled black beard. The remaining eye, under the pressure of the noose, squirted out of its socket.

They say that during the first days after the Emperor's return an unusual agitation reigned in the Palace. Charmen cleaned the floors, sanding soaked-in bloodstains from the parquet. Lackeys took down torn and partly burned curtains, trucks removed heaps of broken furniture and boxes full of empty shells, glaziers installed new windows and mirrors, masons replastered walls pockmarked by bullets. The smell of powder and smoke gradually disappeared. For a long time the ceremonial funerals of those who had preserved their loyalty to the end continued. At the same time the bodies of insurgents were buried at night in hidden, unknown places. Most of the dead had perished accidentally. Hundreds of gaping children, women on the way to market, and men going to work or idly sunning themselves had perished during the street fighting. Once the shooting had died down, the army patrolled the quiet city that only now, long after the fact, was beginning to feel the horror and the shock. They also say that later came weeks of fearsome arrests, exhaustive investigations, and brutal interrogations. Fear and uncertainty reigned. People whispered and gossiped, recalling details of the coup and embellishing them as their fantasy and courage allowed. Yet they embellished in secret, for all discussions of the latest events were officially banned, and the police, with whom one could not joke around even in the best of times (which these assuredly were not), became even more dangerous and efficient than usual in the effort to clear themselves of accusations that they had conspired. There was no lack of those willing to supply the police stations with additional terrified clients.

Everyone was waiting to see what the Emperor would do and declare next. On his return to the fearful, treason-tainted capital, he had expressed his pain and pity over the small group of lost sheep that had recklessly strayed from the flock and lost their way in a stony and bloodstained wilderness.

G. O.-E.:

It had always been an act of punishable impudence to look the Emperor straight in the eye, but now after what had happened even the greatest daredevil in the Palace would not have tried it. Everyone felt ashamed of having allowed the conspiracy to occur and fearful of His Majesty's righteous anger. And this half-frightened, half-shameful inability to look each other in the eye showed in everyone's attitude toward everyone else. Everyone succumbed to it. Because at first no one knew where he stood, which is to say no one knew whom the venerable Emperor would accept and whom he would reject, whose loyalty he would confirm and whose he wouldn't acknowledge, to whom he would give his ear and to whom he would deny all access, and so everyone, unsure of everyone else, preferred not to look anyone in the eye. And so not looking, not seeing, watching the floor, staring at the ceiling, inspecting the tips of one's shoes, and gazing through windows into the distance were the order of the day in the Palace. Now, if I started to look at anyone, it would immediately awaken suspicious, questioning thoughts in him: Why is he watching me so carefully? What does he suspect me of? What does he have against me? If I watch someone else, even in complete innocence or out of mere curiosity, he will not believe in my innocence or curiosity or that I'm simply following the human instinct to gawk. Instead, he will think me too eager, suspicious, and to get the jump on me he will immediately seek to clear himself. And how can he clear himself except by dirtying the one he thought was out to dirty him?

Yes, looking was a provocation, it was blackmail, and everyone was afraid to lift his eyes, afraid that somewhere — in the air, in a corner, behind an arras, in a crack — he would see a shining eye, like a dagger. And still the unanswered questions — Who was guilty? Who had conspired? — hung over the Palace like a thundercloud. To tell the truth, everyone was suspect, and rightly so, if three of the people closest to the Emperor, men of whom the Emperor had been so proud, in whom he had placed his greatest trust, could put a gun to his head. Think about it. Mengistu, Workneh, and Dibou belonged to the chosen handful who always had access to His August Majesty, and even, if the necessity arose, had the unique right to enter the bedchamber and wake him from his sleep. Imagine, my friend, the sort of feelings His Benevolent Majesty went to bed with from then on, never knowing whether he would wake up in the morning. Oh, what ignoble burdens and distresses come with power.

And how could we save ourselves from suspicion? There is no deliverance from suspicion! Every way of behaving, every action, only deepens the suspicions and sinks us the more. If we begin to justify ourselves, alas! Immediately we hear the question, "Why, son, are you rushing to justify yourself? There must be something on your conscience, something you would rather hide, that makes you want to justify yourself." Or if we decide to show an active attitude and goodwill, again we hear the comments, "Why is he showing off so much? He must want to hide his villainy, his shameful deeds. He's out to lie in ambush." Again it's bad, maybe worse. And, as I said, we were all under suspicion, all slandered, even though His Most Gracious Majesty said nothing directly or openly, not a word — but the accusation showed so in his eyes and his way of looking at his subjects that everyone crouched, fell to the ground, and thought in fear, "I am accused." The air became heavy, thick, the pressure low, discouraging, disabling, as if one's wings had been clipped, as if something had broken inside.

His Masterful Highness knew that after such a shock some people would start to become embittered, to grow gloomily silent, to lose enthusiasm, to give in to doubts and questions, to lose hope, to grumble, to surrender to weakness and decay — and that is why he started a purge in the Palace. It was not an instantaneous and complete purge, because His Majesty opposed impious and noisy violence, preferring an exchange in careful doses, thought out, which would keep the old residents in check and in constant fear while at the same time opening the Palace to new people. These were people who wanted to live well and make careers for themselves. They came from all over the land, directed to the Palace by the Emperor's trusted deputies. They had no close knowledge of the capital's aristocracy, but because of their low birth, crudeness, and clumsy thinking, they were held in contempt by the aristocracy and felt fear and aversion for the salons. Therefore they formed their own coterie, keeping close to the person of His Most Unparalleled Highness. The kindly grace of our venerable ruler made them drunk with a feeling of omnipotence, yet how dangerous that feeling of omnipotence could be in someone who wanted to disturb the evening atmosphere of an aristocratic salon or to irritate too long and too importunately the company gathered there! Oh, great wisdom and tact are needed to conquer a salon! Wisdom — or machine-guns, which, my dear friend, you can see for yourself when you look at our tortured city today.

Gradually, these "personal people," our Emperor's chosen ones, began to fill the Palace offices, despite grumbling from members of the Crown Council, who considered the new favorites third-rate, falling far short of what ought to be required to serve the King of Kings. Yet this grumbling only proved the downright shameful naïveté of the Crown Council members, who saw weakness where His Highness saw strength, who could not comprehend the principle of strengthening by depreciating, and who remained oblivious to the fire and smoke raised only yesterday by those who had been elevated long ago and had proved themselves weak.

One important and useful characteristic of the new people was that they had no past, had never taken part in conspiracies, trailed no bedraggled tails behind them, and had nothing shameful to hide in the lining of their clothes. Indeed, they didn't even know anything about conspiracies, and how were they going to find out about them if His Noble Majesty had forbidden the history of Ethiopia to be written? Too young, brought up in distant provinces, they could not know that in 1916 His Highness himself had come to power thanks to a conspiracy; that aided by European embassies, he had staged a coup and eliminated the legal heir to the throne, Lij Yasu. That in the face of the Italian invasion he had sworn publicly to spill his blood for Ethiopia and then, when the invaders marched in, had gone by boat to England and spent the war in the quiet little town of Bath. That later he had developed such a complex about the leaders of the partisans who had remained in the country to fight the Italians that when he returned to the throne he gradually eliminated them or shoved them aside, while granting favor to the collaborators. And that he had done away with, among others, the great commander Betwoded Negash, who came out against the Emperor and wanted to proclaim a republic in the 1950s. Many other events come to mind, but in the Palace it was forbidden to talk about them, and, as I said, the new people could not know about them and did not show much curiosity. And as they had no old connections, their only chance for survival was to keep themselves tied to the throne. Their only support: the Emperor himself. And thus His Most Extraordinary Majesty created a force that, during the last ten years of his reign, propped up the Imperial Throne that Germame had undermined.

Z. S.-K.:

. . . and as the purge went on, every day when the Hour of Assignments — and therefore of demotions — drew near, we old Palace functionaries were overcome by shivering fits as we sat behind our desks. Everyone was trembling for his fate, ready to do anything to keep them from pulling that piece of furniture from under his elbows. During Mengistu's trial, fear reigned behind the desks, fear that the general would start accusing everyone of having been in on the conspiracy. Even very distant participation, even clandestine clapping, led one right to the noose. So when Mengistu pointed at no one, holding his tongue until the Day of Judgment, a winged sigh of relief arose from behind those desks. But a different fear immediately replaced the fear of the gallows: the fear of the purge, of personal destruction. His Most Benevolent Highness no longer hurled people into dungeons, but very simply sent them home from the Palace, and this sending home meant condemnation to oblivion. Until that moment you were a man of the Palace, a prominent figure, a leader, someone important, influential, respected, talked about, and listened to; all this gave one a feeling of existence, of presence in the world, of leading a full, important, useful life. Then His Highness summons you to the Hour of Assignments and sends you home forever. Everything disappears in a second. You stop existing. Nobody will mention you, nobody will put you forward or show you any respect. You may say the same words you said yesterday, but though yesterday people listened to them devoutly, today they don't pay any attention. On the street, people pass you with indifference, and you can already see that the smallest provincial functionary can tell you to go to hell. His Majesty has changed you to a weak, defenseless child and thrown you to a pack of jackals. Good luck!

And then, God forbid, what if they start investigating, sniffing around, poking into things? Although sometimes I think it's better after all if they start to sniff around. Because if they start to sniff around, at least you can come back into existence, if only in a damned and negative way. Still, at least you have being again, you stop drowning, you get your head above water, so that they say, "Look! He's still around." Otherwise, what remains? Superfluity. Nothingness. Doubt that you had ever been alive. There was such a fear of the precipice in the Palace that everyone tried to hold on to His Majesty, still not knowing that the whole court — though slowly and with dignity — was sliding toward the edge of the cliff.

P. M.:

Indeed, my friend, from the moment smoke rose from the Palace a sort of negativism started to flood over us. I have trouble pinning it down, but you could feel negativism all around. You noticed it everywhere on people's faces, faces that seemed diminished and abandoned, without light or energy, in what people did and how they did it. There was negativism in what they said without speaking; in their absent being, as if shrunken, switched off; in their burnt-out existence; in their short-range, small-stuff thinking; in their vegetable-patch, cottage-garden digging; in their weed-grown, overcast look; in the whole atmosphere; in all the immobility — despite the moving around — of the daily grind; in the climate; in the mincing steps. In everything you could feel the negativism flooding over us.

Even though the Emperor went on issuing decrees and striving to get things done, got up early and never rested, all the same the negativism was there, growing all the time, because from the day Germame committed suicide and his brother was captured to be hanged in the main square of the town, a negative system started operating between people and things. People seemed unable to control things; things existed and ceased to exist in their own malicious ways, slipping through people's hands. Everyone felt helpless before the seemingly magic force by which things autonomously appeared and disappeared, and nobody knew how to master or break that force. This feeling of helplessness, of always losing, always falling behind the stronger, drove them deeper into negativism, into numbness, into dejection, into depression, into hiding like partridges. Even conversation deteriorated, losing its vigor and momentum. Conversations started but somehow never seemed to be completed. They always reached an invisible but perceptible point, beyond which silence fell. The silence said, "Everything is already known and clear, but clear in an obscure way, known unfathomably, dominating by being beyond helping." Having confirmed this truth by a moment of silence, the conversation changed its direction and moved on to a different subject, a trivial, second-rate, secondhand subject.

The Palace was sinking, and we all felt it, we veterans in the service of His Venerable Majesty, we whom fate had saved from the purge. We could feel the temperature falling, life becoming more and more precisely framed by ritual but more and more cut-and-dried, banal, negative.

He goes on to say that even though the Emperor considered the December upheaval to be over and done with and never returned to the subject, the coup staged by the Neway brothers continued to have destructive consequences for the Palace. As time passed, these consequences grew more powerful rather than weaker, and they changed the life of the Palace and the Empire. Having suffered such a blow, the Palace would never again know true, sweet peace.

Things were gradually changing in town, too. The first mention of disturbances appeared in the secret reports by the police. Fortunately, as my informant says, these were not yet disturbances on a great, revolutionary scale, but rather — at first — tremors, slight oscillations, ambiguous murmurs, whispers, sniggering, a sort of excessive heaviness in people, lying around, drooping, a certain messiness, all expressing some kind of avoidance and refusal. He admits that cleanup operations couldn't start on the basis of these reports. The information was too vague, even comfortingly innocent; it stated that something was hanging in the air, without saying precisely what and where. And without specifics, where was one to send the tanks, and in what direction order the shooting? Usually the reports stated that these murmurs and whispers came from the university — a new one, the only institution of higher learning in the country — in which, from God knows where, there had appeared skeptical, unfriendly individuals, ready to spread harmful and unverified calumnies for the sole purpose of causing new anxieties for the Emperor. He goes on to say that the monarch, in spite of his advanced age, maintained a perspicacity amazing to those around him, and that he understood better than his closest followers that a new era was coming and it was time to pull together, to bring things up to date, to speed up, to catch up. To catch up, and even to overtake. Yes, he insists, even to overtake. He confesses (today one can talk about it) that a part of the Palace was reluctant to embrace these ambitions, muttering privately that instead of giving in to the temptation of certain novelties and reforms, it would be better to curb the Western inclinations of youth and root out the unreasonable idea that the country should look different, that it should be changed.

The Emperor, however, listened to neither the aristocratic grumbling nor the university whispers, believing as he did that all extremes are harmful and unnatural. Demonstrating innate concern and foresight, the Emperor widened the scope of his power and involved himself in new domains, manifesting these new interests by introducing the Hour of Development, the International Hour, and the Army-Police Hour, between four and seven in the afternoon. With the same goals in mind, the Emperor created appropriate ministries and bureaus, branch offices, and commissions, into which he introduced hosts of new people, well behaved, loyal, devoted. A new generation filled the Palace, energetically carving out careers. It was, recalls P. M., the beginning of the 1960s.

P. M.:

A kind of mania seized this mad and unpredictable world, my friend: a mania for development. Everybody wanted to develop himself! Everyone thought about developing himself, and not simply according to God's law that a man is born, develops, and dies. No, each one wanted to develop himself extraordinarily, dynamically, and powerfully, to develop himself so that everyone would admire, envy, talk, and nod his head. Where it came from, no one knows. Like a flock of sheep, people went crazy with blind greed, and it sufficed that somewhere at the other end of the world someone developed himself; immediately everyone wants to develop himself. Immediately they press, storm, urge that they be developed, too, be raised, that they catch up — and it's enough, my friend, to neglect these voices for you to get mutinies, shouts, rebellions, negativism, frustration, and refusal. Yet our Empire had existed for hundreds, even thousands of years without any noticeable development and all the while its leaders were respected, venerated, worshiped. The Emperors Zera Jakob,

Towodros, Johannes all were worshiped. And who would ever have gotten it into his head to press his face to the floor in front of the Emperor and beg to be developed?

However, the world began to change. Our Emperor, innately infallible, noticed and generously agreed with this, seeing the advantages and charms of costly novelty, and since he had always had a weakness for all progress — indeed, he even liked progress — his most honorably benevolent desire for action manifested itself in the unconcealed desire to have a satiated and happy people cry for years after, with full approval, "Hey! Did he ever develop us!" Thus, in the Hour of Development, between four and five in the afternoon, His Highness showed particular vivacity and keenness. He received processions of planners, economists, and financial specialists, talking, asking questions, encouraging, and praising. One was planning, another was building, and so, in a word, development had started. And how. His Indefatigable Majesty would ride out to open a bridge here, a building there, an airport somewhere else, giving these structures his name: the Haile Selassie Bridge in Ogaden, the Haile Selassie Hospital in Harara, the Haile Selassie Hall in the capital, so that whatever was created bore his name. He also laid cornerstones, supervised construction, cut ribbons, took part in the ceremonial starting of a tractor, and everywhere, as I said, he talked, asked questions, encouraged, and praised. A map of the Empire's development hung in the Palace, on which little arrows, stars, and dots lit up, blinking and twinkling so that the dignitaries could gladden their eyes with the sight when His Venerable Majesty pressed a button, although some saw in all this the proof of the Emperor's growing eccentricity. But foreign delegations, whether African or from the wider world, obviously delighted in the map, and upon hearing the Emperor's explanation of the little lights, arrows, and dots, they too talked, asked questions, encouraged, and praised.

And that is how it would have gone on for years, to the joy of His Supreme Highness and his dignitaries, had it not been for our grumbling students, who, since Germame's death, had started to raise their heads more and more, to tell horrendous stories, and to speak unreasonably and insultingly against the Palace. Instead of showing their gratitude for the benefits of enlightenment, those youngsters launched themselves on the turbid and treacherous waters of slander and faction. Alas, my friend, it is a sad truth that, despite His Majesty's having led the Empire onto the path of development, the students reproached the Palace for demagoguery and hypocrisy. How, they said, can one talk of development in the midst of utter poverty? What sort of development is it when the whole nation is being crushed by misery, whole provinces are starving, few can afford a pair of shoes, only a handful of subjects can read and write, anyone who falls seriously ill dies because there are neither hospitals nor physicians, ignorance and illiteracy hold sway everywhere, barbarity, humiliation, trampling underfoot, despotism, exploitation, desperation, and on and on in this tone, dear visitor. Reproaching, calumniating ever more arrogantly, they spoke out against sweetening and dressing things up — taking advantage of His Clement Highness, who only rarely ordered that the mutinous rabble which spilled from the university gates in a larger mass each year be fired upon.

Finally the time came when they brought out their impudent whim of reforming. Development, they said, is impossible without reform. One should give the peasants land, abolish privileges, democratize society, liquidate feudalism, and free the country from dependence on foreigners. From what dependence? I ask. We were independent. We had been an independent country for three thousand years! That's thoughtlessness and running off at the mouth for you. Besides, I ask, how do you reform, how do you reform without everything falling apart? How do you move something without bringing it all tumbling down? But was one of them ever capable of asking himself such a question? To develop and feed everybody simultaneously is also difficult, because where will the money come from? Nobody runs around the world passing out dollars. The Empire produces little and has nothing to export. So how do you fill the treasury? Our Supreme Leader treated that problem with kindly and provident solicitude, considering it a matter of the utmost importance and manifesting his concern incessantly during the International Hour.

T.:

How wonderful international life is! It suffices to recall our visits: airports, greetings, cascades of flowers, embraces, orchestras, every moment polished by protocol, and then limousines, parties, toasts written out and translated, galas and brilliance, praise, confidential conversations, global themes, etiquette, splendor, presents, suites, and finally tiredness, yes, after a whole day tiredness, but how magnificent and relaxing, how refined and honored, how dignified and proper, how — exactly — international! And the next day: sightseeing, stroking children, accepting gifts, excitement, programs, tension — but tension that is pleasant, significant, that frees one for a moment from Palace troubles, displaces Imperial worries, lets one forget about petitions, coteries, and conspiracies. His Benevolent Highness, however, even when magnificently entertained by his hosts and lit up by the popping flashbulbs, always asked about telegrams with news from the Empire, asked what was with the budget, the army, the police, the students. Even I took part in these worldly splendors, I who was only a member of the sixth decade of the eighth rank of the ninth level.

Please notice, my friend, that our monarch had an exceptional taste for foreign travel. As early as 1924, the first monarch in our history to cross the borders of the Empire, His Gracious Majesty honored the European lands with a visit. There was something of a family inclination to travel, inherited from his father, the late Prince Makonen, who had been sent abroad many times to negotiate with other countries on the orders of the Emperor Menelik. Let me add that His Majesty never lost that inclination, and, even though old age usually makes people inclined to keep close to home, His Indefatigable Majesty traveled more and more as the years went by, inspecting, visiting the most distant countries, losing himself in these peregrinations to such an extent that malicious journalists from the foreign press called him the flying ambassador of his country and asked when he planned to visit his own Empire. This is indeed an appropriate moment, my friend, to pour out all our grievances over the impropriety and maliciousness of the foreign newspapers, which instead of working toward understanding and rapprochement stand ready to commit any baseness and to meddle in internal affairs. And with delight, I may add.

I wonder now why His Venerable Majesty traveled so much in spite of the heavy burden of years that pressed upon his shoulders. It all goes back to the rebellious vanity of the Neway brothers, who forever destroyed the sweet peace of the Empire by pointing out with impious irresponsibility its backwardness and the way it lagged behind everyone else. A few of the journalists picked up such slanders and used them to calumniate His Majesty. Then the students grabbed it and read it, although no one knows how they got their hands on it, because His Most Gracious Majesty forbade the importation of slanders. And so began the pronouncements, criticism, talk of stagnancy and development. His Majesty sensed the spirit of the times, and shortly after the bloody rebellion he ordered complete development. Having done so, he had no choice but to set out on an odyssey from capital to capital, seeking aid, credits, and investment: our Empire was barefoot, skinny, with all its ribs showing. His Majesty demonstrated his superiority over the students by showing them that one can develop without reforming. And how, I hear you asking, is that possible? Well, it is. If you use foreign capital to build the factories, you don't need to reform. So there you are — His Majesty didn't allow reform, yet the factories were going up, they were built. That means development. Just take a ride from downtown toward Debre Zeit. Factories lined up one after the other, modern, automatic!

But now that His Noble Majesty has ended his days in such unseemly abandonment, I can confess that I also had my own thoughts about the Emperor's visits and travels. His Majesty looked more profoundly, more acutely, into things than any of us. He understood that the end was coming and that he was too old to stop the impending avalanche. Older and older, more and more helpless. Tired, exhausted. He needed more relief and freedom from worry. And these visits were a break, a chance for him to rest and catch his breath. At least for a while he didn't have to read the informants' reports, to listen to the roar of crowds and the sound of police gunfire, to look into the faces of toadies and flatterers. He didn't, at least for one day, have to solve the insoluble, repair the irreparable, or cure the incurable. In those foreign countries no one conspired against him, no one was sharpening the knife, no one needed to be hanged. He could go to bed calmly, sure that he would wake up alive. He could sit down with a friendly president and have a relaxing talk, man to man. Yes, my friend, allow me once more to commend the international life. Without it, who could ever bear the burden of governing these days? After all, where is one to look for recognition and understanding if not in the faraway world, in foreign countries, during those intimate conversations with other rulers who will respond to our grief with sympathetic grief, because they have worries and troubles of their own?

But it didn't all seem quite as I'm describing it to you now. Since we've already reached this degree of sincerity, let's admit that in the last years of his reign Our Benefactor had fewer successes and more problems. In spite of every endeavor, his monarchical achievements were not multiplying. And how can anyone justify not having achievements in today's world? Certainly it was possible to invent, to count things twice, to explain, but then troublemakers would immediately stand up and hurl calumnies, and by that time such indecency and perversity had spread that people would rather believe the troublemakers than the Emperor. So His Most Supreme Majesty preferred to set out abroad, to settle disputes, recommend development, lead his brother presidents onto the high road, express concern for the fate of humanity — on the one hand he saved himself from the exhausting troubles at home, and on the other he gained salutary compensation in the form of the splendors and friendly promises of other governments and other courts. You must remember that despite all the hardships of such a long life he never gave up the fight even in the moments of greatest trials and disappointments, and in spite of fatigue and the need for reward he never for a moment considered stepping down from the throne. On the contrary, as adversaries accumulated and the opposition grew, the Emperor observed the Army-Police Hour with exceptional diligence, reinforcing the order and stability necessary to the Empire.

B. H.:

First, I will emphasize that His Majesty, the highest person in the state, was above the law, since he himself constituted the only source of law, and he was not subject to any of its norms and regulations. He was supreme in everything, in all that had been created by God or man, and therefore also he was supreme commander of the army and the police. He had to exercise particular care and discrimination in his supervision of the two institutions, especially since the December events proved that shameful disorder, abusive opinions, and even sacrilegious treason had taken root among the ranks of the Imperial Guard and the police. Fortunately, the army generals had shown their loyalty in that unexpected hour of trial and made possible a dignified though painful return of the Emperor to his Palace. But having saved his throne, they now started to importune the Supreme Benefactor, asking to be paid for that service. Such was the down-to-earth attitude prevalent in the army that they computed their loyalty in money terms and even expected His Benevolent Highness, of his own initiative, to stuff their pockets full, oblivious to the fact that privileges corrupt and corruption stains the honor of the uniform. This impudence and aggressiveness spread from the army generals to the head police officers, who also wanted to be corrupted, to be showered with privileges, to have their pockets stuffed. All because, having observed the progressive weakening of the Palace, they cleverly deduced that our monarch was going to need them often and that in the end they constituted the surest, and in critical moments the only, prop of sovereign power.

And so His Unrivaled Highness had to introduce the Army-Police Hour, during which he bestowed abundant favors on the highest-ranking officers and expressed his concern about the state of those institutions that secured the internal order and stability for which the people thanked heaven. These generals, with His Gracious Majesty's help, arranged such a good life for themselves that in our Empire, which contained thirty million farmers and only a hundred thousand soldiers and police, agriculture received one percent of the national budget and the army and police forty percent. This provided the students with subject matter for their cracker-barrel philosophizing and wisecracks. But were they right? Did not His

Majesty create the first regular army in our history, an army paid out of the Imperial cashbox? Before that our armies always assembled from a levy en masse. When summoned, soldiers set out for the battlefield from all corners of the Empire, stealing whatever they could along the way, plundering the villages in their path, butchering peasants and cattle. After such incidents — and they occurred endlessly — the monarchy was a shambles and couldn't get back on its feet for a long time. So His Venerable Highness punished robbery, forbade the levy en masse, and entrusted to the British the task of forming a regular army, which they did as soon as the Italians had been pushed out.

His Distinguished Majesty had a great fondness for his army. He willingly reviewed parades, and he liked to put on his Emperor-marshall's uniform, to which rows of colorful decorations and medals added splendor. However, his Imperial dignity would not allow him to probe too deeply into the details of barracks life or to investigate the condition of the simple soldier and lower officer, and the Palace machine for deciphering military codes must have been out of order much of the time, because it came out later that the Emperor did not even know what was going on behind army walls, a state of affairs that unfortunately caught up in a disastrous way with the affairs of the Empire.

P. M.:

. . . and as a consequence of Our Benefactor's concern to develop the forces of order and thanks to his great generosity in that area, the number of policemen multiplied during the last years of his reign, and ears appeared everywhere, sticking up out of the ground, glued to the walls, flying through the air, hanging on doorknobs, hiding in offices, lurking in crowds, standing in doorways, jostling in the marketplace. To protect themselves from the plague of informers, people learned — without anyone knowing how or where, or when, without schools, without courses, without records or dictionaries — another language, mastered it, and became so fluent in it that we simple and uneducated folk suddenly became a bilingual nation. It was extremely helpful; it even saved lives and preserved the peace and allowed people to exist. Each of the two languages had a different vocabulary, a different set of meanings, even a different grammar, and yet everyone overcame these difficulties in time and learned to express himself in the proper language. One tongue served for external speech, the other for internal. The first was sweet and the second bitter, the first polished and the second coarse, one allowed to come to the surface and the other kept out of sight. And everybody made his own choice, according to conditions and circumstances, whether to expose his tongue or to hide it, to uncover it or to keep it under wraps.

M.:

And just think, my friend, amid all this flowering development, amid the success and well-being proclaimed by our monarch, suddenly an uprising breaks out. A thunderbolt from a clear blue sky! In the Palace — astonishment, surprise, running back and forth, bustle, His August Majesty asking, "Where did it come from?" And how can we, humble servants, answer him? Accidents happen to people, don't they? So they can also happen to an Empire, and in 1968 this is what happened to us: in Gojam Province the peasants jumped on their rulers' throats. All the notables found it inconceivable, because we had a docile, resigned, God-fearing people not at all inclined to rebellion, and here, as I said, suddenly, for no reason whatever — mutiny! To us humility is uppermost and even His Majesty, as a young lad, kissed his father's shoes. When the elders were eating, children had to stand with their faces to the wall to avoid any ungodly temptation of considering themselves equal to their parents. I mention this, dear friend, to help you understand that if the peasants in such a country go on a rampage, they must have an extraordinary reason.

Let us admit here that the reason was a certain clumsy overzealousness of the Finance Ministry. These were the years of enforced development, which brought us so many worries. Why worries? Because in advocating progress His Highness whetted the appetites and whims of his subjects. Eager to be thus encouraged, the people thought that development meant pleasure and treats, and they kept demanding provender and progress, delicacies in excess. But the greatest troubles sprang from the progress in enlightenment, because the multiplying numbers of school graduates had to be placed in offices, thereby causing the ascendancy of the bureaucracy, which waxed enormous as His Majesty's cashbox waned. And how can you make clerks tighten their belts when they are the most stable and loyal element? A clerk will slander you behind your back, grumble secretly, but when called to order he will shut up and, if need be, turn out to support you. You can't put the courtiers on hard rations, either, because they are the Palace family. Nor the officers — they secure peaceful development. And so during the Hour of the Cashbox a multitude of people showed up, and the purse dwindled away because every day His Benevolent Majesty had to pay more for loyalty.

Since the cost of loyalty was going up, there was an urgent need to increase income, and that's why the Finance Ministry ordered the peasants to pay higher taxes. Today I am free to say that it was His Unrivaled Majesty's decision, but because the Emperor, as a gracious benefactor, could not issue vexatious or plaguing decrees, any proclamation that put a new burden on the shoulders of the people was issued in the name of some ministry. If the people could not shoulder that burden and started a rebellion, His Majesty scolded the ministry and replaced the minister — although he never did so immediately, to avoid creating the humiliating impression that the monarch allows the unbridled mob to put his Palace in order. On the contrary, when he saw the need to demonstrate monarchical supremacy he would raise the most disliked officials to higher positions, as if to say, "Get an eyeload of who's really in charge here, of who makes the impossible possible!" His Noble Majesty asserted his force and authority by benevolently needling his subjects.

Yet now, my gracious sir, reports are coming in from Gojam Province that the peasants are brawling, rebelling, bashing in the skulls of tax collectors, hanging policemen, running dignitaries out of town, burning down estates, uprooting crops. The governor reports that rebels are storming the offices and that whenever they get their hands on the Emperor's people they vilify them, torture them, and quarter them. Obviously, the longer the submissiveness, the silence, and the shouldering of burdens, the greater the hostility and cruelty. And in the capital the students defend the rebels, praising them, pointing a finger at the court, hurling insults. Fortunately that province is so situated that it could be cut off, surrounded by the army, shot up, and bled into submission. But until that was accomplished you could sense a great fear in the Palace, because you never can tell how far boiling water will spill. That is why His Providential Majesty, seeing the Empire wobbling, first sent the strike force to Gojam to take the peasants' heads off, then, confronting the incomprehensible resistance put up by the rebels, ordered the new taxes repealed and scolded the ministry for its overzealousness.

His August Majesty chided the bureaucrats for failing to understand a simple principle: the principle of the second bag.

Because the people never revolt just because they have to carry a heavy load, or because of exploitation. They don't know life without exploitation, they don't even know that such a life exists. How can they desire what they cannot imagine? The people will revolt only when, in a single movement, someone tries to throw a second burden, a second heavy bag, onto their backs. The peasant will fall face down into the mud — and then spring up and grab an ax. He'll grab an ax, my gracious sir, not because he simply can't sustain this new burden — he could carry it — he will rise because he feels that, in throwing the second burden onto his back suddenly and stealthily, you have tried to cheat him, you have treated him like an unthinking animal, you have trampled what remains of his already strangled dignity, taken him for an idiot who doesn't see, feel, or understand. A man doesn't seize an ax in defense of his wallet, but in defense of his dignity, and that, dear sir, is why His Majesty scolded the clerks. For their own convenience and vanity, instead of adding the burden bit by bit, in little bags, they tried to heave a whole big sack on at once.

So, in order to ensure future peace for the Empire, His Majesty immediately set the clerks to work sewing little bags. He had them add to the burden in little bags, taking a break between one bag and the next and keenly watching the expressions on the faces of the burdened, judging whether or not they can stand a little more, whether one should add a wee bit or let them breathe for a while. In that, my dear friend, lay the whole art: in not doing it all at once thickly and blindly, but rather carefully, kindly, reading the faces to know when to add, when to tighten the screw and when to loosen it. Thus, after some time had passed and the blood had soaked into the ground and the wind had blown away the smoke, the clerks started adding taxes again, but this time they dosed it and bagged it gently, carefully, and the peasants bore it all and took no offense.

Z. S.-K.:

A year after the Gojam uprising — which by showing the furious and unrelenting face of the people stirred the Palace and threw a fright into the dignitaries (and not only them: we servants also started getting the creeps) — a singular misfortune happened to me: my son Hailu, a university student in those depressing years, began to think. That's right, he began to think, and I must explain to you, my friend, that in those days thinking was a painful inconvenience and a troubling deformity. His Unexcelled Majesty, in his incessant care for the good and comfort of his subjects, never spared any efforts to protect them from this inconvenience and deformity. Why should they waste the time that ought to be devoted to the cause of development, why should they disturb their internal peace and stuff their heads with all sorts of disloyal ideas? Nothing decent or comforting could result if someone decided to think restlessly and provocatively or mingle with those who were thinking. And yet my harebrained son committed exactly that indiscretion. My wife was the first to notice it. Her maternal instinct told her that dark clouds were gathering over our home, and she said to me one day, "Hailu must have started to think. You can see that he's sad." That's how it was then. Those who surveyed the Empire and pondered their surroundings walked sadly and lost in thought, their eyes full of troubled pensiveness, as if they had a presentiment of something vague and unspeakable. Most often one saw such faces among students, who, let me add, were causing His Majesty a lot of grief. It truly amazes me that the police never caught the scent, the connection between thinking and mood. Had they made that discovery in time they could easily have neutralized these thinkers, who by their snorting and malicious reluctance to show satisfaction brought so many troubles and afflictions on His Venerable Majesty's head.

The Emperor, however, showing more perspicacity than his

police, understood that sadness can drive one to thinking, disappointment, waffling, and shuffling, and so he ordered distractions, merriment, festivities, and masquerades for the whole Empire. His Noble Majesty himself had the Palace illuminated, threw banquets for the poor, and incited people to gaiety. When they had guzzled and gamboled, they gave praise to their King. This went on for years, and the distractions so filled people's heads, so corked them up, that they could talk of nothing but having fun. Our feet are bare, but we're debonair, hey ho! Only the thinkers, who saw everything getting gray, shrunken, mud-splashed, and moldy, skipped the jokes and the merriment. They became a nuisance. The unthinking ones were wiser; they didn't let themselves get taken in, and when the students started holding rallies and talking, the nonthinkers stuffed their ears and made themselves scarce. What's the use of knowing, when it's better not to know? Why do it the hard way, when it can be easy? Why talk, if you're better off keeping your mouth shut? Why get mixed up in the affairs of the Empire, when there's so much to do closer to home, when there's shopping to be done?

Well, my friend, seeing what a dangerous course my son was sailing, I tried to dissuade him, to encourage him to participate in amusements, to send him on excursions. I would even have preferred that he devote himself to nightlife rather than to those damned demonstrations and conspiracies. Just imagine my pain, my distress: the father in the Palace, the son in the anti-Palace. In the streets I'm protected by the police from my own son, who demonstrates and throws rocks. I told him over and over again, "Why don't you give up thinking? It doesn't get you anywhere. Forget it. Fool around instead. Look at other people, those who listen to the wise — how cheerfully they walk around, laugh. No clouds on their foreheads. They devote themselves to the good life, and if they worry about anything it's about how to fill their pockets, and to such concerns and solicitations His Majesty is always kindly inclined, always thinking of how to make things smooth and cozy." "And how," asks Hailu, "can there be a contradiction between a person who thinks and a wise person? If a person doesn't think, he's a fool." "Not at all," I say. "Wise he still is — it's just that he has directed his thoughts to a safe, sheltered place, and not between rumbling, crushing millstones." But it was too late. Hailu was already living in a different world; by then the university, located not far from the Palace, had turned itself into a real anti-Palace where only the brave set foot, and the space between the court and the university increasingly resembled a battlefield on which the fate of the Empire was being decided.

His thoughts return to the December events, when the commander of the Imperial Guard, Mengistu Neway, came to the university to show the students the dry bread with which the rebels had fed those closest to the Emperor. This event was a shock that the students never forgot. One of Haile Selassie's closest and most trusted officers represented the Emperor — a divine being, with supernatural attributes — as a man who tolerated corruption in the Palace, defended a backward system, and accepted the misery of millions of his subjects. That day the fight began, and the university never again knew peace. The tumultuous conflict between the Palace and the university, lasting almost fourteen years, engulfed scores of victims and ended only with the overthrow of the Emperor.

In those years there existed two images of Haile Selassie. One, known to international opinion, presented the Emperor as a rather exotic, gallant monarch, distinguished by indefatigable energy, a sharp mind, and profound sensitivity, a man who made a stand against Mussolini, recovered his Empire and his throne, and had ambitions of developing his country and playing an important role in the world. The other image, formed gradually by a critical and initially small segment of Ethiopian opinion, showed the monarch as a ruler committed to defending his power at any cost, a man who was above all a great demagogue and a theatrical paternalist who used words and gestures to mask the corruption and servility of a ruling elite that he had created and coddled. And, as often happens, both these images were correct. Haile Selassie had a complex personality, and to some he was full of charm while among others he provoked hatred. Some adored him, while others cursed him. He ruled a country that knew only the cruelest methods of fighting for power (or of keeping it), in which free elections were replaced by poison and the dagger, discussions by shooting and the gallows. He was a product of this tradition, and he himself fell back upon it. Yet at the same time he understood that there was an impossibility in it, that it was out of touch with the new world. But he could not change the system that kept him in power, and for him power came first. Hence the flights into demagoguery, into ceremony, into speeches about development — all so very empty in this country of oppressive misery and ignorance. He was a most amiable personage, a shrewd politician, a tragic father, a pathological miser. He condemned innocence to death and pardoned guilt. Whims of power, labyrinths of Palace politics, ambiguity, darkness that no one could penetrate.

Z. S.-K.:

Immediately after the Gojam uprising, Prince Kassa wanted to gather loyal students and stage a demonstration in support of the Emperor. Everything was prepared, portraits and banners, when His Noble Majesty found out about it and rebuked the prince sharply. All demonstrations were out of the question. They begin with support and end up with invective. They start with cheering, and end with shooting. Once more, my friend, you see here the awe-inspiring prescience of His Supreme Highness. In the general confusion they didn't manage to call off the demonstration. When the march of the supporters, composed of policemen disguised as students, started, a great and rebellious mass of real students quickly joined it, this ominous rabble started rolling toward the Palace, and there was no other solution but to bring out the army to enforce the restoration of order. In this unfortunate confrontation, which ended in bloodshed, the leader of the students, Tilahum Gizaw, perished. What an irony it was that several of the policemen died, too, and yet were they not completely innocent? This, I remember, was at the end of 1969.

The next day was awful for me. Hailu and all his friends went to the funeral, and such a crowd gathered at the coffin that it turned into a new demonstration. The continuous ferment and unrest in the capital could no longer be tolerated, so His Distinguished Majesty sent in armored personnel carriers and commanded that order be restored in no uncertain terms. As a result more than twenty students perished and countless others were wounded and arrested. His Highness ordered that the university be closed for a year, thus saving the lives of many young people. Because if they had been studying, demonstrating, and storming the Palace, the Emperor would have had to respond again by clubbing, shooting, and spilling blood.

THE COLLAPSE

It is an amazing thing, the extraordinary feeling of security in which all those tenants of the highest and middle stories of the social edifice were living when the revolution broke out. In all naïveté of spirit they were discoursing on the people's virtues, greatness, and loyalty, of their innocent joys, when the year '93 was hanging over them: a comic and terrible sight.

(de Tocqueville, *The Ancien Régime and the Revolution*)

And something else besides, something invisible, a directing spirit of perdition that dwelt within.

(Conrad, *Lord Jim*)

On the other hand, the courtiers of Justinian who stayed at his side in the palace until the late hours had the impression that, instead of him, they saw a strange phantom. One of them claimed that the Emperor would spring suddenly from the throne and start pacing up and down the chamber (indeed, he could no longer stay in one place); all of a sudden Justinian's head would disappear, but the body would go on pacing. The courtier, thinking his eyesight had betrayed him, stood for a long while helpless and confused. Afterward, however, when the head returned to its place on the torso, he found himself amazed to see what had not been there a moment ago.

(Procopius, *The Secret History*)

Next I ask myself the question, Where is it all now? Smoke, ashes, fable. Or perhaps it is no longer even a fable.

(Marcus Aurelius, *Meditations*)

Nobody's candle keeps burning until the very dawn.

(Ivo Andrić, *The Consuls of Their Imperial Highnesses*)

M. S.:

For many years I served as mortarman to His Most Extraordinary Highness. I used to set up the mortar near the place where the kindly monarch gave feasts for the poor, who craved food. As the banquet was ending, I would fire a series of projectiles. When they burst, these projectiles released a colored cloud that slowly floated to the ground — colored handkerchiefs bearing the likeness of the Emperor. The people crowded, pushing each other, stretching out their hands, everyone wanting to return home with a picture of His Highness that had miraculously dropped from the sky.

A. A.:

Nobody, but nobody, my friend, had any foreboding that the end was drawing near. Or rather, one did sense something, something haunting, but so vague, so indistinct, that it was not like a presentiment of the extraordinary. For a long time there had been a valet de chambre who floated around the Palace, turning off lights here and there. But one's eyes got used to the dimness, and there followed a comfortable inner resignation to the fact that everything had to be turned off, extinguished, obscured. What's more, shameful disorder crept into the Empire, disorder that caused annoyance to the whole Palace, but most of all to our Minister of Information, Mr. Tesfaye Gebre-Egzy, later shot by the rebels who rule today.

This is how it began. In 1973, in the summer, a certain Jonathan Dimbleby, a journalist from London television, came to our country. He had visited the Empire before and made commendable films about His Supreme Majesty, and so it occurred to no one that such a journalist, who had earlier praised, would dare to criticize later. But such is obviously the dastardly nature of people without dignity or faith. Anyway, this time, instead of showing how His Highness attends to development and cares for the prosperity of the little ones, Dimbleby went up north, from where he supposedly returned perturbed and shaken. Right away he left for England. A month hadn't passed when a report came from our embassy there that Mr. Dimbleby had shown a film entitled *Ethiopia: The Unknown Famine* on London TV, in which this unprincipled calumniator pulled the demagogic trick of showing thousands of people dying of hunger, and next to that His Venerable Highness feasting with dignitaries. Then he showed roads on which scores of poor, famished skeletons were lying, and immediately afterward our airplanes bringing champagne and caviar from Europe. Here, whole fields of dying scrags; there, His Highness serving meat to his dogs from a silver platter. This, then that: splendor — misery, riches — despair, corruption — death. In addition, Mr. Dimbleby announced that hunger had already caused the death of a hundred thousand people, perhaps even two hundred thousand, and that twice that number might share their fate in the very near future. The report from the embassy said that after the film was shown, a great scandal broke out in London. There were appeals to Parliament, the newspapers raised alarms, His Royal Highness was condemned.

Here you can see, my friend, the irresponsibility of the foreign press, which like Mr. Dimbleby praised our monarch for years and then suddenly, without any rhyme or reason, condemned him. Why? Why such treason and immorality? The embassy reports that a whole airplaneload of European journalists is taking off from London, to come see death from hunger, to know our reality, and to determine where the money goes that their governments have given to His August Majesty for development, catching up, and surpassing. Bluntly speaking, interference in the internal affairs of the Empire! In the Palace, commotion and indignation, but His Most Singular

Highness counsels calm and discretion. Now we await the highest decisions. Right away voices sound for recalling the ambassador, who sent such unpleasant and alarming reports and brought so much unrest into the Palace. However, the Minister of Foreign Affairs argues that such a recall will put fear into the remaining ambassadors and make them stop reporting, and yet His Venerable Highness needs to know what is said about him in various parts of the world. Next the members of the Crown Council speak up, demanding that the airplane carrying the journalists be turned back and that none of the blasphemous rabble be let into the Empire. But how, asks the Minister of Information, can we not let them in? They'll raise hell and condemn His Gracious Majesty more than ever.

After much deliberation they decide to offer His Benevolent Highness the following solution: let them in, but deny the hunger. Keep them in Addis Ababa, show them the development, and let them write only what can be read in our newspapers. And I'll go so far, my friend, as to say that we had a loyal press — yes, loyal in an exemplary way. To tell the truth, there wasn't much of it, because for over thirty million subjects twenty-five thousand copies were printed daily, but His Highness worked on the assumption that even the most loyal press should not be given in abundance, because that might create a habit of reading, and from there it is only a single step to the habit of thinking, and it is well known what inconveniences, vexations, troubles, and worries thinking causes. For even what is written loyally can be read disloyally. Someone will start to read a loyal text, then he will want a disloyal one, and so he will follow the road that leads him away from the throne, away from development, and straight toward the malcontents. No, no, His Majesty could not allow such demoralization to happen, such straying, and that's why in general he wasn't an enthusiast of excessive reading.

Soon afterward we suffered a real invasion of foreign

correspondents. A press conference took place immediately after their arrival. "What," they ask, "does the problem of death from hunger, which decimates the population, look like?" "I know nothing of any such matter," answers the Minister of Information, and I must tell you, friend, that he wasn't far from the truth. First of all, death from hunger had existed in our Empire for hundreds of years, an everyday, natural thing, and it never occurred to anyone to make any noise about it. Drought would come and the earth would dry up, the cattle would drop dead, the peasants would starve. Ordinary, in accordance with the laws of nature and the eternal order of things. Since this was eternal and normal, none of the dignitaries would dare to bother His Most Exalted Highness with the news that in such and such a province a given person had died of hunger. Of course, His Benevolent Highness visited the provinces himself, but it was not his custom to stop in poor regions where there was hunger, and anyway how much can one see during official visits? Palace people didn't spend much time in the provinces either, because it was enough for a man to leave the Palace and they would gossip about him, report on him, so that when he came back he would find that his enemies had moved him closer to the street. So how were we to know that there was unusual hunger up north?

"Can we," ask the correspondents, "go north?" "No, you can't," explains the minister, "because the roads are full of bandits." Again, I must remark, he wasn't far from the truth, because increased incidents of armed disloyalty near highways all over the Empire had been much reported of late. And then the minister took them for an excursion around the capital, showing them factories and praising the development. But with that gang, forget it! They don't want development, they demand hunger and that's all there is to it. "Well," says the minister, "you won't get hunger. How can there be hunger if there is development?"

But here, my friend, there was a new development. Our rebellious students sent their delegates north, and they came back with photographs and terrible stories about how the nation is dying — and all this they passed along to the correspondents on the sly. So a scandal broke out. You could no longer say that there was no hunger. And once more the correspondents attack, they wave the pictures, they ask what the government has done about hunger. "His Most Supreme Majesty," the minister answers, "has attached the utmost importance to this matter." "But specifically! Specifically what?" this devilish rabble cries disrespectfully. "His Majesty," the minister says calmly, "will announce in due time his intended royal decisions, assignments, and directions, because it is not fitting for ministers to do so." Finally the correspondents flew away, without seeing hunger close up. And this whole affair, conducted so smoothly and in such a dignified manner, the minister considered a success and our press called a victory, which was fine, but we feared that if the minister were to disappear tomorrow we would have nothing but sorrow. And that was exactly what happened later, when the rebels put him against the wall.

Consider also, my dear friend, that — between you and me — it is not bad for national order and a sense of national humility that the subjects be rendered skinnier, thinned down a bit. Our religion ordains a strict fast for half of all the days in the year, and our commandments say that whoever breaks the fast commits a deadly sin and begins to stink all over of hellish sulfur. During a fast day one cannot eat more than once, and then only a piece of unleavened bread with spices for seasoning. Why did our fathers impose such strict rules on us, recommending that mortification of the flesh be practiced unceasingly? It is because man is by nature a bad creature who takes damning pleasure out of giving in to temptations, especially the temptations of disobedience, possessiveness, and licentiousness. Two lusts breed in the soul of man: the lust for aggression, and the lust for telling lies. If one will not allow himself to wrong others, he will wrong himself. If he doesn't come across anyone to lie to, he will lie to himself in his own thoughts. Sweet to man is the bread of untruths, says the Book of Proverbs, and then with sand his mouth is filled up.

How, then, is one to confront this threatening creature that man seems to be, that we all are? How to tame him and daunt him? How to know that beast, how to master it? There is only one way, my friend: by weakening him. Yes, by depriving him of his vitality, because without it he will be incapable of wrong. And to weaken is exactly what fasting does. Such is our Amharic philosophy, and this is what our fathers teach us. Experience confirms it. A man starved all his life will never rebel. Up north there was no rebellion. No one raised his voice or his hand there. But just let the subject start to eat his fill and then try to take the bowl away, and immediately he rises in rebellion. The usefulness of going hungry is that a hungry man thinks only of bread. He's all wrapped up in the thought of food. He loses the remains of his vitality in that thought, and he no longer has either the desire or the will to seek pleasure through the temptation of disobedience. Just think: Who destroyed our Empire? Who reduced it to ruin? Neither those who had too much, nor those who had nothing, but those who had a bit. Yes, one should always beware of those who have a bit, because they are the worst, they are the greediest, it is they who push upward.

Z. S.-K.:

Great discontent, even condemnation and indignation, reigned in the Palace because of the disloyalty of European governments, which allowed Mr. Dimbleby and his ilk to raise such a din on the subject of starvation. Some of the dignitaries wanted to keep on denying, but that was no longer possible since the minister himself had told the correspondents that His Most Sovereign Highness attached the greatest importance to hunger. So we eagerly entered on the new road and asked the foreign benefactors for help. We ourselves do not have, so let others give what they can. Not much time had passed before good news came. Airplanes loaded with wheat landed, ships full of flour and sugar sailed in. Physicians and missionaries came, people from philanthropic organizations, students from foreign colleges, and also correspondents disguised as male nurses. The whole crowd marched north to the provinces of Tigre and Welo, and also east to Ogaden, where, they say, whole tribes had perished of hunger.

International traffic in the Empire! I'll say right off that there wasn't much joy about it in the Palace. It's never good to let so many foreigners in, since they are amazed at everything and they criticize everything. You can imagine, Mr. Richard, that our notables were not disappointed in their fears. When these missionaries, physicians, and so-called nurses reached the north, they saw a thing most amazing to them, namely, thousands dying of hunger right next door to markets and stores full of food. There is food, they say, only there was a bad harvest and the peasants had to give it all to the landowners and that's why they've got nothing left and the speculators took advantage and raised the prices so high that hardly anyone could buy wheat and that's where the misery comes from. An unpleasant affair, Mr. Richard, since it was our notables who were the speculators, and how can one call by such a name the official representatives of His Well-Beloved Highness? Official and speculator? No, no, one can't say that at all!

That's why, when the shouts of these missionaries and nurses reached the capital, voices were immediately raised demanding that these benefactors and philosophers be expelled from the Empire. But how, say the others, can we expel? We cannot possibly stop the action against hunger, since His Benevolent Majesty has attached the greatest importance to it! So once again no one knows what to do: expel — wrong; keep — also wrong. A sort of vacillation and vagueness develops, when suddenly a new thunderbolt strikes. Now the nurses and missionaries are raising hell, saying that the transports of flour and sugar are not reaching those who are starving. Something is happening, say the benefactors, so that the aid is disappearing along the way, and somebody should find out where it is getting lost. They start to poke about, to interfere, to nose around. Once more it turns out that the speculators are packing whole shipments into their warehouses, jacking up the prices, and stuffing their pockets. How this was discovered, it is difficult to say. There must have been some leaks. Things were set up so that the Empire would accept the aid and take care of distribution itself, and no one was to try to figure out where the flour and sugar were going — that would be interference. Now our students get ready for action. They shout in the streets, denounce the corrupt, mount cries for indictments. "Shame!" they scream, proclaiming the death of the Empire. The police club them, arrest them. Upheaval, seething, commotion.

During this period, Mr. Richard, my son Hailu was a rare guest in our home. The university was already engaged in open war with the Palace. This time it started with a completely trivial affair, with a small, insignificant event, so small that nobody would have noticed, nobody would have thought — and yet obviously there come such moments when the smallest event, just a trifle, any bit of nonsense, will provoke a revolution and unleash a war. That is why our police commander, General Yilma Shibeshi, was right when he ordered that no stone be left unturned, that there be no lying around but rather diligent searching with a fine-tooth comb, and that the principle never be forgotten that if a seed starts to sprout, immediately, without waiting for it to grow into something, the plant should be cut down. The general himself looked, and yet, obviously, he found nothing. The trivial event that set things off was a fashion show at the university, organized by the American Peace Corps even though all gatherings and meetings were forbidden. But His Distinguished Majesty could not forbid the Americans a show, could he? And so the students took advantage of this cheerful and carefree event to gather in an enormous crowd and set off for the Palace. And from that moment on they never again let themselves be driven back to their homes. They held meetings, they stormed implacably and vehemently, they did not yield again. And General Shibeshi was tearing his hair out, because not even to him had it occurred that a revolution could start at a fashion show.

But that is exactly how it looked to us. "Father," says Hailu, "this is the beginning of the end for all of you. We cannot live like this any longer. This death up north and the lies of the court have covered us with shame. The country is drowning in corruption, people are dying of hunger, ignorance, and barbarity everywhere. We feel ashamed of this country. And yet we have no other country, we have to dig it out of the mud ourselves. Your Palace has compromised us before the world, and such a Palace can no longer exist. We know that there is unrest in the army and unrest in the city, and now we cannot back down." Yes, Mr. Richard, among these noble but very irresponsible people one was struck by the deep feelings of shame about the state of the fatherland. For them there existed only the twentieth century, or perhaps even this twenty-first century everyone is waiting for, in which blessed justice will reign. Nothing else suited them anymore, everything else irritated them. They didn't see what they wanted to see, and so, apparently, they decided to arrange the world so that they would be able to look at it with contentment. Oh well, Mr. Richard, young people, very young people!

T. L.:

Amid all the people starving, missionaries and nurses clamoring, students rioting, and police cracking heads, His Serene Majesty went to Eritrea, where he was received by his grandson, Fleet Commander Eskinder Desta, with whom he intended to make an official cruise on the flagship *Ethiopia*. They could only manage to start one engine, however, and the cruise had to be called off. His Highness then moved on to the French ship *Protet*, where he was received on board for dinner by Hiele, the well-known admiral from Marseille. The next day, in the port of Massawa, His Most Ineffable Highness raised himself for the occasion to the rank of Grand Admiral of the Imperial Fleet, and made seven cadets officers, thereby increasing our naval power. Also he summoned the wretched notables from the north who had been accused by the missionaries and nurses of speculation and stealing from the starving, and he conferred high distinctions on them to prove that they were innocent and to curb the foreign gossip and slander.

Everything seemed to be moving along well, developing favorably and successfully and most loyally; the Empire was growing and even, as His Supreme Highness stressed, blossoming — when suddenly reports came in that those overseas benefactors who had taken upon themselves the trouble of feeding our ever-insatiable people had rebelled and were suspending shipments because our Finance Minister, Mr. Yelma Deresa, wanting to enrich the Imperial treasury, had ordered the benefactors to pay high customs fees on the aid. "You want to help?" the minister asked. "Please do, but you must pay." And they said, "What do you mean, pay? We give help! And we're supposed to pay?" "Yes," says the minister, "those are the regulations. Do you want to help in such a way that our Empire gains nothing by it?" And here, together with the minister, our press raises its voice to denounce the rebellious benefactors, saying that by suspending aid they condemn our nation to the cruelties of poverty and starvation. They oppose the Emperor and interfere in internal affairs. It was rumored, my friend, that half a million people had died of hunger, which our newspapers blamed on these shameful, infamous missionaries and nurses. Mr. Gebre-Egzy called the strategy of accusing these altruists of waste and starving the nation a success, and the newspapers unanimously confirmed his opinion.

At that very moment, amid all the publicity and writing about the new success, His Venerable Highness, having left the hospitable decks of the French vessel, returned to the capital to be greeted as humbly and thankfully as ever. And yet, if I may now say so, in this humility one sensed a certain vagueness, a sort of obscure duplicity, a sort of, well, humble lack of humility, and the thankfulness was not demonstrated eagerly, but rather reticently and sulkily. True, they did give thanks, but how passive it was, how sluggish, how ungrateful a thanksgiving! This time, as always, people fell on their faces when the procession drove by, but how could it ever compare to the old falling? In the old days, my friend, it used to be real falling — sinking to the point of losing oneself, falling into dust, into ashes, into a shivering, quivering fit on the ground, hands reaching out and beseeching mercy. And now? Sure, they fell, but it was such an unanimated falling, so sleepy, as if imposed on them, as if done only for the sake of peace — slow, lazy, simply negative. Yes, they were falling negatively, awkwardly, grimacing. It seemed to me that, even as their bodies fell, deep down they were standing. They seemed to be lying face to the ground, but in their thoughts they were sitting, acting humbly with hearts that grumbled. Nobody in the procession noticed this, however — and even if anyone had observed a certain indolence and sluggishness, he wouldn't have said anything about it, because any expression of doubt was received badly by the Palace. The nobles had little time, after all, and if one person expressed doubt, everybody else had to put aside what they were doing and dispel these doubts, remove them completely, in fact, and cheer up the doubtful one.

On his return to the Palace, His Prudent Highness accepted a denunciation from the Minister of Commerce, Ketema Yfru, who accused the Finance Minister of interrupting aid to the hungry by imposing the high customs fees. However, His Benevolent Majesty did not reprimand Mr. Yelma Deresa with a single harsh word; on the contrary, manifest satisfaction shone on the royal countenance. His Sovereign Majesty had accepted the aid unwillingly because of all the publicity that accompanied it; all the sighing and headshaking over those who were wasting away spoiled the flourishing and imposing image of the Empire, which, after all, was marching along the road of undisturbed development, catching up and even surpassing. From that moment no aid or contributions were needed. For the starvelings it had to suffice that His Munificent Highness personally attached the greatest importance to their fate, which was a very special kind of attachment, of an order higher than the highest. It provided the subjects with a soothing and uplifting hope that whenever there appeared in their lives an oppressive mischance, some tormenting difficulty, His Most Unrivaled Highness would hearten them — by attaching the greatest importance to that mischance or difficulty.

D.:

The last year! Yes, but who then could have foreseen that 1974 would be our last year? Well, yes, one did feel a sort of vagueness, a melancholy chaotic ineptness, a certain negativity, something heavy in the air, nervousness and tension, flabbiness, now dawning, now growing dark, but how did we go so quickly straight into the abyss? That's it? No more? You can look, but no more Palace. You seek, but you do not find. You ask, but no one can answer. And it began . . . well, that's the point. It began so many times, and yet it never ended. There were so many beginnings but no definite ending, and because of this unending beginning, through so many unfinished starts, your soul grew accustomed to it all. There arose a conviction that we would always wriggle out of it, lift ourselves up again, that we would hold on to whatever we had a grip on and hang on through the worst.

But this growing accustomed to things ended in a mistake. In January 1974 General Beleta Abebe stopped over in the Gode barracks on his way to an inspection in Ogaden. The next day an incredible report came to the Palace: the general has been arrested by the soldiers, who are forcing him to eat what they eat. Food so obviously rotten that some fear the general will fall ill and die. The Emperor sends in the airborne unit of his Guard, which liberates the general and takes him to the hospital. Now, sir, a scandal should break out because His Revered Majesty devoted all his attention to the army during the Army-Police Hour, continually raising its pay and increasing its budget, and suddenly it comes out that the generals have been putting all the raises into their pockets and making great fortunes. However, the Emperor did not scold any of the generals, and he ordered that the soldiers from Gode be dispersed.

After this unpleasant incident, worthy of oblivion, indicating a certain insubordination in the army — we had the biggest army in black Africa, the object of His Majesty's unabashed pride — calm set in. Only for a while, though, because a month later a new report comes in to the Palace, also unheard of! In the southern province of Sidamo, in the Negele garrison, the soldiers start a rebellion and arrest their superiors. It began because the soldiers' wells in this dinky tropical nowhere dried up and their superiors forbade the soldiers to drink from the officers' well. The soldiers lost their sense because of thirst and started a rebellion. The airborne unit of the Imperial Guard should have been sent in to pacify them, but remember, my dear sir, that this was the terrible and unimaginable month of February, when in the capital itself events of such a sudden and revolutionary nature were occurring that everyone forgot about the unruly soldiers in distant Negele, who, having seized the officers' well, were now drinking their fill. It so happened that just then it was necessary to begin stamping out a mutiny that had erupted in the very neighborhood of the Palace.

How very surprising was the cause of this violent unrest that took over the streets! The Minister of Commerce had raised the price of gasoline. In response, the taxi drivers went on strike. The next day the teachers were striking, too. The high school students came out into the streets, attacking and burning buses, and let me mention that His Impeccable Highness owned the bus company. Trying to suppress these pranks, the police catch five high school students, and in a lighthearted mood send them tumbling down a steep hillside and take potshots at the rolling boys. Three of the boys are killed and two seriously wounded. After this incident come the judgment days: confusion, despair, abuse. In support of the high schoolers, the university students move out for a demonstration, no longer thinking of learning or of grateful diligence, but only of sticking their noses into everything and undermining insolently. Now they are heading straight for the Palace, so the police shoot, club, arrest, and set the dogs on them, but nothing avails, and so to please them, to calm them, His Benevolent Highness recommends calling off the gasoline price rise. But the street doesn't want to calm down!

On top of all this, like a bolt from the blue, comes the news that the Second Division has rebelled in Eritrea. They occupy Asmara, arrest their general, lock up the provincial governor, and make a godless proclamation over the radio. They demand justice, pay raises, and humane funerals. It's tough in Eritrea, sir, where the army fights guerrillas and plenty of people die. The problem of burial had existed for a long time, which is to say that in order to limit excessive war expenses, only officers had a right to a funeral, while the bodies of the common soldiers were left to the vultures and hyenas. Such inequality now caused a rebellion. The following day the navy joins the rebels and its commander, the Emperor's grandson, flees to Djibouti. It is a great distress that a member of the royal family has to save himself in such an undignified, unworthy way. But the avalanche rolls on, my dear sir, because that very day the air force mutinies. Airplanes buzz the city and, according to rumor, drop bombs. The next day our biggest and most important division, the Fourth, rebels and immediately surrounds the capital, demanding a raise and insisting that the ministers and other dignitaries be brought to court because, the soldiers say, they corrupted themselves in an ugly way and should stand in the pillory of public opinion. Well, the Fourth Division's bursting into flames means that the conflagration is close to the Palace and everybody had better save himself quickly. That very night, His Magnanimous Highness announces a pay raise, encourages the soldiers to return to their barracks, urges calm and tranquillity. He himself, concerned about the image of the court, orders Premier Aklilu and his government to offer their resignations — that must have been a hard order for him to give because Aklilu, even though disliked and condemned by the majority, was a great favorite and confidant of the Emperor. At the same time, His Highness raised the dignitary Endelkachew, a person considered a liberal and blessed with a talent for well-turned words, to the post of premier.

N. L. E.:

At that time I was titular clerk in the computation department of the office of the grand chamberlain of the court. The change of government loaded us down with work, since our department was responsible for supervising the Emperor's instructions on the number of mentions of particular dignitaries and notables. His Highness had to take care of this matter personally, because every dignitary wanted to be mentioned all the time, and as close to His Unrivaled Majesty's name as possible. There was constant quarreling, envy and intrigue: who is mentioned and who isn't, how many times and in what order. Even though we had strict instructions and norms precisely established by the throne about who is to be mentioned and how many times, such unrestricted greed and freedom arose that we, common clerks, were pressed by the dignitaries to mention them above and beyond the set order, beyond the norms. Mention me, said one and then another, and when you need something you can count on me. Is it surprising, then, that a temptation was born to mention them, in turn, above the limit, and thus gain high-placed patrons for ourselves? The risk was great, however, since adversaries counted how often each of them was mentioned, and if they caught any surplus they immediately lodged an informant's report with His Judicious Highness, who either issued a rebuke or smoothed things over. Finally the grand chamberlain issued an order to introduce cards for the dignitaries, to record the number of times each one was mentioned, and to prepare monthly reports on the basis of which His Benevolent Highness issued additional recommendations about where to subtract and where to add. And now we had to throw away all the cards of the Aklilu cabinet and make up new ones. Special pressures were put on us, since the new ministers strove eagerly to be mentioned and each one tried to take part in receptions and celebrations in order to be mentioned on those occasions.

Very shortly after the change of cabinets, I found myself on the sidewalk because of an incomprehensible and quite unpardonable mental blackout. Once I failed to mention a new minister in the court, Mr. Yohannes Kidane, and he flew into such a rage that, in spite of my appeals for mercy, he had me fired.

March — April — May

S.:

I don't have to explain to you, my friend, that we were beset by a devilish conspiracy. If it hadn't been for that, the Palace would have stood for a thousand more years, because no Palace falls of its own accord. But what I know now, I didn't know yesterday when we were sliding toward ruin — and, in a stupor, blind, in a hellish state of asphyxiation, confident of our power, exalting in ourselves, we didn't look ahead. And all the while the street agitates without interruption. Everybody is demonstrating — students, workers, Muslims, all demand rights, strike, organize meetings, curse the government. A report comes in about a mutiny in the Third Division, stationed in Ogaden. Now our whole army is in ferment, set against authority, and only the Imperial Guard still shows any loyalty. Because of this insolent anarchy and slanderous agitation, dragging on beyond all tolerance, whispering starts in the Palace. Dignitaries watch each other warily, wondering as they watch. What will happen? What to do? The whole court smothers, crushes, fills itself with rumors, psst-psst here, psst-psst there, and they spend all their time mooning about the corridors, gathering in salons, scheming in secret, organizing meetings, cursing the nation. And the cursing, reproaching, envy, and animosity between the Palace and the street are growing reciprocally, poisoning everything.

I would say that slowly, gradually, three factions appear in the Palace. The first, the Jailers, are a fierce and inflexible coterie who demand the restoration of order and insist on arresting the malcontents, putting them behind bars, beating and hanging them. This faction is led by the Emperor's daughter Tenene Work, a sixty-two-year-old lady permanently cross and obstinate, always reproaching His Ineffable Highness for his kindness. A second faction coalesces, the Talkers, a coterie of liberals: weak people, and philosophizers, who think that one should invite the rebels to sit down at a table and talk, listen to what they say, and improve the Empire. Here the greatest voice is that of Prince Mikael Imru, an open mind, a nature ready for concessions, himself a well-traveled man who knows the developed countries. Finally, the third faction is made up of Floaters, who, I would say, are the most numerous group in the Palace. They don't think at all, but hope that like corks in water they will float on the waves of circumstance, that in the end things will somehow settle down and they will arrive successfully in a hospitable port. And when the court divided itself into the Jailers, the Talkers, and the Floaters, each coterie started voicing its arguments, but voicing them secretly, in the underground manner, because His Highness didn't like factions and hated chattering, applying pressure, and any kind of peace-shattering insistence. Yet for the very reason that the factions appeared and began slinging mud and drawing blood, biting and fighting, grinding their jaws and showing their claws, everything in the Palace came to life for a moment, the old verve returned, and it felt like home again.

L. C.:

In those days His Majesty rose from his bed with ever-increasing difficulty. Night after night he slept badly or not at all, and then he would nod off during the day. He said nothing to us, not even during meals, which he ate surrounded by his family. Only during the reports submitted during the Hour of Informants would he come to life, because his people now brought very interesting news that a conspiracy of officers had arisen in the Fourth Division, with agents placed in all the garrisons and in the police all over the Empire, but who was in that conspiracy the informants could not tell because everything was being done in such secrecy. His Venerable Majesty, said the informants afterward, listened to them eagerly but gave no orders, asked no questions. It astonished them that instead of ordering arrests and hangings, His Majesty walked around the gardens, fed the panthers, set out grain for the birds, and remained silent.

In the middle of April, amid the constant unrest in the streets, His Majesty ordered that the ceremony of the succession be organized. Dignitaries gathered in the great throne chamber, waiting and whispering about whom the Emperor would nominate as his successor. This was a new thing, because His Majesty always used to punish and condemn any sort of rumors or sly comments about the succession. Now obviously moved to the highest degree by the affair, so that his quiet voice cracked and could barely be heard, His Most Gracious Majesty announced that, bearing in mind his advanced age and the ever-more-often-heard call of the Lord of Hosts, he was nominating — after his own pious decease — his grandson Zera Yakob as the successor to his throne. This young man, twenty years old, was studying at Oxford. He was sent out of the country some time before because he was leading too free a life, thus causing great worries to his father, Prince Asfa Wossen, the only remaining son of the Emperor, who lived permanently paralyzed in a Geneva hospital. Even though such was His Majesty's will in the matter of the succession, old dignitaries and venerable members of the Crown Council started to complain and even to protest surreptitiously. They said that they would not serve under such a youngster, because to do so would be a humiliation and an offense to their advanced age and their many merits. Right away an antisuccession faction formed, one that pondered ways to summon the Dame Jailer, Tenene Work, daughter of the Emperor, to the throne. And another faction appeared immediately in favor of bringing to the throne another grandson of the Emperor, the Prince Makonen, who was being educated at an officers' school in America.

And so, my friend, in the middle of these suddenly unleashed succession intrigues that plunged the whole court into such bitter fighting that no one thought about what was going on in the Empire, quite unexpectedly and surprisingly the army enters the town at night and arrests all the ministers of the old Aklilu government. They even lock up Aklilu himself, as well as two hundred generals and high-ranking officers distinguished by their unfaltering loyalty to the Emperor. Nobody has had time to recover his senses after this exceptional blow, when news comes that the conspirators have arrested the chief of the General Staff, General Assefa Ayena, the man most loyal to the Emperor and the man who saved the throne during the December events by destroying the Neway brothers and defeating the Imperial Guard. In the Palace — an atmosphere of terror, fear, confusion, depression. The Jailers are pressing the Emperor to do something, to order the rescue of those who have been imprisoned, to drive away the students, and to hang the conspirators. His Benevolent Majesty hears out all the advice, nods his assent, gives comfort. The Talkers say that it's the last chance to sit down at the table, bring the conspirators around to one's own point of view, and repair and improve the Empire. These, too, His

Benevolent Majesty hears out, nodding approval, comforting. Days go by and the conspirators lead first one person, then another, out of the Palace and arrest him. Again the Lady Jailer reproaches His Most Puissant Majesty, saying that he doesn't defend loyal dignitaries. But apparently, my friend, it is the way of the world that the more loyally a person acts, the more of a beating he attracts, because when some faction has him pinned, His Majesty leaves him to twist in the wind. This was something the princess could not comprehend; she wanted to stick with the loyal ones until the bitter end.

May was coming, the last moment to swear in the cabinet of Premier Makonen. However, the Imperial protocol announces that the swearing-in will be difficult because half of the ministers have already been arrested, or have fled abroad, or have stopped coming near the Palace. As for the premier, the students call him names and throw stones at him, because Makonen never knew how to make people like him. Immediately after his promotion he swelled somehow; his gaze became fixed in the distance and so hazed over that he did not recognize anyone. No one could tame him. Some lofty force propelled him through the corridors and made him appear in salons, where he stalked in inaccessible and stalked out unreachable. And wherever he appeared he would start a worship service around himself, for himself. Others kept it going, hosannaing it up, incensing it up, with adoration, incantation, and supplication for mediation. It was already obvious that Makonen could not long remain in power, because neither the soldiers nor the students wanted him. I can't even remember whether the swearing-in finally took place or not, because they kept locking up one minister after another. You must realize, my friend, that the cunning of our conspirators was remarkable. Whenever they arrested someone, they immediately announced that they had done so in the name of the Emperor, and right away they would emphasize their loyalty to His Majesty. This made him very happy, because whenever Tenene Work came to her father to denounce the army, he would scold her, praising the fidelity and devotion of his army. He soon received new proof of this, for in the beginning of May war veterans organized a demonstration of loyalty in front of the Palace, raising their voices in praise of His August Majesty, and the noble monarch came out onto the balcony, thanked his army for its unshakable loyalty, and wished it further prosperity and success.

June — July

U. Z.-W.:

In the Palace, dejection, discouragement, fearful waiting for whatever might happen tomorrow — when suddenly His Majesty summons his counselors, reprimands them for neglecting development, and after giving them a scolding announces that we are going to construct dams on the Nile. But how can we erect dams, the confused advisers grumble, when the provinces are starving, the nation is restless, the Talkers are whispering about straightening out the Empire, and the officers are conspiring and rounding up the notables? Immediately, audacious rumors are heard in the corridors saying that it would be better to help the starving and forget about the dams. To this the Finance Minister replies that if the dams are built, it will be possible to let water into the fields and such an abundant harvest will result that there will be no more death from starvation. Well, yes, murmur those who had been whispering, but how long will it take to build the dams? In the meantime the nation will die of hunger. "The nation isn't going to die," explains the Finance Minister. "It hasn't died yet, so it isn't going to die now. And if we don't build the dams," he asks, "how are we going to catch up and surpass?" "But against whom are we supposed to be racing, anyway?" murmur the whisperers. "What do you mean, whom?" says the Finance Minister. "Egypt, of course." "But Egypt, sir, is wealthier than we are, and even Egypt couldn't put up dams out of its own pocket. Where are we supposed to find the funds for our dams?" Here the minister really lost his temper with the doubting, and began lecturing them, telling them how important it is to sacrifice oneself for development. Besides, His Majesty has ordered, has he not, that we all develop constantly, without resting even for a moment, putting our hearts and souls into it. And the Minister of Information immediately announced His Venerable Majesty's decision as a new success, and I remember that in the twinkling of an eye the following slogan appeared in the streets of the capital:

> As soon as the work on the dams is done,
> Wealth will accrue to everyone!
> Let the slanderers spew their lies and shams—
> They will suffer in hell for opposing our dams!

Nevertheless, this affair so infuriated the conspiring officers that the Imperial Council established by His Unrivaled Highness for the special purpose of supervising the dams was thrown into jail a few days later, on the grounds that nothing could come of the dams but increased corruption and more starvation among the people. I have always been of the opinion, however, that this action on the part of the officers must have brought particular grief to His Majesty. He felt that the years were burdening his shoulders with an ever-increasing weight, and so he wanted to leave an imposing and universally admired monument after himself. That way, many years hence, everyone who could get to the Imperial Dams would cry out, "Behold, all ye! Who but the Emperor could have caused such things to be done, such extraordinary, wondrous things, whole mountains flung across the river!"

Or, to look at it from another angle, were he to give ear to the whispers and murmurs that it would be better to feed the hungry than to build dams . . . well, the hungry, even if they are satiated at last, will eventually die, leaving behind not a trace — neither of themselves, nor of the Emperor.

The one I am talking to ponders for a long time whether the Emperor had already begun to think about his departure. He had appointed his successor to the throne, hadn't he, and ordered the creation of an eternal monument to himself in the form of those dams along the Nile. (How extravagant an idea when juxtaposed with the other, burning needs of the Empire!) However, he thinks there was more to it. In naming his young grandson as his successor to the throne, the Emperor was punishing his son for the disgraceful role he had played in the events of December 1960. By ordering the construction of dams on the Nile, he wanted to prove that the Empire was growing and flourishing and that all the slanders about poverty and corruption were only the malicious chatter of those opposed to monarchy. In reality, the thought of leaving was completely alien to the Emperor's nature; he treated the state as his personal creation, and believed that with his departure the country would fall apart and disappear. Was he to annihilate his own creation? Moreover, was he to leave the walls of the Palace and expose himself of his own free will to the blows of enemies who lurked in waiting? No, departure from the Palace could not be considered; instead, after short attacks of senile depression, the Emperor seemed to rise from the dead, become more lively, acquire new vigor, and it was even possible to see pride on his aged face — that he was so fit, had such presence of mind, and remained so masterful.

June came, the month in which the conspirators, having strengthened themselves, finally renewed their cunning attacks against the Palace. Their cunning consisted in this: they carried out all their destruction of the system with the Emperor's name on their lips, as if executing his will and humbly realizing his thoughts. Now — claiming to do so in the name of the Emperor — they created a commission to investigate corruption among dignitaries, checking their accounts, landholdings, and all other riches. The people of the Palace were overcome by terror because in a poor country, in which the only source of property is not hard work and productivity but extraordinary privilege, no dignitary could have a clear conscience. The more cowardly ones thought of fleeing abroad, but the military closed the airport and put a ban on leaving the country. A new wave of arrests started. People disappeared from the Palace every night; the court became more and more deserted. A great commotion was caused by news of the imprisonment of Prince Asrate Kassa, who presided over the Crown Council and was, after the Emperor, the most important person in the monarchy. The Minister of Foreign Affairs, Minassie Haile, also found himself in prison, as did over a hundred other dignitaries. At the same time, the army occupied the radio station and announced for the first time that a coordinating committee of the armed forces and the police stood at the head of the movement for renewal, acting — as they kept claiming — in the name of the Emperor.

C.:

The whole world stood on its head, my friend, because strange signs appeared in the sky. The moon and Jupiter, stopping in the seventh and twelfth houses instead of turning in the direction of the triangle, began ominously to form the figure of a square. Accordingly, the Indians who explained the signs at court now fled the Palace, probably because they were afraid to disturb His Venerable Majesty with a bad omen. But Princess Tenene Work must still have had meetings with these Indians, because she would run through the Palace perturbed, upsetting His August Majesty, urging him to order imprisonments and hangings. And the remaining Jailers also pressed His Noble Majesty — and even begged him on their knees — to stop the conspirators, to put them behind bars. They were completely dumbfounded, however, completely unable to understand, when they saw that His Most Singular Majesty wore his military uniform all the time (medals jingling), and carried his marshall's baton, as if he wanted to show that he still commanded his army, still stood at its head, and still gave the orders. No matter that this army had designs against the Palace. Well, so it had, but under his command it was a faithful, loyal army, which did everything in the Emperor's name. They rebelled? Yes, but they rebelled loyally!

That's it, my friend — His Venerable Majesty wanted to rule over everything. Even if there was a rebellion, he wanted to rule over the rebellion, to command a mutiny, even if it was directed against his own reign. The Jailers murmur that stupor must have come over His Majesty if he can't understand that by acting the way he does he is supervising his own fall. But His Kindly Majesty does not listen to anyone. He receives in the Palace a delegation of that military committee called "Dergue" in the Amharic language, locks himself in his office with the delegation, and starts conferring with the conspirators! At that moment, my friend, I must confess with shame that one could hear godless and reprehensible rumors in the corridors that His Venerable Majesty has lost his mind, because in this delegation there were common corporals and sergeants, and it is unthinkable that His Majesty could sit down at the table with such low soldiery! Today it is difficult to deduce the subject of His Majesty's conference with these people, but immediately afterward new arrests started and the Palace was even more depopulated. They locked up Prince Mesfin Shileshi, a great lord with his own private army, which they immediately disarmed. They imprisoned Prince Worku Selassie, who had immense landholdings. They imprisoned the emperor's son-in-law General Abiye Abebe, the Minister of Defense. Finally they locked up Premier Endelkachew and several of his ministers. By now they were imprisoning someone every day, insisting that it was in the name of the Emperor.

The Lady Jailer kept urging her venerable father to show some firmness. "Father, stand your ground and unveil your severity!" But, to tell the truth, what sort of firmness can one show at such an advanced age? His Majesty could only use a soft approach now, and he proved his wisdom by displaying a conciliatory attitude instead of trying to overcome the opposition with toughness, intending thus to appease the conspirators. And the more the Lady demanded harshness, the more she regarded his softness with anger, and nothing could calm her or settle her nerves. But His Benevolent Majesty never lost his temper; on the contrary, he always praised her, comforted her, cheered her up. Now conspirators came to the Palace more often, and His Majesty received them, heard them out, praised their loyalty, encouraged them. The Talkers took heart, calling all the time for sitting down at the table, improving the Empire, meeting the demands of the rebels. And whenever the Talkers would present a manifesto in that spirit, His Most Exceptional Majesty would praise them for their loyalty, comfort them, and encourage them. But the Talkers were also being thinned out by the army, so their voices were heard ever more faintly.

The salons, corridors, and galleries grew more deserted each day, and yet nobody took up the defense of the Palace. Nobody gave the call to close the doors and break out the weapons. People looked at one another thinking, "Perhaps they'll take him and leave me alone. And if I raise a hue and cry against the rebels, they'll lock me up right away and leave the others in peace. So it's better to keep quiet and not know anything. Better not to leap, in order not to weep. Better to keep your peace, and avoid an early decease."

At times everybody would go to His Highness asking what to do, and Our Supreme Ruler would listen to our complaints, praise us, and encourage us. Later on, however, it became more and more difficult to gain an audience, because His Noble Majesty grew tired of listening to so much grumbling, demands, and informants' reports. Most willingly he received the ambassadors of foreign countries, and indeed all sorts of foreign representatives, because they brought him relief by praising him, comforting him, encouraging him. These ambassadors, along with the conspirators, were the last people with whom His Majesty talked before his departure, and they confirmed unanimously that he was in good health and had full presence of mind.

D.:

The remainder of the Jailers, those who were still left in the Palace, walked through the corridors calling for action. We must get moving, they said, take the offensive, stand up against the malcontents. Otherwise everything will perish in a deplorable way. But how to take the offensive when the whole court is locked up in defense, how to help if there is such helplessness, how to listen to the Talkers who call for change without saying what change? Change could come only from the monarch. It demanded his support and approval because otherwise it would become faithlessness and would meet reproof. The same was true of all favors — only His Majesty could dispense them, and what someone did not obtain from the throne, he could obtain in no other way. Thus distress reigned among the courtiers: were His Majesty no longer to exist, who would bestow favors and increase their property?

In this Palace beset by troubles and condemnation, how very much one wanted to break the passivity, to come up with something worthy, a brilliant flash that would show vigor. Whoever was still fit paced the corridors wrinkling his brow, searching for that thought, straining his head, until finally just such an idea was born: to organize the celebration of an anniversary! "What?" the Talkers cried, "occupy ourselves with an anniversary now? Nonsense. It's the last moment for us to sit down at the table and save the Empire." But the Floaters considered it a worthy, inspirational sign of vitality, and they enthusiastically started to prepare the anniversary, planning all the festivities, including a gala for the poor. The occasion, my friend, was His Majesty's completion of the eighty-second year of his life, though the students started rummaging through some old papers and set up a cry, claiming it was not eighty-two but ninety-two, because, they shouted, His Majesty had once subtracted a few years from his real age. But the students' venom could not poison the holiday that the Minister of Information — miraculously still at large — called a success and the best example of harmony and loyalty. No adversity could overcome this minister, who had such a sharp mind that in the greatest loss he could spot an advantage and turned everything around so cleverly that in failure he saw success, in unhappiness joy, in misery abundance, and in defeat good fortune. Were it not for such turning around, who could have called that sad holiday a wonderful one?

It was raining that day, a chilly rain, and mist floated in the air as His Majesty stepped out onto the balcony to make his speech. Next to him stood only a handful of soaked, depressed dignitaries — the rest were in prison or had fled the capital. There was no crowd, only the Palace servants and some soldiers from the Imperial Guard standing at the edge of an empty courtyard. His August Majesty expressed his compassion for the starving provinces and said that he would not neglect any chance to keep the Empire developing fruitfully. He also thanked the army for its loyalty, praised his subjects, encouraged them and wished them good luck. But he spoke so quietly that through the steady rain one could hardly make out individual words. And know, my friend, that I will take this memory to the grave with me, because I can still hear how His Majesty's voice breaks, and I can see how tears stream down his venerable face. And then, yes, then, for the first time, I thought to myself that everything was really coming to an end. That on this rainy day all life is seeping away, we are covered with cold, clinging fog, and the moon and Jupiter have stopped in the seventh and the twelfth houses to form a square.

All this time — it is the summer of 1974 — a great contest is going on between two shrewd antagonists: the venerable Emperor and the young officers from the Dergue. For the officers it is a game of hide-and-seek: they are trying to encircle the ancient monarch in his own Palace, in his lair. And the Emperor? His plan is subtle, but let's wait, because in a moment we will come to know his thoughts.

And other players? The other players of this dramatic and absorbing game are drawn in by the course of events; they know little of what's going on. Helpless and frightened, dignitaries and favorites rampage through the corridors of the Palace. We must remember that the Palace was a nest of mediocrity, a collection of second-rate people, and in a time of crisis such people lose their heads and think of nothing but saving their own skins. Mediocrity is dangerous: when it feels itself threatened it becomes ruthless. Such precisely are the Jailers, who are not up to much beyond cracking the whip and spilling blood. Fear and hatred blind them, and the basest forces prod them to action: meanness, fierce egoism, fear of losing their privileges and being condemned. Dialogue with such people is impossible, senseless. The Talkers are the second group — people of goodwill but defensive by nature, wavering, compliant, and incapable of transcending the patterns of Palace thinking. They get beaten worst of all, from every side, shoved out of the way and destroyed. They try to move about in a context that has been torn in half, in which two extreme adversaries — the Jailers and the rebels — don't want their services and treat them as a flabby, superfluous race, as an obstacle, since extremists tend toward battle rather than reconciliation. Thus the Talkers understand nothing and mean nothing; history has outgrown them and passed them by. About the Floaters nothing can be said. They drift along wherever the current drags them, a school of small-fry carried away, pulled in all directions, fighting, striving for even the meanest kind of survival.

That's the fauna of the Palace, against which the group of young officers is acting — bright, intelligent men, ambitious and embittered patriots conscious of the terrible state of affairs in their fatherland, of the stupidity and helplessness of the elite, of the corruption and depravity, the misery and the humiliating dependence of the country on stronger states. They themselves, as part of the Imperial army, belong to the lower ranks of the elite; they, too, have taken advantage of privileges, so it is not poverty — which they have never experienced directly — that goads them to action, but rather the feeling of moral shame and responsibility. They have weapons, and they decide to make the best use of them. The conspiracy comes into being in the headquarters of the Fourth Division, whose barracks lie in the suburbs of Addis Ababa, actually fairly close to the Emperor's Palace. For a long time the conspirators act in the strictest secrecy — even the slightest suggestive leak could bring repressions and executions. Gradually the conspiracy penetrates other garrisons, and later the ranks of the police.

The event that hastened the confrontation between the army and the Palace was the starvation in the northern provinces. Usually it is said that periodic droughts cause bad crops and therefore starvation. But it is the elites of starving countries that propagate this idea. It is a false idea. The unjust or mistaken allocation of funds and national property is the most frequent source of hunger. There was a lot of grain in Ethiopia, but it had first been hidden by the rich and then thrown on the market at a doubled price, inaccessible to peasants and the poor. Figures about the hundreds of thousands who starved next to abundantly stocked granaries were published. On the orders of local dignitaries, the police finished off whole clans of still-living human skeletons. This situation of intense evil, of horror, of desperate absurdity, became the signal for the conspiring officers to go to work. The mutiny involved all the divisions in turn, and it was probably the army that had been the main prop of Imperial power. After a short period of bewilderment, shock, and hesitation, H. S. began to realize that he was losing his most important instrument.

At the beginning the Dergue acted in darkness, hidden in conspiracy; they didn't know how much of the army would back them.

They had workers and students behind them — that was important, but the majority of generals and higher-ranking officers were against the conspirators, and it was the generals who still commanded, still gave the orders. Step by step — that was the tactic of this revolution. If they had come out openly and at once, the disoriented part of the army might have refused to support them or might even have destroyed them. There would have been a repeat performance of the drama of 1960, when the army fired on the army and the Palace was thus preserved for another thirteen years. In any case, the Dergue itself lacked unity; sure, everyone wanted to liquidate the Palace, they wanted to change the anachronistic, worn-out, helplessly vegetating system, but quarrels went on about what to do with the person of the monarch. The Emperor had created around himself a myth, the force and vitality of which it was impossible to ascertain. He was well-liked in the world, full of personal charm, universally respected. What's more, he was the head of the Church, the Chosen One of God, the ruler of men's souls. Raise one's hand against him? It always ended in anathema and the gallows.

The members of the Dergue were people of great courage. And also, to some extent, desperadoes, since they recalled afterward that even when they had decided to stand up against the Emperor, they still didn't believe in their own chances of success. Perhaps H. S. knew something about the doubts and divisions that consumed the Dergue; after all, he possessed an extraordinarily well-developed intelligence service. Perhaps he was guided only by instinct, by his penetrating sense of tactics, by his great experience. And what if it was something else again? What if he simply didn't feel the strength to continue the battle? It seems that he alone, of the whole ruling circle, understood that the wave that had arisen could no longer be withstood. Everything crumbled; his hands were empty. So he began to yield, and more — he stopped ruling. He feigned his existence, but the ones closest to him knew that he really wasn't doing anything; he wasn't in action.

His associates are confused by this inactivity, and they lose themselves in conjectures. First one faction, then the other, presents its arguments to him, each viewpoint at odds with the other. He listens to everyone with the same attention, nods his approval, praises everyone, comforts, and encourages. Haughty, distant, reserved, aloof, he allows events to run their course, as if he were already living in a different space, a different time. Perhaps he wants to stand above the conflict as a means of giving way to the new forces, which he can't stop anyway. Perhaps he reckons that in exchange for this service these new forces will later respect and accept him. Left alone, he, an old man with one foot in the grave, won't be a danger to them, will he? And so he wants to stay? To save himself? The military begin with a small provocation: on charges of corruption, they arrest a few of the already-dismissed ministers from Aklilu's government. They wait anxiously for the Emperor's reaction. But H. S. is silent. That means that the move was successful, the first step taken. Emboldened, they go on — henceforth they put into motion the tactic of gradually dismantling the elite, of slowly and meticulously emptying the Palace. Dignitaries and notables disappear one after the other. Passive, torpid, they await their turn. Later, they all meet in the jail of the Fourth Division, in a new, peculiar, inhospitable anti-Palace. In front of the barracks gates, right next to where the Addis Ababa–Djibouti railway line passes, stands a long line of limousines — these are the princesses, the ministers' and generals' wives, shocked and terrified, bringing food and clothing to their incarcerated husbands and brothers, the prisoners of the coming order. A crowd of disturbed and excited spectators gapes at these scenes, because the street doesn't yet know what's going on; it hasn't really got through yet. The Emperor is still in the Palace and the officers are still deliberating in the division headquarters, planning the next move. The great game goes on, but its last act is approaching.

August — September

M. W. Y.:

Amid all the depression, with the sense of being crushed and pushed against a wall — a feeling that filled the Palace and all the courtiers with mournful gloom — there suddenly arrived the Swedish physicians whom His Most Exceptional Majesty had summoned long ago. Delayed by some inexplicable sluggishness they had come only now — to lead calisthenics at court. And please remember, my friend, that things were already in ruins, and whoever hadn't been thrown in the clink was awaiting his hour, stealthily making his covert way through the Palace — afraid to show his face because the rebels were clearing out the place, taking people to prison day and night. No one could slip through a net so tight. And here you were in the middle of all this rounding up and hunting down, and you had to show up for calisthenics! Who on earth can think of calisthenics, the Talkers want to know, when this is the last moment to sit down at the table and put the Empire straight, season it, make it palatable? But it was the desire of His Majesty and the Crown Council, just then, that all the Palace people should take very good care of their health, take full advantage of the blessings of nature, rest as much as necessary in comfort and affluence, breathe good — and preferably foreign — air. His Benevolent Majesty forbade any economizing in this regard, saying often that the life of the Palace people is the greatest treasure of the Empire and the most valuable resource of the monarchy. A decree to just this effect had been issued long before by His Majesty, a decree requiring the performance of these calisthenics, and since the decree was never annulled in spite of the pervasive tumult and growing commotion, we now — we, the last handful of people remaining in the Palace — had to fall in for morning calisthenics and force the greatest treasure of the Empire into supple fitness by moving our arms and our legs about. Since the calisthenics went on, as if to spite the impudent invaders who were slowly taking over the Palace, the Minister of Information called it a success and a heartening proof of the inviolable unity of our court.

The Imperial decree I spoke of also ordered anyone who exerts himself in the slightest in his governmental duties to take a little rest immediately, to go to a secluded and comfortable spot, loosen up, take deep breaths, and, having adorned himself with everyday clothing and made himself casual, to get closer to nature. And anyone who neglected these vacations, whether out of forgetfulness or overzealousness, was scolded by His August Majesty and admonished by other courtiers not to waste the treasure of the Empire, but instead to preserve the most valuable resource of the monarchy. Yet how could you get closer to nature and enjoy your rest if the officers were not letting anyone out of the Palace? If someone managed to sneak home, the rebels would be lying in ambush and seize him and throw him into jail. But the worst thing about the calisthenics was that when a group of courtiers gathered in a salon to wave their arms and legs about, the conspirators would march in and drive everyone off to jail. "People whose days are numbered doing calisthenics!" the officers snickered, making impudent jokes. This was the best proof that the officers had no respect for values and acted against the good of the Empire. Even the Swedish physicians had a fright. Eventually they lost their contracts — though they were lucky to get away with their lives. To prevent the rebels from capturing everyone at once, the grand chamberlain of the court pulled off a cunning trick by ordering that calisthenics be done in small groups. So if some fell into the trap, others would be saved, and having persevered through the worst, they would keep the Palace under their control. However, my friend, not even this cautious and ingenious stratagem helped much in the end, because by then the rebellion had grown arrogant, pounding fiercely at the Palace with a battering ram and persecuting us with exceptional relentlessness.

And so came the month of August, the last weeks of power for our supreme ruler. But do I really express myself well, using the word "power" about those last days of decline? It's so very difficult to establish where the borderline runs between true power that subdues everything, power that creates the world or destroys it — where the borderline is between living power, great, even terrifying, and the appearance of power, the empty pantomime of ruling, being one's own dummy, only playing the role, not seeing the world, not hearing it, merely looking into oneself. And it is still more difficult to say when omnipotence becomes powerlessness; good fortune, adversity, luster, tarnish. That is exactly what no one in the Palace could sense, since all gazes were so fixed that in powerlessness they saw omnipotence, in adversity good fortune, in tarnish luster. And even if someone had a different perception, how could he, without risking his head, fall to the ground at our monarch's feet and say, "Your Majesty, you are already powerless, surrounded by adversity, becoming tarnished!" The problem in the Palace was that we had no access to the truth, and we didn't recover our senses until we were behind prison fences. In each person things were comfortably divided, seeing from thinking, thinking from speaking, and no man had a place for these three faculties to meet and produce an audible voice. But in my eyes, friend, our misfortunes all started when His Most Exceptional Majesty allowed the students to gather at that fashion show and thereby gave them a chance to form a crowd and begin a demonstration, setting off the whole dissent movement. That's where the big mistake was: no movement should have been permitted, since we could exist only in immobility. The more immobile immobility is, the longer and surer its duration. And His Majesty's action was strange because he himself knew this truth very well, which was evident, for example, from the fact that his favorite stone was marble. Marble, with its silent, immobile, painstakingly polished surface, expressed His Majesty's dream that everything around him be immobile and silent, and just as smooth, evenly cut, forever settled, to adorn majesty.

A. G.:

You must know, Mr. Richard, that by early August the inside of the Palace had lost its stateliness and its awe-inspiring solemnity. There was such confusion everywhere that the remaining ceremony officials could not introduce any order. The Palace had become the last refuge for the dignitaries and notables, who came here from the whole Empire, hoping to be safer at His Majesty's side, hoping that the Emperor would save them and obtain their freedom through his entreaties to the arrogant officers. Without respect for their honors and titles, dignitaries and favorites of all ranks, levels, and distinctions now slept side by side on the carpets, sofas, and armchairs, covering themselves with curtains and drapes — over which they got into constant quarrels, since some didn't want the curtains taken down from the windows, for fear the rebellious air force would bomb the Palace if it were not kept blacked out. The others maintained that they couldn't fall asleep without covers (you have to admit that the nights then were exceptionally cold), and they selfishly pulled down the curtains and covered themselves. All these squabbles and gibes were meaningless, however, because the officers soon reconciled everyone by taking them to jail, where the contentious dignitaries couldn't count on any covers.

In those days, patrols from the Fourth Division would come to the Palace every morning. The rebellious officers would get out of their cars and order a meeting of dignitaries in the throne room. "Meeting of dignitaries! Meeting of dignitaries!" the cries of the ceremony officials resounded through the corridors. These officials were already sucking up to the officers. At the sound of this call some of the dignitaries hid in corners, but the rest, wrapped in curtains and drapes, showed up. Then the officers read their list and those whose names had been called were taken to jail.

One must remark, Mr. Richard, that His Majesty was now always dressed in his uniform, sometimes in the ceremonial uniform, sometimes in the field uniform, the battle dress in which he used to watch maneuvers. He would appear in the salons where the terrified dignitaries lay on the carpets and lounged on the sofas, asking each other what fate would descend on them when their waiting came to an end. He would comfort them, wish them success, attach the greatest importance, treat them with personal care. However, if he met a patrol of officers in the corridor, he encouraged them as well, wished them success, thanked the army for its loyalty to him; he assured them that army affairs were the object of his personal care. At this point the Jailers would angrily and venomously whisper that the officers should be hanged because they had destroyed the Empire. The kindly monarch would hear them out attentively, encourage, wish them luck, and thank them for their loyalty, underlining the fact that he valued them highly. And the indefatigable mobility of His Venerable Majesty, by which he contributed to the general welfare, never sparing his advice or directives, was called a success by Mr. Gebre-Egzy, who saw in it proof of the monarchy's resilience. Unfortunately, by calling everything a success, the minister so infuriated the officers that they dragged him from the hall and gagged him once and for all, throwing him in jail.

I lived through the blackest days of that last month as an official in the Ministry of Palace Provisions, Mr. Richard. And let me tell you that it was impossible to ascertain the number of people in our court, since the roster of dignitaries changed every day — some sneaked into the Palace counting on help, others were taken off to jail, and often someone who had sneaked in overnight would be in jail by noon. So I didn't know how much food to order from the warehouses. Sometimes there were too few servings, and the gentlemen dignitaries would have a fit, asserting that the ministry is in collusion with the rebels and wants to break down the court by hunger. On the other hand, if there were too many servings the officers would scold me for letting wastefulness reign at court. So I was planning to offer my resignation, but this gesture proved to be unnecessary since they drove us all out of the Palace anyway.

Y. Y.:

We were by now only a handful, waiting for the final and most terrible verdict, when — praise be to God! — a ray of hope appeared in the form of the lawyers who at last, after long deliberations, had prepared a revised constitution and come to His Majesty with their proposal. The proposal consisted in changing our autocratic Empire into a constitutional monarchy, creating a strong government and leaving to His Venerable Highness only as much power as the British kings have. The distinguished gentlemen started reading the proposal immediately, dividing into small groups and hiding in secret corners, because whenever the officers noticed a larger gathering they jailed them right away. Unfortunately, my friend, the Jailers opposed this proposal, insisting that absolute monarchy should be preserved, the full power by notables and dignitaries in the provinces maintained, and the delusions about constitutional monarchy, coming as they did from the moribund British Empire, thrown to the dogs. Here, however, the Talkers started jumping down the Jailers' throats, saying that it was the last moment to improve the Empire through constitutional change, season it, make it palatable. And so, quarreling, they went to His Merciful Highness, who was just then receiving the delegation of lawyers and looking into the details of their proposal with personal attention, attaching the greatest importance to their ideas. Now, having listened to the sulking of the Jailers and the flattery of the Talkers, he praised all, encouraged, and wished everyone success. But someone must have run off to the officers and informed, because hardly had the lawyers emerged from His Enlightened Majesty's office when they ran into the military, who immediately snatched the proposal from them, ordered them to go home, and forbade them to return to the Palace.

Life inside the Palace seemed strange, as if existing only of itself and for itself. When I went to town as an official of the Palace post office, I would see normal life — cars driving through the streets, children playing, people selling and buying, old men sitting, talking away — and every day I would pass from one existence to another, no longer knowing which one was real, and feeling that it was sufficient for me to go into the city, to mingle with the crowds, for the whole Palace to vanish from memory. It would disappear, as if it didn't exist, to the point of making me anxious that when I came back I wouldn't find it there.

E.:

He spent the last days alone in the Palace, with only his old valet de chambre for company. Apparently the group in favor of closing the Palace and dethroning the Emperor had gained the upper hand in the Dergue. None of the names of the officers was known, none was announced — they acted in total secrecy until the end. Now they say that this group was headed by a young major named Mengistu Haile-Mariam. There were other officers, too, but they are all dead. I remember when this Mariam would come to the Palace as a captain. His mother was a servant at the court. I cannot tell who made it possible for him to graduate from the officers' school. Slender, slight, always tense, but in control of himself — anyway, that was the impression he gave. He knew the structure of the court, he knew who was who, he knew whom to arrest and when in order to prevent the Palace from functioning, to make it lose its power and strength, change it into a useless simulacrum that today stands abandoned and deteriorating.

The crucial decisions in the Dergue must have been taken sometime around the first of August. The military committee — that is, the Dergue — was composed of a hundred and twenty delegates elected at meetings in divisions and garrisons. They had a list of five hundred dignitaries and courtiers whom they gradually arrested, creating a sinking emptiness around the Emperor until finally he was left alone in the Palace. The last group, members of the Emperor's inner circle, was jailed in the middle of August. That's when they took the chief of the Imperial bodyguards, Colonel Tassew Wajo; our monarch's aide-de-camp, General Assefa Demissie; the commander of the Imperial Guard, General Tadesse Lemma; the personal secretary to H. S., Solomon Gebre-Mariam; the premier, Endelkachew; the Minister of the Highest Privileges, Admassu Retta; and perhaps twenty others. At the same time they dissolved the Crown Council and other institutions directly subordinate to the Emperor.

Then the officers made detailed searches of the Palace. The most compromising documents were found in the Office of Highest Privileges, and found with all the more ease because Admassu Retta himself started to spill the beans. Once only the monarch distributed privileges, but as the Empire began to fall apart the grabbing and snatching grew so strong among the notables that H. S. was unable to keep things under control, and he handed over some of the distribution of privileges to Admassu Retta. But Admassu Retta was not such a mnemonic genius as the Emperor, who never needed to write anything down, so he kept detailed accounts of his disbursements of land, enterprises, foreign currencies, and the other gratuities given to the dignitaries. All this fell into the hands of the military, who used these gravely compromising documents in a major propaganda campaign about the corruption in the Palace. They awakened anger and hatred in the people. Demonstrations flared up, the street demanded hangings in an atmosphere of horror and apocalypse. It turned out well that the military drove us all from the Palace — maybe that was what saved my head.

T. W.:

I'll tell you, sir, I knew things were going under just from watching the dignitaries sticking together in a close little pack, slapping each other on the back, telling each other they were right and the rest of the world could go to hell. They didn't even bother to ask us servants for news, because they knew what we said would give them the blues. Anyway, they said, what can we do? Everything's falling apart. And you should have seen the Floaters — all consolation. Everything will work out, they said, because we're in a state of inertia and inertia always wins. We'll hang on in the Palace and the common people will never wake up, they'll never overcome the weight of inertia. If we learn how to give a little here and there, at just the right moments, they'll go on sleeping. We should let sleeping dogs lie. The trick is not to resist evil, but to humor it. And the Floaters might have been right, except for those officers, they had a real burr in their tail, and they just sliced into the Palace, cutting off great hunks of dignitaries, until in the end the Palace was picked clean, flushed out, and there was nobody left except for His Most Extraordinary Majesty and one servant.

That servant was the most difficult to find. As old as his former master, he lived buried in such oblivion that when I asked people about him they would shrug their shoulders and say he had died long ago. He served the Emperor until the last day, the moment when the military led the monarch out of the Palace. Then they told the servant to gather up his belongings and go home.

In the second half of August the officers arrest the last of H. S.'s circle. They still don't touch the Emperor, because they need time to prepare public opinion: the capital must understand why the monarch is being removed. The officers know about the magical element in popular thinking, and about the dangers it contains. The magical aspect is that the highest one is endowed, often unconsciously, with divine characteristics. The supreme one is wise and noble, unblemished and kindly. Only the dignitaries are bad; they cause all the misery. Moreover, if the one on the top knew what his people were up to, he would immediately repair the damage and life would be better. Unfortunately, these crafty villains pull the wool over their master's eyes, and that is why life is so hard, so low and miserable. This is magical thinking because, in reality, in an autocratic system it is precisely the one on the top who is the primary cause of what happens. He knows what is going on, and if he doesn't know, it's because he doesn't want to know. It was no accident that the majority of the people around the Emperor were mean and servile. Meanness and servility were the conditions of ennoblement, the criteria by which the monarch chose his favorites, rewarded them, bestowed privileges on them. Not one step was taken, not one word said, without his knowledge and consent. Everyone spoke with his voice, even if they said diverse things, because he himself said diverse things. The condition for remaining in the Emperor's circle was practicing the cult of the Emperor, and whoever grew weak and lost eagerness in the practice of this cult lost his place, dropped out, disappeared. Haile Selassie lived among shadows of himself, for what was the Imperial suite if not a multiplication of the Emperor's shadow? Who were gentlemen like Aklilu, Gebre-Egzy, Admassu Retta, aside from being H. S.'s ministers? Nobodies. But it was precisely such people the Emperor wanted around him. Only they could satisfy his vanity, his self-love, his passion for the stage and the mirror, for gestures and the pedestal.

And now the officers meet the Emperor alone, they confront him face-to-face, the final duel begins. The moment has come for everyone to remove the mask and show his face. This action generates anxiety and tension because the two sides form a new geometry. The Emperor has nothing to gain, but he can still defend himself by his defenselessness, by inactivity, by the unique virtue of occupying the Palace, by virtue of his being long-established — and also because he performed an extraordinary service: he was silent, was he not, when the rebels claimed that they were carrying out the revolution in his name. He never protested, he never called it a lie, and yet it was precisely this charade of loyalty, acted out for months by the military, that made their task so eminently easy. But the officers decide to go further, to follow through to the very end: they want to unmask the deity. In a society so crushed by misery, by privation and worry, nothing will speak more eloquently to the imagination, nothing cause greater unrest, anger, and hatred than the picture of corruption and privilege among the elite. Even an incompetent and sterile government, if it lived a spartan life, could exist for years basking in the esteem of the people. The attitude of the people to the Palace is normally kindhearted and understanding. But all tolerance has its limits, which in its swaggering arrogance the Palace often and easily violates. And the mood of the street changes violently from submission to defiance, from patience to rebelliousness.

Now comes the moment when the officers decide to lay bare the King of Kings, to turn his pockets inside out, to reveal to the people the secret hiding places in the Emperor's closet. All the while the ancient H. S. wanders through the deserted Palace, accompanied by his valet, L. M.

L. M.:

This, my gracious sir, was when they were taking away the last of the dignitaries, inviting the gentlemen to the trucks. An officer tells me to remain with His Venerable Majesty and perform all the services I had always performed. Having said this, he drove away. Immediately I made for the Supreme Office, to lend my ear to the will of His Omnipotent Highness. I found no one in the office. I was walking through the corridors, wondering where my lord had gone, when I discovered him standing in the main reception gallery, watching the soldiers of his Guard loading their backpacks and duffel bags, readying themselves to leave. How can this be? I think — they are all going, leaving His Majesty unprotected in a town full of thieves and unrest. So I go up to them and ask, "And you, my gracious sirs, are you leaving like this, altogether?" "Altogether," they answer, "but the sentry at the gate stays so that if some dignitary tries to sneak into the Palace, they'll capture him." His Venerable Majesty is standing, watching, not saying a word. Then they bow to His Majesty and leave with their bundles, and His Most Reverend Majesty looks on in silence as they go, and in silence he returns to his chamber.

Unfortunately, L. M.'s story is chaotic. The old man cannot turn his images, his experiences, and his expressions into a coherent entity. "Please try to remember more details, father!" urges Teferra Gebrewold. (He calls L. M. "father" because of his age, not of kinship.) So L. M. remembers the following scene: One day he found the Emperor standing in a chamber, looking out the window. He came closer and also looked out the window, and saw cows grazing in the Palace garden. Someone must have told herdsmen that the Emperor is no longer important and that everyone can share his property, or at least the Palace grass.

The Emperor now devoted himself to long periods of meditation ("In this the Hindus once gave him instructions, ordering him to stand on one leg, forbidding him to breathe, making him close his eyes.") Immobile, he would meditate for hours in his office (at least the valet thinks he meditated — perhaps he dozed). L. M. did not dare to disturb him. The rainy season wore on. It rained for days on end; trees stood in water. Mornings were foggy and nights cold. H. S. still wore his uniform, over which he would throw a warm woolen cape. They got up as they had in the old days, as they had for years, at daybreak, and they went to the Palace chapel, where each day L. M. read aloud different verses from the Book of Psalms. "Lord, how they are increased that trouble me! many are they that rise up against me." "Hold up my goings in thy paths, that my footsteps slip not." "Be not far from me; for trouble is near; for there is none to help."

Afterward, H. S. would go to his office and sit down at his desk, on which more than a dozen telephones were perched. All of them silent — perhaps they had been cut off. L. M. would sit by the door, waiting for the bell to ring, summoning him to receive orders from his monarch.

L. M.:

So, my gracious sir, in those days, only the officers intruded. First they would come to me, asking to be announced to His Unparalleled Majesty, and then they would enter the office, where His Highness would seat them in comfortable armchairs. Then they would read a proclamation demanding that His Benevolent Majesty give back the money that, they claim, he has been illegally appropriating for fifty years, depositing in banks around the world and concealing in the Palace and in the homes of dignitaries and notables. This, they say, should be returned, because it is the property of the people, from whose blood and sweat it came. "What money are you talking about?" His Benevolent Majesty asks. "Everything went for development, for catching up and surpassing, and the development was proclaimed a success, was it not? We had no money for ourselves." "Some development!" cry the officers. "All this is empty demagoguery, a smoke screen." And they get up from the armchairs, lift the great Persian carpet from the floor, and there under the carpet are rolls of dollar bills stuck together, one next to the other, so that the floor looked green. In the presence of His August Majesty they order the sergeants to count the money, write down the amount, and carry it off to be nationalized.

They leave soon afterward, and His Dignified Majesty calls me into his office and orders me to hide among his books the money he used to keep in his desk. Since His Majesty, as the designated descendant of Solomon, had a great collection of the Holy Scriptures, translated into many languages, that's where we stashed the money. Ah, those officers, clever sharks they were! The following day they come, read their proclamation, and demand the return of the money, because, they say, it's needed to buy flour for the starving. His Majesty, sitting at his desk, shows them the empty drawers. At which the officers spring from their armchairs, grab all those Bibles from the bookcases, and shake the dollars out, whereupon the sergeants count them, write down the figures, and take them away to be nationalized.

All this is nothing, say the officers. The rest of the money should be returned, especially the amounts in the Swiss and British banks in His Majesty's private account, estimated at half a billion dollars. They persuade His Majesty to sign the appropriate checks, and thus, they claim, the money will be returned to the nation. "Where am I to come up with all this money?" asks His Venerable Majesty. "All I have is a few pennies for the care of my ailing son in a Swiss hospital." "Pretty pennies they are, too," answer the officers, and they read aloud a letter from the Swiss embassy which says that His Majesty has on account in banks there the sum of one hundred million dollars. So they go on quarrelling until finally His Majesty falls into meditation, closes his eyes, and stops breathing. Then the officers withdraw, promising to return.

Silence fell on the Palace, but a bad silence, in which one could hear the shouts from the street. Demonstrators were marching through the town, all sorts of rabble loitering about, cursing His Majesty, calling him a thief, wanting to string him up from a tree. "Crook! Give back our money!" they cried. "Hang the Emperor! Hang the Emperor!" Then I would close all the windows in the Palace, to prevent these indecent and slanderous cries from reaching His Venerable Majesty's ears, from stirring his blood. And I would quickly lead my lord to the chapel, which was in the most secluded place, and to muffle the blasphemous roar, I would read aloud to him the words of the prophets. "Also take no heed unto all words that are spoken; lest thou hear thy servant curse thee." "They are vanity and the work of errors: in the time of their visitation they shall perish." "Remember, O Lord, what is come upon us: consider, and behold our reproach. The joy of our heart is ceased: our dance is turned into mourning. The crown is fallen from our head: For this our heart is faint; for these things our eyes are dim." "How is the gold become dim! how is the most fine gold changed! the stones of the sanctuary are poured out in the top of every street. They that did feed delicately are desolate in the streets: they that were brought up in scarlet embrace dunghills." "Thou hast seen all their vengeance and all their imaginations against me. Thou hast heard their reproach, O Lord; The lips of those that rose up against me; I am their musick. They have cut off my life in the dungeon, and cast a stone upon me."

And as His August Majesty listened, gracious sir, he would doze off. There I would leave him, proceeding to my lodgings to hear what was being said on the radio. In those days the radio was the only link between the Palace and the Empire.

Everybody listened to the radio then, and those who could afford a television set (still the greatest symbol of luxury in this country) watched. During this period, late August and early September, every day brought an abundance of revelations about the Emperor and the life of the Palace. There was a shower of names and figures, of bank account numbers, of the names of properties and private firms. Dignitaries' houses were shown: the riches gathered there, the contents of secret safes, piles of jewelry. One often heard the voice of the Minister of Highest Privileges, Admassu Retta, who testified before the Commission for Investigating Corruption about which of the dignitaries received what and when, where he himself received it, and what its value was. The difficulty, however, was that it was impossible to determine the borderline between the state budget and the Emperor's private treasury; everything was blurred, muddled, ambiguous. With state money the dignitaries built themselves palaces, bought estates, traveled abroad. The Emperor himself amassed the greatest riches. The older he grew, the greater became his greed, his pitiable cupidity. One could talk about it with sadness and indulgence, were it not for the fact that H. S. — he and his people — took millions from the state treasury amid cemeteries full of people who had died of hunger, cemeteries visible from the windows of the royal Palace.

At the end of August the military proclaimed the nationalization of all the Emperor's Palaces. There were fifteen of them. His private enterprises met the same fate, among them the Saint George Brewery, the Addis Ababa metropolitan bus company, the mineral-water factory in Ambo. The officers kept paying their visits to the Emperor, having long talks with him, urging him to withdraw his money from foreign banks and transfer it to the national treasury. The exact sum in the Emperor's accounts will probably never be known. The propaganda bulletins spoke of four billion dollars, but this was probably a gross exaggeration. It was rather a matter of hundreds of millions. The insistent demands of the military ended in failure: the Emperor never gave his money to the state, and it remains in foreign banks to this day.

L. M. recalls that the officers came to the Palace one day and announced that in the evening the television would show a film that H. S. should watch. The valet passed on this information to the Emperor, and the monarch willingly agreed to fulfil the request of his army. In the evening he sat down in his armchair in front of the television and the program began. They were showing Jonathan Dimbleby's film Ethiopia: The Unknown Famine. *L. M. assures me that the Emperor watched the film to the end and then became lost in thought. That night, September 11, the servant and his master — two old men in an abandoned Palace — did not sleep, because it was New Year's Eve according to the Ethiopian calendar. For this occasion L. M. lit candles in chandeliers all through the Palace.*

At daybreak they heard the throbbing of motors and the clank of tank treads on asphalt. Then silence. At six o'clock military trucks pulled up in front of the Palace. Three officers in combat uniforms made their way to the chamber where the Emperor had been since dawn. After a preliminary bow, one of them read the act of dethronement. The text, published later in the press and read over the radio, went as follows: "Even though the people treated the throne in good faith as a symbol of unity, Haile Selassie I took advantage of its authority, dignity, and honor for his own personal ends. As a result, the country found itself in a state of poverty and disintegration. Moreover, an eighty-two-year-old monarch, because of his age, is incapable of meeting his responsibilities. Therefore His Imperial Majesty Haile Selassie I is being deposed as of September 12, 1974, and power assumed by the Provisional Military Committee. Ethiopia above all!"

The Emperor, standing, heard out the officer's words, and then he expressed his thanks to everyone, stated that the army had never disappointed him, and added that if the revolution is good for the people then he, too, supports the revolution and would not oppose the dethronement. "In that case," said the officer (he was wearing a major's uniform), "His Imperial Majesty will please follow us." "Where to?" H. S. asked. "To a safe place," explained the major.

"His Imperial Highness will see." Everybody left the Palace. In the driveway stood a green Volkswagen. Behind the wheel sat an officer, who opened the door and held the front seat, so that the Emperor could get into the back. "You can't be serious!" the Emperor bridled. "I'm supposed to go like this?" It was his only gesture of protest that morning. However, he presently fell silent and sat down in the back seat of the car. The Volkswagen set off, preceded by a jeep full of armed soldiers, with an identical jeep following. It wasn't seven o'clock yet. The curfew was still in force. They were driving through empty streets. With a gesture of his hand, H. S. greeted those few people they passed along the way. Finally the column disappeared through the gates of the Fourth Division barracks.

On the orders of the officers, L. M. packed his belongings in the Palace and then went out into the street with his bundle on his back. He flagged down a passing taxi and had himself driven home, to Jimma Road. Teferra Gebrewold says that two lieutenants came that same day at noon and locked the Palace. One of them put the key into his pocket. They climbed into their jeep and left. Two tanks, which had stood before the Palace gates during the night and been showered with flowers by the people during the day, returned to their base.

HAILE SELASSIE STILL BELIEVES HE IS EMPEROR OF ETHIOPIA

Addis Ababa, February 7, 1975 (Agence France Presse). Imprisoned in the rooms of the Menelik Palace on the hills above Addis Ababa, Haile Selassie is spending the last months of his life surrounded by soldiers. According to eyewitness accounts, these soldiers, as in the best times of the Empire, still bow before the King of Kings. Thanks to such gestures, as a representative of an international aid organization discovered recently when he paid a visit to the Emperor and other prisoners remaining in the Palace, Haile Selassie still believes that he is the Emperor of Ethiopia.

The Negus is in good health, has begun to read a lot — in spite of his years he still reads without glasses — and from time to time gives advice to the soldiers who guard him. It bears mentioning that these soldiers are changed every week, because the aged monarch has retained his gift of winning allies. As in the past, each of the ex-Emperor's days is arranged within the framework of an inviolable program and proceeds according to protocol.

The King of Kings gets up at dawn, attends morning mass, and afterward plunges into his reading. The former supreme ruler still repeats what he said on the day of his deposition: "If the revolution is good for the people, then I am for the revolution."

In the Emperor's old chamber, several meters from the building where Haile Selassie is staying, the ten members of the Dergue hold continuous conferences on saving the revolution. New dangers threaten because of the outbreak of war in Eritrea. Close by, the Emperor's lions, locked in their cages and growling threateningly, demand their daily portion of meat.

On the other side of the Palace, near the building occupied by Haile Selassie, stand lodgings for the former court, where dignitaries and notables await their fates in the basements where they are imprisoned.

The Ethiopian Herald

Addis Ababa, August 28, 1975 (ENA). Yesterday Haile Selassie I, the former Emperor of Ethiopia, died. The cause of death was circulatory failure.

SHAH OF SHAHS

CONTENTS

CARDS, FACES, FIELDS OF FLOWERS

Everything is in confusion, as though the police have just finished a violent, nervous search. Newspapers, local and foreign, are scattered everywhere, special editions, big attention-getting headlines,

HE HAS LEFT

large photos of a gaunt, elongated face, its controlled features so bent on showing neither anxiety nor defeat that it no longer expresses anything at all. Copies of later editions proclaim in fervor and triumph:

HE HAS RETURNED

A severe patriarchal face that has no intention of expressing anything at all fills the rest of the page.

(And between that departure and that return, what heights of emotion and fervor, rage and terror, how many conflagrations!)

On the floor, chairs, table, desk lie heaps of index cards, scraps of paper, notes so hastily scrawled and chaotic, I have to stop and think where I jotted down the sentence "He will deceive you and make promises to you, but don't let yourself be fooled." Who said that? When? To whom?

Or, covering a whole sheet of paper in red pencil: "Must call 64–12–18." But so much time has passed, I can't remember whose number it is or why it was so important to call.

Unfinished letter, never mailed. I could go on at length about what I've seen and lived through here, but it is difficult to organize my impressions . . .

The worst chaos is on the big round table: photos of various sizes, cassettes, 8-mm film, newsletters, photocopies of leaflets — all piled, mixed up together, helter-skelter, like a flea market. And more posters and albums, records and books acquired or given by people, the collected remnants of an era just ended but still able to be seen and heard because it has been preserved here on film — flowing, agitated rivers of people; on cassettes — the wail of the muezzins, shouted orders, conversations, monologues; in photos — faces in ecstasy, exaltation.

Now, at the very thought of trying to put everything in order (because the day I'm to leave is approaching), I am overcome by both aversion and profound fatigue. When I stay in a hotel (which is quite often) I like the room to be a mess because then the ambience has the illusion of some kind of life, a substitute warmth and intimacy, a proof (though illusory) that such a strange uncozy place, as all hotel rooms in essence are, has been at least partially conquered and tamed. In a room arranged into antiseptic order, I feel numb and lonely, pinched by all the straight lines, corners of furniture, flat walls, all that indifferent, stiff geometry, a strained, meticulous arrangement existing only for its own sake, without a trace of human presence. Fortunately, within a few hours of my arrival, influenced by my unconscious actions (the result of haste or laziness), the existing order breaks down, disappears, objects come to life, begin moving from place to place, and enter into ever changing configurations and connections; things take on a cramped, baroque look, and, all at once, the room's atmosphere becomes friendlier and more familiar. Then I can take a deep breath and relax.

Right now I cannot summon up enough strength to do anything with the room, so I go downstairs, where four young men are drinking tea and playing cards in a gloomy, empty hall. They've abandoned themselves to some intricate game — neither bridge nor poker, blackjack nor pinochle — whose rules I'll probably never grasp. They use two sets of cards at once, playing in silence, until at a certain moment one of them takes all the cards, a delighted expression on his face. After a pause they deal, lay dozens of cards on the table, ponder, count, and begin quarreling as they count.

These four, the reception staff, live off me. I am supporting them because I am the only guest in the hotel. I also support the cleaning woman, cooks, waiters, launderers, janitors, gardener, and for all I know several other people and their families, too. I don't mean to say that if I delayed settling my bill they would all starve, but I try to keep my account paid just in case. Only a few months ago it was an achievement, like winning a lottery, to get a room in this city. Despite the many many hotels, there was such an avalanche of people that new arrivals had to rent beds in private hospitals just to have a place to stay. Now the boom of easy money and dazzling transactions is over, the local businessmen are lying low, and the foreign partners have fled, leaving everything behind. Tourism has fallen to zero; all international traffic has frozen. Some hotels were burned down, others are closed or empty, and in one of them, guerrillas have set up their headquarters. Today the city is engrossed in its own affairs, it doesn't need foreigners, it doesn't need the world.

The cardplayers take a break from their game to offer me tea. Here they drink only tea or yogurt, not coffee or alcohol. For drinking alcohol you can get forty or even sixty lashes, and if someone brawny does the whipping (that type is often the most enthusiastic flogger) your back will be pulp. So we slurp our tea and watch the TV below the window at the other end of the hall.

Khomeini's face appears on the screen.

Khomeini is seated in a simple wooden armchair on a simple wooden platform in one of the squares of (to judge from the shabbiness of the buildings) a poor section of Qom. A small, flat, gray, charmless city, Qom lies a hundred miles south of Teheran in a vacant, wearying, parched, sunbaked desert. Nothing in that murderous climate would seem to favor reflection and contemplation, yet Qom is a place of religious fervor, rabid orthodoxy, mysticism, and faith militant. It contains five hundred mosques and the nation's biggest seminaries. Koranic scholars and the guardians of tradition quarrel in Qom; the venerable ayatollahs convene their councils there; Khomeini rules the country from Qom. He never leaves, never goes to the capital, never goes anywhere. He neither sightsees nor pays visits. He used to live with his wife and five children in Qom in a small house on a cramped, dusty, unpaved little street with a gutter running down the middle. Now he's moved to his daughter's house, from whose balcony he appears to the crowds in the street below (usually, zealous pilgrims visiting the mosques of the holy city and, most important of all, the tomb, forbidden to non-Muslims, of the Immaculate Fatima, sister of the eighth Imam Reza). Khomeini leads an ascetic life, eating only rice, yogurt, and fruit, and occupying but one room, bare walls, no furniture, only a bedroll on the floor, and a pile of books. Here, sitting on a blanket spread on the floor, leaning back against the wall, he receives his guests, including the most formal official foreign delegations. From the window he can see the domes of the mosques and the spacious courtyard of the medresh — an enclosed world of turquoise mosaics, bluish-green minarets, coolness and shade. All day a steady stream of guests and petitioners passes through this room. When there is a break, Khomeini goes off to pray or stays in his room, devoting the time to reflection or simply — as is natural for a man of eighty — taking a nap. The one with the most access to him is his younger son Ahmed, like his father a cleric. The other son, the first-born and the hope of his father's life, perished in mysterious circumstances — treacherously killed, people say, by Savak, the Shah's secret police.

The camera shows the square packed with people standing shoulder to shoulder. It shows curious and solemn faces. Off to the side, separated from the men in a clearly marked enclosure, stand women wrapped in chadors. It's a gray cloudy day, the crowd is charcoal-colored and, where the women stand, black. As always, Khomeini is dressed in loose-fitting dark clothes, a black turban on his head. He sits stiffly. His face is pale and still above his white beard. He does not gesticulate when he speaks; his hands rest on the arms of the chair. Once in a while he wrinkles his high forehead and raises his eyebrows; otherwise, not a muscle moves in the face of this man of immense stubborn, unretreating, unhesitating, implacable will. In this face, which seems to have been composed once and for all, yielding to neither emotions nor moods, expressing nothing but taut attentiveness and internal concentration, only the eyes move constantly. Their lively, incisive glance slides over the sea of curly heads, measures the depth of the square and the distance to its limits and continues its meticulous inspection as if insistently searching for a specific person. I listen to his monotonous voice, with its measured slow rhythm — a strong voice, but a voice that never leaps or flies, never betrays a mood, never sparkles.

"What is he talking about?" I ask the cardplayers, when Khomeini pauses for a moment to consider his next sentence.

"He is saying that we must preserve our dignity," one of them answers.

The cameraman pans across the roofs of the nearby houses where young people, with checkered scarves wrapped around their heads, stand, holding automatic rifles.

"And now what is he saying?" I ask again, because I don't understand Farsi.

"He is saying," one of the young men tells me, "in our country there is no room for foreign influence."

Khomeini goes on speaking and everyone follows attentively. On the screen someone's trying to quiet a group of children at the base of the platform.

"What is he saying?" I ask again after a while.

"He is saying that nobody will tell us what to do in our own home or impose anything on us, and he is saying: 'Be brothers to one another, be united.' "

That is all they can tell me in their halting English. Everyone learning English should understand that it is getting harder and harder to communicate in that language around the world. The same is true of French and, generally, of all European languages. Once Europe ruled the world, sending its merchants, soldiers, and missionaries to every continent, imposing on others its own interests and culture (this in usually rather bogus versions). Even in the remotest corners of the world, knowing a European language was a mark of distinction, testifying to an ambitious upbringing, and was often a necessity of life, the basis for career and promotion, and sometimes even a condition for being considered human. Those languages were taught in African schools, used in commerce, spoken in exotic parliaments, Asian courts, and Arab coffeehouses. Traveling almost anywhere in the world, Europeans could feel at home. They could express their opinions and understand what others were saying to them. Today the world is different. Hundreds of patriotisms have blossomed. Every nation wants to control and organize its own population, territory, resources, and culture according to native traditions. Every nation thinks it is or wants to be free, independent, cherishes its own values, and insists upon (and is particularly sensitive about getting) respect for them. Even small and weak nations — these especially — hate to be preached to, and rebel against anyone who tries to rule them or force often suspect values on them. People may admire the strength of others — but preferably at a safe remove and certainly not when used against them. Every power has its own dynamics, its own domineering, expansionist tendencies, its bullying obsessive need to trample the weak. This is the law of power, as everyone knows. But what can the weaker ones do? They can only fence themselves off, afraid of being swallowed up, stripped, regimented into a conformity of gait, face, expression, tongue, thought, response, ordered to give their life's blood for an alien cause, and of finally being crushed altogether. Hence their dissent and revolt, their struggle for independent existence, their struggle for their own language. In Syria the French newspaper was closed down;

in Vietnam after the Americans left, the English-language paper, and now in Iran both French and English ones. On radio and television and during press conferences, only Farsi, their own language, is used. A man who can't read the Farsi sign on a woman's clothing store in Teheran — "Entry to this store by men is forbidden under penalty of arrest" — will go to jail. Someone else who cannot read the inscription near Isfahan that warns "Keep out — Mines!" may die.

I used to carry a small transistor radio and listen to the local stations. No matter which continent I was on, I could always find out what was happening in the world. Now that radio is worthless. When I turn the dial I get ten stations, each using a different language, and I can't understand a word. If I travel a thousand miles, I get ten new equally incomprehensible stations. Are they saying that the money in my pocket is no longer any good? Are they saying that war has broken out?

Television is the same.

All over the world, at any hour, on a million screens an infinite number of people are saying something to us, trying to convince us of something, gesturing, making faces, getting excited, smiling, nodding their heads, pointing their fingers, and we don't know what it's about, what they want from us, what they are summoning us to. They might as well have come from a distant planet — an enormous army of public relations experts from Venus or Mars — yet they are our kin, with the same bones and blood as ours, with lips that move and audible voices, but we cannot understand a word. In what language will the universal dialogue of humanity be carried out? Several hundred languages are fighting for recognition and promotion; the language barriers are rising. Deafness and incomprehension are multiplying.

After a short break (during which they show fields of flowers — they love flowers here and plant colorful, luxuriant gardens around the tombs of their greatest poets) the photo of a young man appears on the screen. An announcer says something.

"What's he saying?" I ask my cardplayers.

"He's giving the name of the man in the photo. And telling who he was."

Then another photograph appears, and another — photos from student identity cards, framed pictures, snapshots from automatic photo machines, photographs with ruins in the background, one family portrait with an arrow pointing to a barely visible girl to show who is being described. Each photograph appears for a few moments; the list of names the announcer is reading goes on and on.

The parents are asking for information. They have been doing this for months, hoping against hope. The people in the photographs disappeared in September, December, January, that is, in the months of heaviest fighting, when the glow of fires over the city never died. They must have marched in the front ranks of the demonstration, right into the machine-gun fire. Or sharpshooters on nearby rooftops picked them off. We can suppose that each of these faces was last seen in the gun-sight of a soldier taking aim. Every evening, during this program, we listen to the announcer's matter-of-fact voice and meet more and more people who no longer exist.

More fields of flowers appear, followed by the evening's next program, also presenting photographs; but the people here are completely different. These are, for the most part, elderly men, sloppily dressed (with wrinkled collars and rumpled denim jackets), their desperate faces sunken and unshaven, some bearded. A big piece of cardboard with his name written on it hangs from the neck of each. When a particular face appears, one of the cardplayers exclaims, "Aha, so *that's* the one!" and everybody looks intently at the screen. The announcer is reading the personal data of each and the list of crimes that each committed. General Mohammed Zand gave the order to fire on an unarmed demonstration in Tabriz:

hundreds were killed. Major Hossein Farzin tortured prisoners by burning their eyelids and pulling out their fingernails. A few hours ago, the announcer says, the firing squad of the Islamic Militia carried out the sentence of the tribunal against them.

The hall feels stuffy and oppressive during this parade of good then evil absent ones — all the more so because the wheel of death that's been turning for so long keeps spinning and throwing off hundreds of new people (faded photographs and ones just taken, graduation pictures, prison mug shots). This procession of still, silent faces flowing past in fits and starts becomes depressing but at the same time so absorbing that I expect suddenly to see my cardplayers' faces on the screen, then my own, and hear the announcer reading our names.

I walk back upstairs, through the empty corridor, and lock myself in my cluttered room. As usual at this hour I can hear gunfire from the depths of an invisible city. The shooting starts regularly at nine as if custom or tradition had fixed the hour. Then the city falls silent. Then there are more shots and muffled explosions. No one's upset, no one pays attention or feels directly threatened (no one except those who are shot). Since the middle of February, when the uprising broke out in the city and the crowds seized the army munitions depots, Teheran has been armed, intensely charged, while in streets and houses, under cover of darkness, the drama of assassination is enacted. The underground keeps a low profile during the day, but at night it sends masked combat squads into the city.

These uneasy nights force people to lock themselves in their own homes. There is no curfew, but getting anywhere between midnight and dawn is difficult and risky. The Islamic Militia or the independent combat squads rule the looming, motionless city between those hours. Both are groups of well-armed boys who point their guns at people, cross-examine them, confer among themselves, and occasionally, just to be on the safe side, take those they've stopped to jail — from which it is difficult to get out. What's more, you are never sure who has locked you up, since no identifying marks differentiate the various representatives of violence whom you encounter, no uniforms or caps, no armbands or badges — these are simply armed civilians whose authority must be accepted unquestioningly if you care about your life. After a few days, though, we grow used to them and learn to tell them apart. This distinguished-looking man, in his well-made white shirt and carefully matched tie, walking down the street shouldering a rifle is certainly a militiaman in one of the ministries or central offices. On the other hand, this masked boy (a woolen stocking pulled over his head and holes cut out at eyes and mouth) is a local fedayeen no one's supposed to know by sight or name. We can't be sure about these people dressed in green US Army fatigue jackets, rushing by in cars, barrels of guns pointed out the windows. They might be from the militia, but then again they might belong to one of the opposition combat groups (religious fanatics, anarchists, last remnants of Savak) hurrying with suicidal determination to carry out an act of sabotage or revenge.

But finally it's no fun trying to predict just whose ambush is awaiting you, whose trap you'll fall into. People don't like surprises, so they barricade themselves in their homes at night. My hotel is also locked (at this hour the sound of gunfire mingles with the creaking of shutters rolling down and the slamming shut of gates and doors). No friends will drop by; nothing like that will happen. I have no one to talk to. I'm sitting alone looking through notes and pictures on the table, listening to taped conversations.

DAGUERREOTYPES

PHOTOGRAPH 1

Here's the oldest picture I've managed to obtain. A soldier, holding a chain in his right hand, and a man, at the end of the chain. The two gaze intently into the lens. This is clearly an important moment in their lives. The soldier is an older man, on the short side, a simple, obedient peasant, wearing an oversized, clumsily stitched uniform, trousers, rumpled like an accordion, a big cap tilted onto protruding ears — in sum, an amusing figure reminiscent of the good soldier Schweik. The man on the chain: thin, pale face, sunken eyes, bandaged head, obviously wounded. The photo's caption says the soldier is the grandfather of Shah Mohammed Reza Pahlavi (the last Shah of Iran) and the wounded man is the assassin of Shah Nasr-ed-Din. Accordingly, the photo must date from 1896, when Nasr-ed-Din, after reigning for forty-nine years, was killed. The grandfather and the murderer look tired, which is understandable, since they have been wandering for days from Qom to the place of public execution in Teheran. They have been trudging down the desert road in scorching heat and stifling air, the soldier at the rear and the gaunt killer before him on his chain, like a member of an old-time circus troupe and his trained bear working their way from village to village, earning food for themselves. At times the assassin complains about the pain in his injured head but for the most part they are silent, because finally they have nothing to talk about. The murderer has killed, and the grandfather is leading him to his execution. Persia is a country of extreme poverty; it has no railroads, only the aristocracy own horse-drawn conveyances, and thus these two men must walk to the distant goal established by sentence and order. From time to time they come across a few clay huts where haggard peasants surround the dusty travelers. "Who is that you're leading, sir?" they shyly ask the soldier. "Who?" the soldier repeats the question and holds his tongue for a moment to heighten the suspense. "This," he says finally, pointing to the prisoner, "is the Shah's murderer." The grandfather's voice betrays a note of unconcealed pride. The peasants gape at the assassin in horror and admiration. Because he's killed someone great, he also seems somehow great. His crime has elevated him to a higher realm of existence. The peasants cannot decide between glowering indignantly and falling to their knees. Meanwhile, the soldier ties the chain to a stake driven into the ground at the roadside, unslings his rifle (which is so long it almost touches the ground when slung over his shoulder), and orders the peasants to bring water and food. They scratch their heads. There is almost nothing to eat in the village, because a famine is raging. We should add that the soldier himself is a peasant, just like them, and no more than they does he even have a surname of his own — he calls himself Savad-Kuhi, the name of his village — but he has a carbine and a uniform and has been singled out to lead the Shah's assassin to the place of execution, so he takes advantage of his high position and again commands the peasants to bring water and food, since he is excruciatingly hungry and, furthermore, cannot allow the man on the chain to perish of thirst or exhaustion. If that happened, the extraordinary spectacle of hanging the Shah's assassin in a crowded Teheran square would have to be canceled. Badgered ruthlessly by the soldier, the peasants end up bringing what they themselves would have eaten: withered rootlets dug from the ground and a canvas pouch full of dried locusts. The grandfather and the murderer sit down in the shade to eat, eagerly popping locusts into their mouths, spitting out the wings, and washing the remains down with water, while the peasants look on in silent envy. As evening draws near, the soldier chooses the best hut, throws out its owners, and turns it into a temporary jail. He winds the prisoner's chain around his own body, then, tired from countless hours of marching under the blazing sun, the two stretch out on the clay floor black with cockroaches and fall into deep sleep. In the morning they get up and continue on the road to the goal established by sentence and order, northward, to Teheran, across the same desert, in the same quivering heat, the murderer with his bandaged head, his long swinging tail of iron chain held up by the hand of the escorting soldier, in his clumsily sewn uniform, looking so comical with his large cap resting askew on his protruding ears that when I first saw him in this photo I thought it was Schweik himself.

PHOTOGRAPH 2

Here we see a young officer of the Persian Cossack Brigade standing next to a machine-gun and explaining the principles of the deadly weapon to his colleagues. This particular weapon is the updated 1910 model of the Maxim gun, so the photograph must be from about that year. The young officer, named Reza Khan and born in 1878, is the son of the soldier-escort we met leading the Shah's murderer across the desert less than two decades earlier. If we compare the two pictures, we immediately notice that Reza Khan, unlike his father, is a physical giant. He is taller than his colleagues by at least a head, has a bulging chest, and looks like the sort of muscleman who could break a horseshoe with ease. He has a military mien, a cold, piercing look, a wide, massive jaw, and clenched lips on which even the faintest smile would be out of the question. On his head sits a broad cap of black caracul, for he is, as I have mentioned, an officer of the Persian Cossack Brigade (the only army that the Shah of those days had) commanded by Vsevolod Lyakhov, a Tsarist colonel from St. Petersburg. Reza Khan is the protégé of Colonel Lyakhov, who has a fondness for born soldiers, and our young officer is the model of the born soldier. He joined the Brigade as an illiterate boy of fourteen (he will never learn to read and write well) and climbed gradually through the echelons of professional soldiery thanks to his obedience, discipline, decisiveness, innate intelligence, and what the military likes to call leadership quality. Great promotions come his way only after 1917, however, when the Shah (quite mistakenly) suspecting Lyakhov of Bolshevik sympathies, sends him back to Russia. Now Reza Khan becomes a colonel and the commander of the Cossack Brigade, which soon falls under British protection. At a reception the British general Sir Edmund Ironside stands on tiptoe to reach Reza Khan's ear and whispers, "Colonel, you are a man of great possibilities." They walk out into the garden where the general, in the course of their stroll, suggests a *coup d'état* and conveys London's blessings. In February, 1921, Reza Khan enters Teheran at the head of his brigade, arrests the capital's politicians (it is winter, snow is falling; the politicians will later complain about their cold damp cells), and forms a new government, in which he serves first as Minister of War and then as Prime Minister. In December, 1925, the obedient Constitutional Assembly (which fears the colonel and the Englishmen standing behind him) proclaims the cossack commander Shah of Persia. From now on our young officer — in the photograph explaining the principles of the updated 1910-model Maxim machine-gun to his colleagues (all wearing belted Russian peasant shirts and quilted jackets) — will be known as Shah Reza the Great, King of Kings, Shadow of the Almighty, God's Vicar and the Center of the Universe, and also as founder of the Pahlavi dynasty, which begins with him and, destiny decrees, ends with his son, who, on a winter morning as chilly as the day his father seized power and throne, fifty-eight years later, will depart the palace and Teheran, by jet, to an ambiguous fate.

Photograph 3

Whoever scrutinizes this photo of father and son, taken in 1926, will understand a lot. The father is forty-eight and the son seven. The contrast between them is striking in every respect. The huge, powerful Shah-father stands sulkily, peremptorily, hands on his hips, and beside him the small pale boy, frail, nervous, obediently standing at attention, barely reaches his father's waist. They are wearing the same uniforms and caps, the same shoes and belts, and the same number of buttons: fourteen. The father, who wants his son — so essentially unlike him — to resemble him in as many details as possible, thought up this identity of apparel. The son senses this intention, and, though he is by nature weak and hesitant, he will try at all costs to resemble his despotic, ruthless father. From that moment two natures begin to develop and coexist in the boy: the inborn one and the parental one that, because of his ambitions, he starts to acquire. Finally he falls so totally under his father's domination that when he becomes Shah many years later, he automatically (but also, often, consciously) repeats Daddy's behavior and even, toward the end of his reign, invokes his father's authority. But at this moment the father is assuming power with all his inborn energy and drive. He has an acute sense of mission and knows what he is after — in his own brutal words, he wants to put the ignorant mob to work and build a strong modern state before which all will beshit themselves in fear. His are the Prussian's iron hand, the slavedriver's simple methods. Ancient, slumbering, loafing Iran (on the Shah's orders, Persia will hereafter be called Iran) trembles to its foundations. He begins by creating an imposing army. A hundred and fifty thousand men get uniforms and guns. The army is the apple of the Shah's eye, his great passion. The army must always have money. It must have everything. The army will make the nation modern, disciplined, obedient. Everyone: *Attention!*

The Shah issues an order forbidding Iranian dress. Everyone, wear European suits! Everyone, don European hats! The Shah bans chadors. In the streets, police tear them off terrified women. The faithful protest in the mosques of Meshed. He sends in the artillery to level the mosques and massacre the rebels. He orders that the nomadic tribes be settled permanently. The nomads protest. He orders their wells poisoned, threatening them with death by thirst and starvation. The nomads keep protesting, so he sends out punitive expeditions that turn vast regions into uninhabited land. A lot of blood flows. He forbids the photographing of that symbolically backward beast, the camel. In Qom a mullah preaches a critical sermon, so, armed with a cane, the Shah enters the mosque and pummels the critic. He imprisons the great Ayatollah Madresi, who had raised his voice in complaint, in a dungeon for years. The liberals protest timorously in the newspapers, so the Shah closes down the newspapers and imprisons the liberals. He orders several of them walled up in a tower. Those he considers malcontents must report daily to the police. Aristocratic ladies faint in terror at receptions when this gruff unapproachable giant turns his harsh gaze on them. Until the end Reza Khan preserves many of the habits of his village childhood and his barracks youth. He lives in a palace but still sleeps on the floor; he always goes around in uniform; he eats with his soldiers from the same pot. One of the boys! At the same time, he covets land and money. Taking advantage of his power, he accumulates incredible wealth. He becomes the biggest landowner, proprietor of nearly three thousand villages and the two hundred and fifty thousand peasants living in them; he owns stock in factories and banks, receives tribute, counts, totes, adds, calculates — if a splendid forest, green valley, or fertile plantation so much as catches his eye, it must be his — indefatigably, insatiably he increases his estates, multiplying his enormous fortune. No one may even approach the borders of the Shah's lands. One day there is a public execution: On the Shah's orders a firing squad kills a donkey that, ignoring all warning signs, entered a meadow belonging to Reza Khan. Peasants from neighboring villages are herded to the place of execution to learn respect for the master's property. But apart from his cruelty, greed, and outlandishness, the old Shah deserves credit for saving Iran from the dissolution that threatened after the First World War. In his efforts to modernize the country he built roads and railways, schools and offices, airports and new residential quarters in the cities. The nation remained poor and apathetic, however, and when Reza Khan departed, an exultant people celebrated the event for a long time.

Photograph 4

Here's a picture that circulated around the world in its time: Stalin, Roosevelt, and Churchill sitting in armchairs on a spacious veranda. Stalin and Churchill are wearing uniforms, Roosevelt a dark suit. Teheran, a sunny December morning, 1943. Everybody in this picture is putting on a serene face meant to cheer us; after all, we know that the worst war in history is underway and the expression on these faces is crucial: It has to encourage us. The photographers finish, and the three great ones move into the hall for a moment of private conversation. Roosevelt asks Churchill what has become of the ruler of this country, Shah Reza (if, Roosevelt adds, I'm pronouncing it correctly). Churchill shrugs his shoulders and speaks reluctantly. The Shah admired Hitler and surrounded himself with Hitler's people. There were Germans all over Iran, in the palace, the ministries, the army. The Abwehr became a force to reckon with in Teheran, and the Shah looked on approvingly — Hitler was at war with England and Russia, and our monarch could not tolerate England and Russia; he rubbed his hands gleefully as the Führer's armies advanced.

London was worried about Iranian oil, which fueled the British fleet, and Moscow was afraid the Germans would land in Iran and attack in the region of the Caspian Sea. But the major concern remained the trans-Iranian railroad, which the Americans and the British needed to transport food and weapons to Stalin. Then, at a moment of crisis, as German divisions were advancing farther and farther eastward, the Shah suddenly refused the Allies use of the railroad. They moved decisively: Units of the British and Red armies entered Iran in August, 1941. The Shah received with disbelief, as a personal humiliation and defeat, news that fifteen Iranian divisions had surrendered without much resistance. Some of his troops dispersed and went home, while others were locked up in their barracks by the Allies. Deprived of his soldiers the Shah no longer mattered, no longer existed. The British, who respect even those monarchs who betray them, left Reza Khan an honorable way out: Would His Highness kindly abdicate in favor of his son, the heir to the throne? We have a high opinion of him and will ensure his position. But His Highness should not think there is any other solution. The Shah agreed and in September of that year, 1941, his twenty-two-year-old son Mohammed Reza Pahlavi ascended the throne. The old autocrat was a private person now, and for the first time in his adult life he put on civilian clothes. The British sent him to Africa, to Johannesburg (where he died after three years of a dull, comfortable life about which there is not much to say). Empire giveth; empire taketh away.

From the notes 1

I see I'm missing or have misplaced a few pictures. I don't have the shots of the last Shah in his early youth. I don't have the one from 1939 when he was attending officers' school in Teheran: On his twentieth birthday his father promoted him to general. I don't have a picture of his first wife, Fawzia, bathing in milk. Yes, Fawzia, King Farouk's sister and a girl of striking beauty, bathed in milk — but Princess Ashraf, the young Shah's twin sister and, as some say, his evil genius, his black conscience, poured caustic detergent into the bathtub: yet another palace scandal. But I do have a picture of the last Shah on September 16, 1941, when he succeeded his father and was crowned Shah Mohammed Reza Pahlavi. Slender, in a dress uniform, a sword at his side, he is standing in the chambers of parliament and reading the text of the oath from a sheet of paper. This picture was repeated in all the published commemorative albums devoted to the Shah, of which there were scores, if not hundreds. He loved reading books about himself and looking through albums published in his honor. He loved unveiling his monuments and portraits. Catching a glimpse of the monarch's likeness was nearly unavoidable. To stand in any given place and open your eyes was enough: The Shah was everywhere. Since height was not his strong point, photographers always shot from angles that made him seem the tallest person in the picture. He furthered this illusion by wearing elevator shoes. His subjects kissed his shoes. I have just such a picture, where they are prostrating themselves and kissing his elevator shoes. On the other hand, I don't have a photo of a certain uniform of his, from 1949. That apparel, pocked with bullet holes and stained with blood, was displayed in a glass case at the officers' club in Teheran as relic and reminder. The Shah was wearing it when a young man pretending to be a photographer but with a gun built into his camera got off a series of shots that wounded the monarch gravely. There were five attempts on his life, in all. Thus around him grew an atmosphere of danger (finally real), and he had to be surrounded by policemen wherever he went. The Iranians resented the fact that, for security reasons, only foreigners were invited to certain celebrations in which the Shah took part. His compatriots also said bitingly that since he traveled almost exclusively by airplane and helicopter, he saw his country only from a lofty vantage point that obliterated all contrasts. I don't have any photographs of Khomeini in his early years. When he appears in my collection, he is already an old man, and so it is as if he had never been young or middle-aged. The local fanatics believe Khomeini is the Twelfth Imam, the Awaited One, who disappeared in the ninth century and has now returned, more than a thousand years later, to deliver them from misery and persecution. That Khomeini almost always appears in photographs only as an aged man could be taken as confirmation of this belief.

Photograph 5

This is undoubtedly the greatest day in the long life of Doctor Mossadegh. He is leaving parliament high on the shoulders of an elated crowd. He is smiling and holding up his right hand in greeting to the people. Three days earlier, on April 28, 1951, he became Prime Minister, and today parliament has passed his bill nationalizing the country's oil. Iran's greatest treasure has become the property of the nation. We have to enter into the spirit of that epoch, because the world has changed a great deal since. In those days, to dare the sort of act that Doctor Mossadegh just performed was tantamount to dropping a bomb suddenly and unexpectedly on Washington or London. The psychological effect was the same: shock, fear, anger, outrage. Somewhere in Iran, some old lawyer who must be a half-cocked demagogue has pillaged Anglo-Iranian — the pillar of the Empire! Unheard of, unforgivable! In those years, colonial property was a sacred value, the ultimate taboo. But that day, whose exalted atmosphere the faces in the photograph reflect, the Iranians do not yet know they have committed a crime for which they will have to suffer bitter painful punishment. Right now, all Teheran is living joyous hours of its great day of liberation from a foreign and hated past. Oil is our blood! the crowds chant enthusiastically. Oil is our freedom! The palace shares the mood of the city, and the Shah signs the act of nationalization. It is a moment when all feel like brothers, a rare instant that quickly turns into a memory because accord in the national family is not going to last long. Mossadegh never had good relations with the Pahlavis, father and son. Mossadegh's ideas had been formed by French culture: A liberal and a democrat, he believed in institutions like parliament and a free press and lamented the state of dependence in which his homeland found itself. The fall of Reza Khan presented a great opportunity for him and those like him. The young monarch, meanwhile, takes more interest in good times and sports than in politics, so there is a chance for democracy in Iran, a chance for the country to win full independence. Mossadegh's power is so great and his slogans are so popular that the Shah ends up on the sidelines. He plays soccer, flies his private airplane, organizes masked balls, divorces and remarries, and goes skiing in Switzerland.

Photograph 6

Here are the Shah and his new wife Soraya Esfandiari in Rome. But this is no honeymoon, no fun-filled carefree adventure far from the worries and routines of everyday life; no, this is their exile. Even in this posed shot the thirty-four-year-old Shah (tanned, dressed in a light double-breasted suit) cannot hide his edginess — small wonder, since he doesn't know whether he is going to return to the throne he left so hurriedly, or lead the life of an émigré wandering the globe. Soraya, a woman of conspicuous but cold beauty, daughter of the tribal leader of the Bakhtiars and of a German woman who settled in Iran, looks more in control: Her face reveals little, especially with dark glasses hiding her eyes. Yesterday, August 17, 1953, they flew here from their homeland in their own airplane (with the Shah at the controls; flying always relaxed him) and checked into the swank Hotel Excelsior, to which dozens of paparazzi have flocked to immortalize each appearance by the imperial couple. Rome is full of tourists in this summer vacation season and the Italian beaches are packed (the bikini is just coming into fashion). Europe is resting, vacationing, sightseeing, dining well in good restaurants, hiking in the mountains, pitching tents, gathering strength for the chill autumn and snowy winter. Teheran, in the meantime, has neither calm moments nor relaxation because everyone can already smell the gunpowder and hear the knives being sharpened. Everyone is saying that something must happen, will happen (everyone senses the wearying pressure of ever thickening air portending explosion), but only a handful of conspirators knows who will begin it and how. Doctor Mossadegh's two years of rule are drawing to a close. Constantly threatened with coups (the democrats, the liberals, the Shah's people, and the Islamic fanatics all are plotting against him), the Doctor has transferred his bed, a briefcase full of pajamas (he is used to working in his pajamas), and a bag full of medicines to parliament, where he thinks he will be safe. He lives and works here, never venturing out, already so broken that those who visit him always tell of the tears in his eyes. All his hopes have vanished, all his calculations have proven wrong. He has eliminated the English from the oilfields, for each nation has the right to its own resources, but he forgot that might makes right. The West proclaims a blockade of Iran and a boycott of the country's oil, which becomes forbidden fruit on the world market. The Shah cannot decide: Should he obey those officers closest to the palace who are advising him to eliminate Mossadegh so as to save the monarchy and the army? For a long time he has been unable to take the final step that would burn once and for all his flimsy bridges to the Prime Minister (they are bound in a struggle that admits of no compromise because it is the conflict between two principles: the autocracy of the Shah and the democracy of Mossadegh), and perhaps the Shah is continuing to delay because he feels some sort of respect for the old Doctor, or perhaps simply because, unsure of himself, of his own will to uncompromising action, he lacks the courage to declare war on Mossadegh. The Shah would doubtless prefer that someone else carry out the whole painful, even brutal operation for him. Still undecided and continually anguished, he travels from Teheran to his summer residence in Ramsar on the Caspian Sea, where in the end he signs a sentence against the Prime Minister. But when it develops that the first attempt to finish off the Doctor has come to light and ended in a setback for the palace, the Shah does not wait for further (and, as it turns out, favorable) events but instead flees to Rome with his young bride. He returns to Teheran a few weeks later, only after the army has deposed Mossadegh and delivered all authority into the monarch's hands.

CASSETTE 1

Yes, of course — you can record. Today he is no longer a prohibited subject. Before, he was. Do you know that for twenty-five years it was forbidden to utter his name in public? That the name "Mossadegh" was purged from all books, all history texts? And just imagine: Today, young people, who, it was assumed, should know nothing about him, go to their deaths carrying his portrait. There you have the best proof of what such expunging and rewriting history leads to. But the Shah didn't understand that. He did not understand that even though you can destroy a man, destroying him does not make him cease to exist. On the contrary, if I can put it this way, he begins to exist all the more. These are paradoxes no tyrant can deal with. The scythe swings, and at once the grass starts to grow back. Cut again and the grass grows faster than ever. A very comforting law of nature. Mossadegh! The English nicknamed him "Old Mossy." He drove them crazy, and yet they respected him in a way. No Englishman ever took a shot at him. In the end it was necessary to summon our own uniformed goons. And it took them only a few days to establish their kind of order! Mossy went off to prison for three years. Five thousand people went up against the wall or died in the streets — the price of rescuing the throne. A sad, bloody, dirty re-entry. You ask if Mossy was fated to lose? He didn't lose. He won. Such a man can't be erased from people's memories; so he can be thrown out of office but never out of history. The memory is a private possession to which no authority has access. Mossy said the land we walk on belongs to us and everything we find in that land is ours. Nobody in this country had ever put it that way. He also said, Let everybody speak out — I want to hear their ideas. Do you understand this? After two and a half millennia of tyrannical degradation he pointed out to the Iranian that he is a thinking being. No ruler had ever done that! People remembered what Mossy said. It stayed in their minds and remains alive to this day. Words that open our eyes to the world are always the easiest to remember. And so it was with those words. Could anyone say that Mossy was wrong in what he did and said? Today everyone says that he was right, but that the problem is he was right too early. You can't be right too early, because then you risk your own career and at times your own life. It takes a long time for a truth to mature, and in the meantime people suffer or blunder around in ignorance. But suddenly along comes a man who speaks that truth too soon, before it has become universal, and then the ruling powers strike out at the heretic and burn him at the stake or lock him up or hang him because he threatens their interests or disturbs their peace. Mossy came out against the monarchical dictatorship and against the country's subjugation. Today monarchies are falling one after the other and subjugation has to be masked with a thousand disguises because it arouses such opposition. But he came out against it thirty years ago, when nobody here dared says these obvious things. I saw him two weeks before his death. When was that? It must have been in February, '67. He had spent the last ten years of his life under house arrest on a little farm outside Teheran. Visiting him was forbidden, of course, and the police watched the whole area. But you can arrange anything in this country if you know the right people and have the money. Money changes all the iron rules into rubber bands. Mossy must have been close to ninety then. I think he lasted so long because he wanted to see the time when life would admit he had been right. He was a hard man, hard on others because he never wanted to back down. But such a man couldn't back down even if he wished to. Until the end he thought clearly and knew exactly what was going on. Yet he could get around only with difficulty, leaning on a cane. He would stop and lie down on the ground to rest. The police who watched him said later that he was out walking like that one morning and lay down on the ground to rest, but he stayed there for a long time and when they went up to him they could see he was dead.

From the notes 2

Oil kindles extraordinary emotions and hopes, since oil is above all a great temptation. It is the temptation of ease, wealth, strength, fortune, power. It is a filthy, foul-smelling liquid that squirts obligingly up into the air and falls back to earth as a rustling shower of money. To discover and possess the source of oil is to feel as if, after wandering long underground, you have suddenly stumbled upon royal treasure. Not only do you become rich, but you are also visited by the mystical conviction that some higher power has looked upon you with the eye of grace and magnanimously elevated you above others, electing you its favorite. Many photographs preserve the moment when the first oil spurts from the well: people jumping for joy, falling into each other's arms, weeping. Oil creates the illusion of a completely changed life, life without work, life for free. Oil is a resource that anesthetizes thought, blurs vision, corrupts. People from poor countries go around thinking: God, if only we had oil! The concept of oil expresses perfectly the eternal human dream of wealth achieved through lucky accident, through a kiss of fortune and not by sweat, anguish, hard work. In this sense oil is a fairy tale and, like every fairy tale, a bit of a lie. Oil fills us with such arrogance that we begin believing we can easily overcome such unyielding obstacles as time. With oil, the last Shah used to say, I will create a second America in a generation! He never created it. Oil, though powerful, has its defects. It does not replace thinking or wisdom. For rulers, one of its most alluring qualities is that it strengthens authority. Oil produces great profits without putting a lot of people to work. Oil causes few social problems because it creates neither a numerous proletariat nor a sizable bourgeoisie. Thus the government, freed from the need of splitting the profits with anyone, can dispose of them according to its own ideas and desires. Look at the ministers from oil countries, how high they hold their heads, what a sense of power they have, they, the lords of energy, who decide whether we will be driving cars tomorrow or walking. And oil's relation to the mosque? What vigor, glory, and significance this new wealth has given to its religion, Islam, which is enjoying a period of accelerated expansion and attracting new crowds of the faithful.

From the notes 3

He says that what later happened with the Shah was quintessentially Iranian. Since time immemorial the reigns of every monarch have ended in lamentable, shameful ways. They died beheaded or with knives in their backs or — if they were luckier — had to flee the country, to die, exiled, abandoned, forgotten. He does not remember, although there may have been such exceptions, a Shah ending his days on the throne surrounded by respect and love, dying a natural death. He cannot remember the nation weeping for one of its rulers and bearing him to the grave with tearful eyes. In the last century all the Shahs, and there were quite a few of them, lost their crowns and their lives in unpleasant circumstances. The people regarded them as monsters, denounced their vilenesses, accompanied their departures with the curses and abuse of the crowd, and made news of their deaths the occasion for joyful holidays.

Of course, he says, we have had excellent Shahs like Cyrus and Abbas, but that was long ago. The last two dynasties spilled a great deal of innocent blood in order to win or keep the throne. Imagine the monarch Agha Mohammed Khan, who orders the entire population of the city of Kerman murdered or blinded — no exceptions. His praetorians set energetically to work. They line up the inhabitants, slice off the heads of the adults, gouge out the eyes of the children. In the end, despite taking regular breaks, the praetorians grow too exhausted to lift their swords or knives anymore. Only thanks to this fatigue do a remnant of the people preserve their lives and eyesight. Later, processions of blinded children leave the city. Some, wandering around the countryside, lose their way in the desert and die of thirst. Other groups reach inhabited settlements and, singing songs about the extermination of the citizens of Kerman, beg for food. News travels slowly in these days, so the people they meet are shocked to hear a chorus of barefoot, blinded children singing about whistling swords and tumbling heads. They ask what crime Kerman committed to earn such cruel punishment. At that question, the children break into a song about the offense, which was this: Because their fathers had sheltered the previous Shah, the new ruler could not forgive them. The spectacle of processions of blinded children arouses universal pity and the people do not refuse them sustenance, but the wanderers have to be fed discreetly and even secretly, since the little blinded ones, having been punished and stigmatized by the Shah, constitute a sort of peripatetic opposition and all support for the opposition is punishable to the highest degree. Gradually, sighted urchins attach themselves to these processions as guides for the blind children. Then they wander together, seeking food and protection from the cold and carrying the tale of the destruction of Kerman to the farthest villages.

These, he says, are the grim and brutal histories we hoard in our national memory. Tyrants won the throne by force, climbing toward it over corpses, amid maternal lamentations and the moans of the mortally wounded. The issue of succession was often settled in distant capitals, and the new pretender to the crown would enter Teheran with the British and Russian envoys supporting his elbows on either side. People treated such Shahs as usurpers and occupiers, and when one knows about that tradition one can understand how the mullahs managed to spark off so many uprisings against them. The mullahs would say: He, the one sitting in the palace, is a foreigner taking his orders from foreign powers. He is causing all your miseries; he's making a fortune at your expense and selling out the country. The people paid attention to this because the words of the mullahs struck them as the most obvious truths. I don't mean that the mullahs were saints. Far from it! Many dark forces lurk in the shadows of the mosque. But the abuses of power and the lawlessness of the palace made the mullahs into advocates of the national interest.

He returns to the fate of the last Shah. Back then, in Rome during his exile of a few days, Mohammed Reza has to face the fact that he could lose the throne forever and swell the exotic regiment of dispossessed royalty. That thought sobers him up. He wants to cast off the life that he has been squandering amid pleasures and distractions. (Later, he writes in his book that in Rome the sainted Ali appeared to him in a dream and said: Return to your homeland so that you can save the nation.) Now a great ambition is born in him, a yearning to demonstrate his strength and superiority. This trait, too, my interlocutor says, is most Iranian. One Iranian will never yield to another. Each believes in his own superiority, wants to be first and foremost, wants to impose his own exclusive *I. I! I! I* know better, *I* have more, *I* can do everything. The world begins with me, *I* am the whole world in myself. *I! I!* (To demonstrate, he stands up, rears his head high, peering down at me with exaggerated, haughty, oriental pride in his eyes.) Any group of Iranians immediately organizes itself according to hierarchical principles. I'm first, you're second, you're third. The second and third ones don't go for that, but immediately start trying to nose ahead, intriguing and maneuvering to unseat number one. Number one has to dig in to keep on top.

Dig in and get out the automatic rifles!

Similar rules apply elsewhere — for example, in the family. Because the man has to be superior, the woman must be inferior. Outside the home I might be a nonentity, but under my own roof I make up for it — here I am everything. Here my power admits of no division, and the more numerous the family, the wider and mightier my authority. The more children, the better: They give a man more to rule over. He becomes the monarch of a domestic state, commanding respect and admiration, deciding the fate of his subjects, settling disputes, imposing his will, ruling. (He stops to see what sort of an impression he is making on me. I protest energetically: I oppose such stereotypes. I know many of his fellow countrymen who are modest and polite, who have never made me feel inferior.) Quite true, he agrees, but only because you don't threaten us. You're not playing our game of seeing whose *I* is superior. This game made it impossible to create any solid parties because quarrels about leadership always broke out immediately and everyone would want to set up his own party. But now, upon his return from Rome, the Shah too throws himself body and soul into the game of trying to be the supreme *I*.

Since losing face is a great humiliation, he tells me, the Shah first of all tries to recoup his lost face. Imagine, under our system of values, a monarch — the father of his country — who flees at the most critical moment, and is shown buying jewelry with his wife! No, he has to erase that impression somehow. So when Zahedi, whose army has overthrown the Mossadegh government, sends the Shah a telegram saying that the tanks have done their job and it is safe for the monarch to return, the Shah first heads for Iraq to have himself photographed leaning on the tomb of Ali, patron saint of the Shiites.

A religious gesture — that's how to get back in our nation's good graces.

So the Shah returns, but Iran is still far from calm — students on strike, streets full of demonstrations, gun battles, funerals. In the army itself, conflicts, plots, contention. The monarch thinks it safer to stay in the palace; too many people want his head. He surrounds himself with his family, courtiers, and generals. Now, with Mossadegh out of the way, Washington starts sending big bucks and the Shah sets aside half of the take for the military.

So the soldiers get meat and bread. You have to remember how miserably our people live and what it means for a soldier to have meat and bread, how that raises him above others.

In those days there were children everywhere with big swollen bellies; they'd been eating only grass.

I remember a man who burned his child's eyelid with a cigarette. The eye puffed up with pus, and the face looked terrible. This man smeared his own arm with axle grease, so the arm swelled up and turned black. He only wanted people to feel sorry for him and his child, so that somebody would feed them.

The only toys of my childhood were stones. I pulled a stone with a string — I was the horse, and the stone was the Gilded Chariot of the Shah.

From the notes 4

Every pretext, he says, was good for rising up against the Shah. The people wanted to get rid of the dictator, and they flexed their muscles whenever they had the chance.

Everybody looked toward Qom. That's the way it had always been in our history. Whenever there was unhappiness and a crisis, people always started listening for the first signals from Qom.

And Qom was rumbling.

This was when the Shah extended diplomatic immunity to all US military personnel and their families. Our army was already full of American experts. And the mullahs came right out and said that the Shah's move offended the principle of sovereignty. Now, for the first time, Iran would hear Ayatollah Khomeini. Before that, no one knew of him — nobody but the people of Qom, that is. He was already over sixty, old enough to be the Shah's father. Later he would often call the ruler "son," but of course in an ironic and wrathful tone. Khomeini attacked him ruthlessly. My people, he would cry, don't trust him. He's not your man! He's not thinking of you — he's only thinking of himself and of the ones who give him orders. He's selling out our country, selling us all out! *The Shah must go!*

The police arrest Khomeini. Demonstrations begin in Qom. People call for his freedom. Next, other cities take to the streets — Teheran, Tabriz, Meshed, Isfahan. Then the Shah sends the army into the streets and the slaughter begins. (He stands up, stretches out his arms, and curls his hands as though gripping the stock of a machine-gun. He squints his right eye and makes a machine-gun *rattattat.*) That, he says, was June, 1963. The uprising went on for five months. Democrats from Mossadegh's party and the clerics led it. More than ten thousand people were killed or wounded. Then came a few years of funereal but never total quiet since some sort of rebellion and fighting was already breaking out. Khomeini was thrown out of the country and went to live in Iraq, in An Najaf, in the greatest Shiite city, site of Caliph Ali's tomb.

Now I wonder just what conditions created Khomeini. In those days, after all, there were plenty of more important, better-known ayatollahs as well as prominent political opponents of the Shah. We were all writing protests, manifestos, letters, statements. Only a small group of intellectuals read them because such materials could not be printed legally and, besides, most people didn't know how to read. We were criticizing the monarch, saying things were bad, demanding changes, reform, democratization, and justice. It never entered anyone's head to come out the way Khomeini did — to reject all that scribbling, all those petitions, resolutions, proposals. To stand before the people, and cry, *The Shah must go!*

That was the gist of what Khomeini said then, and he kept on saying it for fifteen years. It was the simplest thing, and everyone could remember it — but it took them fifteen years to understand what it really meant. After all, people took the institution of the monarchy as much for granted as the air. No one could imagine life without it.

The Shah must go!

Don't debate it, don't gab, don't reform or forgive. There's no sense in it, it won't change anything, it's a vain effort, it's a delusion. We can go forward only over the ruins of the monarchy. There's no other way.

The Shah must go!

Don't wait, don't stall, don't sleep.

The Shah must go!

The first time he said it, it sounded like a maniac's entreaties, like the keening of a madman. The monarchy had not yet exhausted the possibilities of endurance.

PHOTOGRAPH 7

Here we see a group of people standing at a bus stop on a Teheran street. People waiting for a bus look the same all over the world, which is to say that they have the same tired, apathetic expression on their faces, the same posture of sluggishness and defeat, the same dullness and antipathy in their eyes. The man who gave me the photograph, whenever that was, asked me if I noticed anything strange in it. I thought it over and said, no, I couldn't spot anything. He replied that the picture had been taken under cover, from a window across the street. I was to note, he said as he showed it to me, the guy (with the anonymous face of a lower-level bureaucrat) standing near, inclining his ear toward three other men talking. That guy was from Savak and he was always on duty at the bus stop, eavesdropping as people waited for the bus and absent-mindedly bantered about this and that. People could discuss only innocuous matters, but even then it was necessary to stay away from subjects in which the police could pick out significant allusions. Savak had a good ear for all allusions. One scorching afternoon an old man with a bad heart turned up at the bus stop and gasped, "It's so oppressive you can't catch your breath." "So it is," the Savak agent replied immediately, edging closer to the winded stranger; "it's getting more and more oppressive and people are fighting for air." "Too true," replied the naive old man, clapping his hand over his heart, "such heavy air, so oppressive." Immediately, the Savak agent barked, "Now you'll have a chance to regain your strength," and marched him off. The other people at the bus stop had been listening in dread, for they had sensed from the beginning that the feeble elderly man was committing an unpardonable error by saying "oppressive" to a stranger. Experience had taught them to avoid uttering such terms as *oppressiveness, darkness, burden, abyss, collapse, quagmire, putrefaction, cage, bars, chain, gag, truncheon, boot, claptrap, screw, pocket, paw, madness,* and expressions like *lie down, lie flat, spreadeagle, fall on your face, wither away, gotten flabby, go blind, go deaf, wallow in it, something's out of kilter, something's wrong, all screwed up, something's got to give* — because all of them, these nouns, verbs, adjectives, and pronouns, could hide allusions to the Shah's regime, and thus formed a connotative minefield where you could get blown to bits with one slip of the tongue. For a moment, for just an instant, a new doubt flashed through the heads of the people standing at the bus stop: What if the sick old man was a Savak agent too? Because he had criticized the regime (by using "oppressive" in conversation), he must have been free to criticize. If he hadn't been, wouldn't he have kept his mouth shut or spoken about such agreeable topics as the fact that the sun was shining and the bus was sure to come along any minute? And who had the right to criticize? Only Savak agents, whose job it was to provoke reckless babblers, then cart them off to jail. The ubiquitous terror drove people crazy, made them so paranoid they couldn't credit anyone with being honest, pure, or courageous. After all, they considered themselves honest and yet they couldn't bring themselves to express an opinion or a judgment, to make any sort of accusation, because they knew punishment lay ruthlessly in wait for them. Thus, if someone verbally attacked and condemned the monarch, everybody thought he was an agent provocateur, acting maliciously to uncover those who agreed with him, to destroy them. The more incisively and lucidly he spoke the views that they kept hidden inside themselves, the more suspect he seemed and the more violently they backed away from him, warning their friends: Watch out, something fishy about this guy, he's acting too brave. In this way terror carried off its quarry — it condemned to mistrust and isolation anyone who, from the highest motives, opposed coercion. Fear so debased people's thinking, they saw deceit in bravery, collaboration in courage. This time, however, seeing how roughly the Savak agent led his victim away, the people at the bus stop had to admit that the ailing old man could not have been connected with the police. In any case, the captor and his prey were soon out of sight, and the sole remaining question was, Where did they go? Nobody actually knew where Savak was located. The organization had no headquarters. Dispersed all over the city (and all over the country), it was everywhere and nowhere. It occupied houses, villas, and apartments no one ever paid any attention to. Its doors stood blank or bore the names of nonexistent firms and institutions. Only those who were in on the secret knew its telephone numbers. Savak might rent quarters in an ordinary apartment house, or you might enter its interrogation rooms through a store, a laundry, a nightclub. In such a situation, all walls can have ears and every door or gate can lead to the secret police. Whoever fell into the grip of that organization disappeared without a trace, sometimes forever. People would vanish suddenly and nobody would know what had happened to them, where to go, whom to ask, whom to appeal to. They might be locked up in a prison, but which one? There were six thousand. An invisible, adamant wall would rise up, before which you stood helpless, unable to take a step forward. Iran belonged to Savak, but within the country the police acted like an underground organization that appeared then disappeared, hiding its tracks, leaving no forwarding address. Yet, at the same time, some of its sections existed officially. Savak censored the press, books, and films (it was Savak that banned the plays of Shakespeare and Molière because they criticized monarchical and aristocratic vices). Savak ruled in the universities, offices, and factories. A monstrously overgrown cephalopod, it entangled everything, crept into every crack and corner, glued its suckers everywhere, ferreted and sniffed in all directions, scratched and bored through every level of existence. Savak numbered sixty thousand agents. It also controlled, someone calculated, three million informants, who denounced other people from such varied motives as money, self-preservation, or the desire for a job or promotion. Savak bought people or condemned them to torture, appointed them to positions or clapped them into the dungeons. It defined the enemy and thus decided who should be destroyed. Of such a sentence there could be no review, no appeal. Only the Shah could save the condemned. Savak answered to the Shah alone, and those upon whom the monarchy rested quailed helplessly before the police. The people waiting at the bus stop knew all this and therefore remained silent once the Savak agent and the old man had gone. They watched each other out of the corners of their eyes, for all they knew the one standing next to them might have to inform. He might have just returned from an interview in which Savak told him that if by chance he noticed or heard something and reported it, his son would gain admission to the university. Or that if he noticed or heard something, the entry about his belonging to the opposition would be erased from the records. "For God's sake, I'm not in the opposition," he says in self-defense. "Yes you are; it's written down right here that you are." Without wanting to (even though some of them try to hide it so as not to provoke any aggressive outbursts), the people at the bus stop look at each other with loathing. They are inclined to neurotic, disproportionate reactions. Something gets on their nerves, something smells bad, and they move away from each other, waiting to see who goes after whom, who attacks someone first. This reciprocal distrust is the work of Savak, which has been whispering into all ears that everyone belongs to Savak. This one, this one, and that one. That one too? Sure, of course. Everybody. But on the other hand these people waiting for the bus might be decent folk, and their inward agitation, which they mask with silence and stony expressions, might stem from the fact that a moment earlier they felt the quick surge of fear that a close brush with Savak causes. Had their instinct failed them only for a moment, and had they begun discussing some ambiguous subject like the way that fish spoils quickly in the heat and the amazing fact that a rotting fish's head begins to stink first and has to be cut off immediately if you want to save the rest — had they broached such a culinary theme they might have shared the hapless lot of the man who held his hand over his heart. But they are safe for the moment and they stand at the bus stop wiping their sweat away and fanning their wet shirts.

From the Notes 5

Whisky sipped in conspiratorial circumstances (and you really have to conspire now, with Khomeini's prohibition in effect) has, like all forbidden fruits, an additional, enticing tang. Yet the glass holds just a few drops of liquid — the host has drawn his last bottle from deep in hiding and knows he won't be able to buy a next one. Iran's remaining alcoholics are dying: Unable to purchase vodka, wine, or beer, they gulp one of a variety of chemical solvents, which finishes them off.

We are sitting on the ground floor of a small, comfortable, well-cared-for townhouse, looking through the open glass doors onto the garden and the wall separating the property from the street. Ten feet high, this wall multiplies the territory of intimacy and constitutes a sort of outer boundary of the house, within which the living space has been built. My host and hostess are both around forty; they studied in Teheran and work in one of the travel agencies (of which, due to their compatriots' wanderlust, there are hundreds).

"We've been married more than twelve years," says the man, whose hair is just beginning to gray, "but only now, for the first time, have my wife and I been discussing politics. We'd never before spoken to each other on the subject. It's the same with all the other couples we know."

No, he doesn't want to imply they lacked faith in each other. Nor had they ever made any sort of agreement about the matter. Yet they had an unspoken compact that they accepted mutually and almost unconsciously, which resulted from a certain sober reflection on human nature: namely, that you never know how someone is going to behave in an extreme predicament, what he can be forced into, what calumny, what betrayal.

"The worst of it," his wife suggests, "is that no one can predict how much torture he'll be able to stand. And Savak meant, above all, torture of the most horrible kind. They would kidnap a man as he walked along the street, blindfold him, and lead him straight into the torture chamber without asking a single question. There they would start in with the whole macabre routine — breaking bones, pulling out fingernails, forcing hands into hot ovens, drilling into the living skull, and scores of other brutalities — in the end, when the victim had gone mad with pain and become a smashed, bloody mass, they would proceed to establish his identity. Name? Address? What have you been saying against the Shah? Come on, what have you been saying? And you know, he might not have said anything, ever. He might have been completely innocent. But to Savak, that was nothing, being innocent. This way everyone will be afraid, innocent and guilty alike, everyone will feel the intimidation, no one will feel safe. The terror of Savak depended on this ability to strike at everyone, on everyone's being accused, since accusations had to do not with deeds but with the sort of intentions that

Savak could ascribe to anyone. Were you against the Shah? No, I wasn't. But you wanted to be, you shit! That was all it took.

"Sometimes they would hold a trial. For political acts (but what is a political act? Here, everything is a political act), they used only military courts: closed sessions, no counsel, no witnesses, and an instantaneous sentence. The execution took place later. Has anyone added up the number of people that Savak shot? Hundreds, for sure. Our great poet Khosrow Golesorkhi was shot. Our great director Keramat Denachian was shot. Dozens of writers, professors, and artists were imprisoned. Dozens of others had to emigrate to save themselves. Unbelievably ignorant and barbarous scum made up Savak, and when they got their hands on someone in the habit of reading books they worked him over with particular malice.

'Savak avoided trials and tribunals. They preferred other methods and did most of their killing in secret. Nothing could be established afterward. Who did the killing? Nobody knew. Who was guilty? There were no guilty ones.

"People went after the army and the police with their bare hands because they reached a point at which they could no longer stand the terror. It might look like desperation to you, but to us it was all the same.

"Do you know that if anyone mentioned Savak, whoever was talking to that person would look at him hours afterward and start thinking. Perhaps he's an agent? The one I was talking to might have been my father, my husband, my best friend. I would tell myself, Keep cool, it's nonsense, but nothing helped and the thought kept returning. Everything was sick — the whole regime was sick, and I have to say, I don't know when we will recover our health, our equilibrium. Years of a dictatorship like that broke us, psychologically, and I think it'll take a long time before we can begin living normally."

PHOTOGRAPH 8

This picture was hanging alongside slogans, proclamations, and a few other photographs on the bulletin board in front of a revolutionary committee building in Shiraz. I asked a student to translate the handwritten statement thumbtacked below the photo. "It's written here," he said, "that this little boy, three years old, Habib Fardust, was a prisoner of Savak." "What?" I asked. "Three years old and a prisoner?" He answered that sometimes Savak locked up a whole family, which is what happened in this case. He read the statement to the end and added that the boy's parents had died during torture. Now, a lot of books are being published about Savak's crimes, along with various police documents and personal accounts by people who survived torture. And, the most shocking thing for me, I saw color postcards being sold in front of the university showing the bodies of Savak victims. Six hundred years after Tamburlaine, the same pathological cruelty remains, unchanged except perhaps for the degree of mechanization. The most common instrument discovered in Savak quarters was an electrically heated metal table called "the frying pan," on which the victim was tied down by his hands and feet. Many died on these tables. Often, the accused was already raving by the time he entered the torture chamber — few people could bear the screams they heard while they waited, and the smell of burning flesh. But technological progress could not displace medieval methods in this nightmare world. In Isfahan, people were thrown into huge bags full of cats crazed with hunger, or among poisonous snakes. Accounts of such horrors, sometimes, of course, propagated by Savak itself, circulated among the populace for years. They were so threatening, and the definition of an enemy of the state was so loose and arbitrary, that everyone could imagine ending up in such a torture chamber.

PHOTOGRAPH 9

This was taken in Teheran on December 23, 1973: The Shah, surrounded by a bank of microphones, is giving a speech in a hall crowded with journalists. On this occasion Mohammed Reza, usually marked by a careful, studied reticence, cannot hide his emotion, his excitement, even — as the reporters note — his feverishness. In fact, the moment is important and fraught with consequences for the whole world: The Shah is announcing a new price for oil. The price had quadrupled in less than two months, and Iran, which used to earn five billion dollars a year from its petroleum exports, will now be bringing in twenty billion. What's more, control of this great pile of money will belong to the Shah alone. In his autocratic kingdom he can use it however he likes. He can throw it into the sea, spend it on ice cream, or lock it up in a golden safe. No wonder he looks so excited — how would any of us behave if we suddenly found twenty billion dollars in our pockets and knew, additionally, there would be twenty billion more each and every year, and eventually even greater sums? No wonder the Shah acted as he did, which was to lose his head. Instead of assembling his family, loyal generals, and trusted advisers to think over together the most reasonable way of using such a fortune, the ruler — who claims to have suddenly been blessed with a shining vision — announces to one and all that within a generation he will make Iran (which is a backward, disorganized, half-illiterate, barefoot country) into the fifth greatest power on earth. At the same time the monarch awakens high hopes among his people with the attractive slogan "Prosperity for All." Initially, with everyone aware that the Shah is in the really big money, these hopes do not seem completely vain.

A few days after the press conference shown in our photograph, the monarch grants an interview to *Der Spiegel* and says, "In ten years we will have the same living standard that you Germans, French, and English have now."

"Do you think, sir," the correspondent asks incredulously, "you will be really able to accomplish this within ten years?"

"Yes, of course."

But, says the astonished journalist, the West needed many generations to achieve its present standard of living. Will you be able to skip all that?

Of course.

I think of this interview now, when Mohammed Reza is no longer in the country and, surrounded by half-naked shivering children, I am wading through mud and dung among the squalid clay huts of a little village outside Shiraz. In front of one of the huts a woman is forming cow patties into circular cakes that, once dried, will serve (in this country of oil and gas!) as the only fuel for her home. Well, walking through this sad medieval village and remembering that interview of a few years back, the most banal of reflections comes into my head: Not even the greatest nonsense is beyond the reach of human invention.

For the time being, however, the autocrat locks himself in his palace and begins issuing the hundreds of decisions that convulse his homeland and lead to his overthrow five years later. He orders investment doubled, begins the great importing of technology, and creates the third most advanced army in the world. He commands that the most up-to-date equipment be ordered, installed, and put in use. Modern machines produce modern merchandise, and Iran is going to swamp the world with its superior output. He decides to build atomic power plants, electronics factories, steel mills, and great industrial complexes. Then, since there is a delicious winter in Europe, he leaves to ski in St. Moritz. But his charming, elegant residence in St. Moritz suddenly stops being a quiet hideaway and retreat, because word of the new Eldorado has spread around the world by this time and excited the power centers, where everyone immediately has begun calculating the amounts of money to be plucked in Iran. The premiers and ministers of otherwise respectable and affluent governments from serious, respected countries have begun to line up outside the Shah's Swiss domicile. The ruler sat in an armchair, warming his hands at the fireplace and listening to a deluge of propositions, offers, and declarations. Now the whole world was at his feet. Before him were bowed heads, inclined necks, and outstretched hands. "Now look," he'd tell the premiers and ministers, "you don't know how to govern and that's why you don't have any money." He lectured London and Rome, advised Paris, scolded Madrid. The world heard him out meekly and swallowed even the bitterest admonitions because it couldn't take its eyes off the gold pyramid piling up in the Iranian desert. Ambassadors in Teheran went crazy under the barrage of telegrams that their ministers turned on them, all dealing with money: How much can the Shah give us? When and on what conditions? You say he won't? Then insist, Your Excellency! We offer guaranteed service and will ensure favorable publicity! Instead of elegance and seriousness, pushing and shoving without end, feverish glances and sweaty hands filled the waiting rooms of even the most petty Iranian ministers. People crowding each other, pulling at each other's sleeves, shouting, Get in line, wait your turn! These are the presidents of multinational corporations, directors of great conglomerates, representatives of famous companies, and finally the delegates of more or less respectable governments. One after another they are proposing, offering, pushing this or that factory for airplanes, cars, televisions, watches. And besides these notable and — under normal circumstances — distinguished lords of world capital and industry, the country is being flooded with smaller fry, penny-ante speculators and crooks, specialists in gold, gems, discotheques, strip joints, opium, bars, razor cuts, and surfing. These operators are scrambling to get into Iran, and they are unimpressed when, in some European airport, hooded students try to hand them pamphlets saying that people are dying of torture in their homeland, that no one knows whether the victims carried off by the Savak are dead or alive. Who cares, when the pickings are good and when, furthermore, everything is happening under the Shah's exulted slogan about building a Great Civilization? In the meantime, Mohammed Reza has returned from his winter vacation, well rested and satisfied. Everyone is praising him at last; the whole world is writing about him as an exemplar, puffing up his splendid qualities, constantly pointing out that everywhere, wherever you turn, there are so many foulups and cheats, whereas, in his land — not a one.

Unfortunately, the monarch's satisfaction is not to last long. Development is a treacherous river, as everyone who plunges into its currents knows. On the surface the water flows smoothly and quickly, but if the captain makes one careless or thoughtless move he finds out how many whirlpools and wide shoals the river contains. As the ship comes upon more and more of these hazards the captain's brow gets more and more furrowed. He keeps singing and whistling to keep his spirits up. The ship looks as if it is still traveling forward, yet it is stuck in one place. The prow has settled on a sandbar. All this, however, happens later. In the meantime the Shah is making purchases costing billions, and ships full of merchandise are steaming toward Iran from all the continents. But when they reach the Gulf, it turns out that the small obsolete ports are unable to handle such a mass of cargo (the Shah hadn't realized this). Several hundred ships line up at sea and stay there for up to six months, for which delay Iran pays the shipping companies a billion dollars annually. Somehow the ships are gradually unloaded, but then it turns out that there are no warehouses (the Shah hadn't realized). In the open air, in the desert, in nightmarish tropical heat, lie millions of tons of all sorts of cargo. Half of it, consisting of perishable foodstuffs and chemicals, ends up being thrown away. The remaining cargo now has to be transported into the depths of the country, and at this moment it turns out that there is no transport (the Shah hadn't realized). Or rather, there are a few trucks and trailers, but only a crumb in comparison to the need. Two thousand tractor-trailers are thus ordered from Europe, but then it turns out there are no drivers (the Shah hadn't realized). After much consultation, an airliner flies off to bring South Korean truckers from Seoul. Now the tractor-trailers start rolling and begin to transport the cargo, but once the truckdrivers pick up a few words of Farsi, they discover they're making only half as much as native truckers. Outraged, they abandon their rigs and return to Korea. The trucks, unused to this day, still sit, covered with sand, along the Bander Abbas–Teheran highway. With time and the help of foreign freight companies, however, the factories and machines purchased abroad finally reach their appointed destinations. Then comes the time to assemble them. But it turns out that Iran has no engineers or technicians (the Shah hadn't realized). From a logical point of view, anyone who sets out to create a Great Civilization ought to begin with people, with training cadres of experts in order to form a native intelligentsia. But it was precisely that kind of thinking that was unacceptable. Open new universities and polytechnics, every one a hornets' nest, every student a rebel, a good-for-nothing, a freethinker? Is it any wonder the Shah didn't want to braid the whip that would flay his own skin? The monarch had a better way — he kept the majority of his students far from home. From this point of view the country was unique. More than a hundred thousand young Iranians were studying in Europe and America. This policy cost much more than it would have taken to create national universities. But it guaranteed the regime a degree of calm and security. The majority of these young people never returned. Today more Iranian doctors practice in San Francisco or Hamburg than in Tebriz or Meshed. They did not return even for the generous salaries the Shah offered. They feared Savak and didn't want to go back to kissing anyone's shoes. An Iranian at home could not read the books of the country's best writers (because they came out only abroad), could not see the films of its outstanding directors (because they were not allowed to be shown in Iran), could not listen to the voices of its intellectuals (because they were condemned to silence). The Shah left people a choice between Savak and the mullahs. And they chose the mullahs. When thinking about the fall of any dictatorship, one should have no illusions that the whole system comes to an end like a bad dream with that fall. The physical existence of the system does indeed cease. But its psychological and social results live on for years, and even survive in the form of subconsciously continued behavior. A dictatorship that destroys the intelligentsia and culture leaves behind itself an empty, sour field on which the tree of thought won't grow quickly. It is not always the best people who emerge from hiding, from the corners and cracks of that farmed-out field, but often those who have proven themselves strongest, not always those who will create new values but rather those whose thick skin and internal resilience have ensured their survival. In such circumstances history begins to turn in a tragic, vicious circle from which it can sometimes take a whole epoch to break free. But we should stop here or even go back a few years, because by jumping ahead of events we have already destroyed the Great Civilization, and first we have to build it. And yet how do we build it here, where there are no experts and the nation, even if it is eager to learn, has nowhere to study? In order to fulfill his vision, the Shah needed at least 700,000 specialists immediately. Somebody hit upon the safest and best way out — import them. The issue of security carried great weight here since foreigners, concerned about doing their jobs, making money, and getting home, would clearly not organize plots and rebellions or contest and rail against Savak. In general, revolutions would stop breaking out around the world if, for example, Ecuadorans built Paraguay and Indians built Saudi Arabia. Stir, mix together, relocate, disperse, and you will have peace. Tens of thousands of foreigners thus begin arriving. Airplane after airplane land at Teheran airport: domestic servants from the Philippines, hydraulic engineers from Greece, electricians from Norway, accountants from Pakistan, mechanics from Italy, military men from the United States. Let us look at the pictures of the Shah from this period: He's talking to an engineer from Munich, a foreman from Milan, a crane operator from Boston, a technician from Kuznetsk. And who are the only Iranians in these pictures? Ministers and Savak agents guarding the monarch. Their countrymen, absent from the pictures, observe it all with ever-widening eyes. This army of foreigners, by the very strength of its technical expertise, its knowing which buttons to press, which levers to pull, which cables to connect, even if it behaves in the humblest way, begins to dominate and starts crowding the Iranians into an inferiority complex. The foreigner knows how, and I don't. This is a proud people, extremely sensitive about its dignity. An Iranian will never admit he can't do something; to him, such an admission constitutes a great shame and a loss of face. He'll suffer, grow depressed, and finally begin to hate. He understood quickly the concept that was guiding his ruler: All of you just sit there in the shadow of the mosque and tend your sheep, because it will take a century for you to be of any use! I on the other hand have to build a global empire in ten years with the help of foreigners. This is why the Great Civilization struck Iranians as above all a great humiliation.

Photograph 10

This is not exactly a photograph but rather a reproduction of an oil painting in which a panegyrist-dauber portrays the

Shah in a Napoleonic pose (as when the French emperor, mounted, was directing one of his victorious battles). The Iranian Ministry of Information distributed this picture, and the Shah, who gloried in such comparisons, must therefore have approved. With galloons in giddy profusion, a plenitude of medals, and an intricate arrangement of cords across the chest, the well-cut uniform accentuates the attractive, athletic silhouette of Mohammed Reza. The image depicts him in his favorite role: commander of the army. The Shah, of course, always concerned himself with the welfare of his subjects, occupied himself with accelerated development, and so on, but these were all burdensome obligations resulting from the fact that he was the father of his country, while his true hobby, his real passion, was the army. Nor was this an entirely disinterested fascination. The army had always constituted the main prop of the throne and, as the years passed, it became more and more the sole support. At the moment that the army scattered, the Shah ceased to exist. And yet I hesitate to use the term "army," which can lead to mistaken associations — this was nothing but an instrument of domestic terror, a kind of police that lived in barracks. For this reason the nation looked upon any further development of the army with fear and terror, realizing that the Shah was swinging an ever thicker and more painful whip that would fall sooner or later across the backs of the people. The division between army and police (of which there were eight varieties) was merely formal. Army generals, intimates of the dictator, commanded each type of police. No less than Savak, the army enjoyed all the privileges. ("After studying in France," one doctor recalled, "I returned to Iran. My wife and I went to a movie and we were waiting on line to buy tickets. A noncommissioned officer appeared and went past everyone, straight to the box office. I made a remark about this. He walked back to me and slapped my face. I had to stand there and take it, because my neighbors in the line were warning me that any protest would land me in prison.") And so the Shah felt best in uniform and devoted the better part of his time to the military. For years his favorite occupation had been reading the magazines that the West produces in such profusion, displaying the newest varieties of weapons as advertised by their merchandisers and manufacturers. Mohammed Reza subscribed to all these periodicals and read them from cover to cover. For many years, before he had the money to buy every deadly toy that caught his fancy, he could only daydream, while engrossed in his reading, that the Americans would give him this tank or that airplane. And to be sure the Americans gave him a lot, but some Senator would always stand up to criticize the Pentagon for sending the Shah too many arms. Then the shipments would stop for a while. But now that the monarch was getting all that oil money, his problems were over. He immersed himself even more deeply in reading his magazines and arms catalogues. A stream of the most fantastic orders flowed out from Teheran. How many tanks does Great Britain have? Fifteen hundred? Fine, said the Shah — I'm ordering two thousand. How many artillery pieces does the Bundeswehr have? A thousand? Good, put us down for fifteen hundred. And why always more than the British army and the Bundeswehr? Because we've got to have the third best army in the world. It's a shame that we can't have the first or the second, but the third is within reach and we're going to have it. So once again the ships steamed, the airplanes flew, and the trucks rolled in the direction of Iran bearing the most modern weapons that man could devise and produce. The more trouble it is to build factories, the more attractive the supply of tanks looks. So Iran quickly transforms itself into a great showplace for all types of weapons and military equipment. "Showplace" is the right word, because the country lacks the warehouses, magazines, and hangars to protect and secure it all. The spectacle has no precedent. If you drive from Shiraz to Isfahan even today you'll see hundreds of helicopters parked off to the right of the highway. Sand is gradually covering the inert machines.

PHOTOGRAPH 11

A Lufthansa airliner at Mehrabad airport in Teheran. It looks like an ad, but in this case no advertising is needed because all the seats are sold. This plane flies out of Teheran every day and lands at Munich at noon. Waiting limousines carry the passengers to elegant restaurants for lunch. After lunch they all fly back to Teheran in the same airplane and eat their suppers at home. Hardly an expensive entertainment, the jaunt costs only two thousand dollars a head. For people in the Shah's favor, such a sum is nothing. In fact, it is the palace plebeians who only go to Munich for lunch. Those in somewhat higher positions don't always feel like enduring the travails of such long journeys. For them an Air France plane brings lunch, complete with cooks and waiters, from Maxim's of Paris. Even such fancies have nothing extraordinary about them. They cost hardly a penny when compared to a fairy-tale fortune like the one that Mohammed Reza and his people are amassing. In the eyes of the average Iranian the Great Civilization, the Shah's Revolution, was above all a Great Pillage at which the elite busied itself. Everyone in authority stole. Whoever held office and did not steal created a desert around himself; he made everybody suspicious. Other people regarded him as a spy sent to report on who was stealing how much, because their enemies needed such information. Whenever possible they got rid of someone like that in short order — he spoiled the game. All values thus came to have a reversed meaning. Whoever tried to be honest looked like a paid stoolie. If someone had clean hands, he had to keep them deeply hidden because there was something shameful and ambivalent about purity. The higher up, the fuller the pockets. Anyone who wanted to build a factory, open a business, or grow cotton had to give a piece of the action as a present to the Shah's family or one of the dignitaries. And they gave willingly, because you could get a business going only with the backing of the court. With money and influence you would overcome every obstacle. You could buy influence and use it afterward to multiply your fortune further. It is hard to imagine the river of money that flowed into the till of the Shah, his family, and the whole court elite. Bribes to the Shah's family generally ran to a hundred million dollars and more. Prime ministers and generals took bribes of from thirty to fifty million dollars. Lower down, the bribe was smaller, but it was always there! As prices rose, the bribes got bigger and ordinary people complained that more and more of their earnings went to feed the moloch of corruption. In earlier times Iran had known a custom of auctioning off positions. The Shah would announce a floor price for the office of governor and whoever bid highest became governor. Later, in office, the governor would plunder his subjects to recover (with interest) the money that had gone to the monarch. Now this custom was revived in a new form: The ruler would buy people by sending them to negotiate contracts, usually military ones.

The Shah's big money enabled him to breathe life into a new class, previously unknown to historians and sociologists: the petro-bourgeoisie. An unusual social phenomenon, the petro-bourgeoisie produces nothing, and unbridled consumption makes up its whole occupation. Promotion to this class depends on neither social conflict (as in feudalism) nor on competition (as in industry and trade), but only on conflict and competition for the Shah's grace and favor. This promotion can occur in the course of a single day, or even in a few minutes: The Shah's word or signature suffices. Whoever most pleases the ruler, whoever can best and most ardently flatter him, whoever can convince him of his loyalty and submission, receives promotion to the petro-bourgeoisie. This class of freeloaders quickly makes a significant part of the oil revenues its own and becomes proprietor of the country. At their elegant villas its members entertain visitors to Iran and shape their guests' opinions of the country (though the hosts themselves often have scant familiarity with their own culture). They have international manners and speak European languages — what better reasons for the Europeans to depend on them? But how misleading these encounters can be, how far these villas are from the local realities that will soon find a voice to shock the world! This class we are speaking about, guided by the instinct of self-preservation, has premonitions that its own career will be as short-lived as it is glittering. Thus, it sits on its suitcases from the start, exporting money and buying property in Europe and America. But since it has such big money, it can earmark a part of its fortunes for a comfortable life at home. Superluxurious neighborhoods, with enough conveniences and ostentation to stupefy any sightseer, begin to spring up in Teheran. Many of the houses cost more than a million dollars. These neighborhoods take root only a few streets away from districts where whole families huddle in narrow, crowded hovels without electricity or running water. This privileged consumption, this great hogging, should go on quietly and discreetly — take it, hide it, and leave nothing showing. Have a feast, but draw the curtains first. Build for yourself, but deep in the forest so as not to provoke others. So it should be — but not here. Here, custom ordains that you dazzle, knock the wind out of people, put everything on display, light all the lights, stun them, bring them to their knees, devastate them, pulverize them! Why have it at all, if it's to be on the sly, some alleged thing that somebody has seen or heard about? No! To have it like that is not to have it at all! To really have it is to blow your horn, shout it, let others come and gawk at it until their eyes pop out. And so, in plain sight of a silent and increasingly hostile people, the new class mounts an exhibition of the Iranian *dolce vita,* knowing no measure in its dissoluteness, rapacity, and cynicism. This provokes a fire in which the class itself, along with its creator and protector, will perish.

PHOTOGRAPH 12

This is a reproduction of a caricature that some opposition artist drew during the revolution. It shows a Teheran street. Big American cars, gas-guzzling roadhogs, are slinking along the avenue. On the sidewalks stand people with disappointed faces. Each of them is holding a part of a car: a door handle, fanbelt, or gearshift. The caption under the cartoon reads: "A Peykan for Everyone" (the Peykan is an Iranian economy car). When the Shah got into the big money he claimed that every Iranian would be able to buy his own car. The caricature shows how this pledge was fulfilled. Above the street, an angry Shah is sitting on a cloud with this inscription running above his head: "Mohammed Reza is furious with a nation that will not admit it feels an improvement." This is an interesting drawing, which tells how the Iranians interpreted the Great Civilization — as a Great Injustice. It created even bigger gulfs in a society that had never known equality. The Shahs, of course, had always had more than others, but it was hard to think of them as magnates. They had to sell concessions to keep the court in respectable shape. Shah Nasr-ed-Din ran up such debts in Paris brothels that, in order to bail himself out and get back home, he sold the French the rights to carry out archaeological expeditions and keep whatever artifacts they found. But that was in the past. Now, in the mid-seventies, Iran has become a behemoth of riches. And what does the Shah do? Half the money goes to the army, some to the elite, the rest for development. But what does that word mean? "Development" is no indifferent, abstract concept. It always applies to someone, in the name of something. Development can make a society richer and life better, freer, more just — but it can also do exactly the opposite. So it is in autocratic societies (where the elite identifies its interests with those of the state that guarantees its control); in such societies, development, aiming at strengthening the state and its apparatus of repression, reinforces dictatorship, subjugation, barrenness, vagueness, and the emptiness of existence. The development packaged and sold in Iran as the Great Civilization worked in just that way. Can anyone blame the Iranians for rising up at the cost of great sacrifices and destroying that model of development?

From the Notes 6

A Shiite is, first of all, a rabid oppositionist. At first the Shiites were a small group of the friends and backers of Ali, the son-in-law of Mohammed and husband of the Prophet's beloved daughter Fatima. When Mohammed died without a male heir and without clearly designating his successor, the Muslims began struggling over the Prophet's inheritance, over who would be caliph, or leader of the believers in Allah and thus the most important person in the Islamic world. Ali's party (*Shi'a* means "party") supports its leader for this position, maintaining that Ali is the sole representative of the Prophet's family, the father of Mohammed's two grandsons Hassan and Hussein. The Sunni Muslim majority, however, ignores the voices of the Shiites for twenty-four years and chooses Abu Bakr, Umar, and Utman as the next three caliphs. Ali finally becomes caliph, but his caliphate ends after five years, when an assassin splits his skull with a poisoned saber. Of Ali's two sons, Hassan will be poisoned and Hussein will fall in battle. The death of Ali's family deprives the Shiites of the chance to win power, which passes to the Sunni Omayyad, Abassid, and Ottoman dynasties. The caliphate, which Mohammed had conceived as a simple and modest institution, becomes a hereditary monarchy. In this situation the plebeian, pious, poverty-stricken Shiites, appalled by the nouveau-riche style of the victorious caliphs, go over to the opposition.

All this happens in the middle of the seventh century, but it has remained a living and passionately dwelt-on history to this day. When a devout Shiite talks about his faith he will constantly return to those remote histories and relate tearfully the massacre at Karbala in which Hussein had his head cut off. A skeptical, ironic European will think, God, what can any of that mean today? But if he expresses such thoughts aloud, he provokes the anger and hatred of the Shiite.

The Shiites have indeed had a tragic fate, and the sense of tragedy, of the historical wrongs and misfortunes that accompany them, is encoded deep within their consciousness. The world contains communities for whom nothing has gone right for centuries — everything has slipped through their hands, and every ray of hope has faded as soon as it began to shine — these people seem to bear some sort of fatal brand. So it is with the Shiites. For this reason, perhaps, they have an air of dead seriousness, of fervent unsettling adherence to their arguments and principles, and also (this is only an impression, of course) of sadness.

As soon as the Shiites (who constitute barely a tenth of all Muslims, the rest being Sunnis) go into opposition, the persecution begins. To this day they live the memory of the centuries of pogroms against them, and so they close themselves off in ghettoes, use signals only they understand, and devise conspiratorial forms of behavior. But the blows keep falling on their heads.

Gradually they start to look for safer places where they will have a better chance of survival. In those times of difficult and slow communication, in which distance and space constitute an efficient isolator, a separating wall, the Shiites try to move as far as possible from the center of power (which lies first in Damascus and later in Baghdad). They scatter throughout the world, across mountains and deserts, and descend step by step underground. So the Shiite diaspora, which has lasted till today, comes into being. The epic of the Shiites is full of acts of incredible abjuration, courage, and spiritual strength. A part of the wandering community heads east. Crossing the Tigris and the Euphrates, it passes through the mountains of Zagros and reaches the Iranian desert plateau.

At this time, Iran, exhausted and laid waste by centuries of war with Byzantium, has been conquered by Arabs who are spreading the new faith, Islam. This process is going on slowly, amid continual fighting. Until now the Iranians have had an official religion, Zoroastrianism, related to the ruling Sassanid dynasty. Now comes the attempt to impose upon them another official religion, associated with a new and, what's more, a foreign regime — Sunni Islam. It seems like jumping from the frying pan into the fire.

But exactly at this moment the poor, exhausted, wretched Shiites, still bearing the visible traces of the Gehenna they have lived through, appear. The Iranians discover that these Shiites are Muslims and, additionally (as they claim), the only legitimate Muslims, the only preservers of a pure faith for which they are ready to give their lives. Well, fine, say the Iranians — but what about your Arab brothers who have conquered us? Brothers? cry the outraged Shiites. Those Arabs are Sunnis, usurpers and our persecutors. They murdered Ali and seized power. No, we don't acknowledge them. We are in opposition! Having made this proclamation, the Shiites ask if they might rest after their long journey and request a jug of cold water.

This pronouncement by the barefoot newcomers sets the Iranians thinking along important lines. You can be a Muslim without being an establishment Muslim. What's more, you can be an opposition Muslim! And that makes you an even better Muslim! They feel empathy for these poor, wronged Shiites. At this moment the Iranians themselves are poor and feel wronged. They have been ruined by war, and an invader controls their country. So they quickly find a common language with these exiles who are looking for shelter and counting on their hospitality. The Iranians begin to listen to the Shiite preachers and finally accept their faith.

In this adroit maneuver one can see all the intelligence and independence of the Iranians. They have a particular talent for preserving their independence under conditions of subjugation. For hundreds of years the Iranians have been the victims of conquest, aggression, and partition. They have been ruled for centuries on end by foreigners or local regimes dependent on foreign powers, and yet they have preserved their culture and language, their impressive personality and so much spiritual fortitude that in propitious circumstances they can arise reborn from the ashes. During the twenty-five centuries of their recorded history the Iranians have always, sooner or later, managed to outwit anyone with the impudence to try ruling them. Sometimes they have to resort to the weapons of uprising and revolution to obtain their goal, and then they pay the tragic levy of blood. Sometimes they use the tactic of passive resistance, which they apply in a particularly consistent and radical way. When they get fed up with an authority that has become unbearable, the whole country freezes, the whole nation does a disappearing act. Authority gives orders but no one is listening, it frowns but no one is looking, it raises its voice but that voice is as one crying in the wilderness. Then authority falls apart like a house of cards. The most common Iranian technique, however, is absorption, active assimilation, in a way that turns the foreign sword into the Iranians' own weapon.

And so it is after the Arab conquest. You want Islam, they tell the conquerors, so Islam you'll get — but in our own national form and in an independent, rebellious version. It will be faith, but an Iranian faith that expresses our spirit, our culture, and our independence. This philosophy underlies the Iranian decision to accept Islam. They accept it in the Shiite variant, which at that time is the faith of the wronged and the conquered, an instrument of contestation and resistance, the ideology of the unhumbled who are ready to suffer but will not renounce their principles because they want to preserve their distinctness and dignity. Shiism will become not only the national religion of the Iranians but also their refuge and shelter, a form of national survival and, at the right moments, of struggle and liberation.

Iran transforms itself into the most restless province of the Muslim empire. Someone is always plotting here, there is always some uprising, masked messengers appear and disappear, secret leaflets and brochures circulate. The representatives of the occupying authorities, the Arab governors, spread terror and end up with results opposite to what they'd intended. In answer to the official terror the Iranian Shiites begin to fight back, but not in a frontal assault, for which they are too weak. An element of the Shiite community from now on will be — if one can use such a term — the terrorist fringe. Down to the present day, small, conspiratorial terrorist organizations that know neither fear nor pity operate in Iran. Half of the killings blamed on the ayatollahs are performed on the sentences of these groups. Generally, history regards the Shiites as the founders of the theory and practice of individual terror as a means of combat.

Fervor, orthodoxy, and an obsessive, fanatic concern for doctrinal purity characterize the Shiites as they characterize every group that is persecuted, condemned to the ghetto, and made to fight for its survival. A persecuted man cannot survive without an unshakable faith in the correctness of his choice. He must protect the values that led him to that choice. Thus, all the schisms — and Shiism has lived through dozens of them — had one thing in common: They were all, as we would put it, ultra-leftist. A fanatical branch was always springing up to accuse the remainder of its co-religionists of atrophied zeal, of treating lightly the dictates of faith, of expediency and taking the easy way out. Once the split took place the most fervid of the schismatics would take up arms to finish off the enemies of Islam, redeeming in blood (because they themselves often perished) the treachery and laziness of their backsliding brothers.

The Iranian Shiites have been living underground, in the catacombs, for eight hundred years. Their life recalls the suffering and trials of the first Christians. Sometimes it seems that they will be extirpated completely, that a final annihilation awaits them. For years they have been taking refuge in the mountains, holing up in caves, dying of hunger. Their songs that survive from these years, full of rue and despair, prophesy the end of the world.

But there have also been calmer periods, and then Iran became the refuge of all the oppositionists in the Muslim empire, who arrive from all corners of the world to find shelter, encouragement, and support among the plotting Shiites. They could also take lessons in the great Shiite school of conspiracy. They might, for example, master the principle of dissembling (*taqija*), which facilitates survival. This principle allows the Shiite, when he finds himself up against a stronger opponent, seemingly to accept the prevailing religion and acclaim himself a believer as long as doing so will save him and his people. Shiism also teaches *kitman*, the art of disorienting one's enemies, which allows the Shiite to contradict his own assurances and pretend that he is an idiot when danger threatens. Iran thus becomes a medieval mecca of malcontents, rebels, strange varieties of hermits, prophets, ecstatics, shady heretics, stigmatics, mystics, and fortune-tellers, who pour in along every road to teach, contemplate, pray, and soothsay. All this creates the atmosphere of religiosity, exaltation, and mysticism so characteristic of the country. I was very devout in school, says an Iranian, and all the kids thought I had a radiant halo around my head. Try imagining a European leader who writes that once when he was out riding he fell over a cliff and would have died except that a saint reached out a hand to save him. Yet the last Shah described such a scene in a book of his and all Iran read it seriously. Superstitious beliefs, such as faith in numbers, omens, symbols, prophecies, and revelations, have deep roots here.

In the sixteenth century the rulers of the Safavid dynasty raised Shiism to the dignity of official religion. What had been the ideology of mass opposition became the ideology of a state in opposition — for the Iranian state opposed the Sunni domination of the Ottoman Empire. But with time the relations between the monarchy and Shiism grew worse and worse.

The point is that Shiites not only reject the authority of the caliphs; they barely tolerate any lay authority at all. Iran constitutes the unique case of a country whose people believe only in the reign of their religious leaders, the imams, one of whom, the last, left this world (according to rational, if not to Shiite, criteria) in the ninth century.

Here we reach the essence of Shiite doctrine, the main act of faith for its believers. Deprived of any chance to win the caliphate, the Shiites turn their backs on the caliphs and henceforth acknowledge only the leaders of their own faith, the imams. Ali is the first imam, Hassan and Hussein his sons the second and third, and so on until the twelfth. All these imams died violent deaths at the hands of caliphs who saw them as dangerous rivals. The Shiites believe, however, that the twelfth and last imam, Mohammed, did not perish but disappeared into the cave under the great mosque at Samarra, in Iraq. This happened in 878. He is the Hidden Imam, the Awaited One, who will appear at the appropriate time as Mahdi (The One Led By God) to establish the kingdom of righteousness on earth. Afterward comes the end of the world. The Shiites believe that if the Twelfth Imam were not a living presence, the world would cease to be. They draw their spiritual strength from their faith in the Awaited One, they live and die for that faith. This is the simple human longing of a wronged, suffering community that finds hope and, above all, its sense of life, in that idea. We do not know when that Awaited One will appear; it could happen at any moment, even today. Then the tears will cease and each will take his seat at the table of plenty.

The Awaited One is the only leader the Shiites are willing to submit themselves to totally. To a lesser degree they acknowledge their religious helmsmen, the ayatollahs, and to a still lesser degree, the Shah. Because the Awaited One is the Adored, the focus of a cult, the Shah can be at best the Tolerated One.

From the time of the Safavids a dual authority, of the monarchy and the mosque, has existed in Iran. The relations between these two forces have varied but have never been overly friendly. If something disturbs this balance of forces, however, if, as happened, the Shah tries to impose total authority (with, to boot, the help of foreign backers), then the people gather in the mosques and the fighting starts.

For Shiites, the mosque is far more than a place of worship. It is also a haven where they can weather a storm and even save their lives. It is a territory protected by immunity, where authority has no right to enter. It used to be the custom that if a rebel pursued by the police took refuge in a mosque, he was safe and could not be removed by force.

There are marked differences in the construction of a mosque and a Christian church. A church is a closed space, a place of prayer, meditation, and silence. If someone starts talking, others rebuke him. A mosque is different. Its largest component is an open courtyard where people can pray, walk, discuss, even hold meetings. An exuberant social and political life goes on there. The Iranian who has been harassed at work, who encounters only grumpy bureaucrats looking for bribes, who is everywhere spied on by the police, comes to the mosque to find balance and calm, to recover his dignity. Here no one hurries him or calls him names. Hierarchies disappear, all are equal, all are brothers, and — because the mosque is also a place of conversation and dialogue — a man can speak his mind, grumble, and listen to what others have to say. What a relief it is, how much everyone needs it. This is why, as the dictatorship turns the screws and an ever more oppressive silence clouds the streets and workplaces, the mosque fills more and more with people and the hum of voices. Not all those who come here are fervent Muslims, not all are drawn by a sudden wave of devotion — they come because they want to breathe, because they want to feel like people. Even Savak has limited freedom of action on the grounds of the mosque. Nevertheless, the police arrest and torture many clerics who speak out against the abuse of power. Ayatollah Saidi dies during torture, on "the frying pan." Ayatollah Azarshari dies soon afterward, when Savak agents throw him into a pot of boiling oil. Ayatollah Teleghani emerges from prison with only a short time to live because of the way he has been treated. He has no eyelids. As he watched, Savak agents raped Teleghani's daughter, and when the ayatollah closed his eyes, they burned his eyelids with cigarettes so he would have to watch. All this goes on in the 1970s. But in his policy toward the mosque, the Shah entangles himself in no small web of contradictions. On the one hand he persecutes the clerical opposition and, on the other — always courting public favor — he declares himself a fervent Muslim, perpetually makes pilgrimages to the holy places, immerses himself in prayer, and solicits the blessing of the mullahs. How, then, can he declare open war on the mosques?

The Shiite also visits the mosque because it is always close, in the neighborhood, on the way to everywhere. Teheran contains a thousand mosques. The tourist's uninstructed eye spots only a few of the most impressive ones. But the majority of them, especially in the poorer neighborhoods, are modest buildings difficult to distinguish from the flimsily constructed little houses in which the underclass lives. Built of the same clay, they melt into the monotonous faces of the lanes, back alleys, and street corners, resulting in a working, intimate climate between the Shiite and his mosque. No need to make long treks, no need to get dressed up: The mosque is everyday life, life itself.

The first Shiites to reach Iran were city people, small merchants and craftsmen. They would enclose themselves in their ghettoes, build mosques, and set up their market stands and little shops next door. Craftsmen opened workshops nearby. Because Muslims should wash before they pray, baths appeared as well. And because a Muslim likes to drink tea or coffee and have a bite to eat after praying, there were also restaurants and coffee shops close at hand. Thus comes into being that phenomenon of the Iranian cityscape, the bazaar — a colorful, crowded, noisy mystical-commercial-gustatory nexus. If someone says, "I'm going to the bazaar," he does not necessarily mean that he needs his shopping bag. You go to the bazaar to pray, to meet friends, to do business, to sit in a café. You can go there to catch up on gossip and take part in an opposition rally. Without having to run all over town, the Shiite finds in one place, the bazaar, all that is indispensable for earthly existence and, through prayer and offerings, also ensures his eternal life.

From the Notes

Mahmud Azari returned to Iran at the beginning of 1977. He had lived in London for eight years, supporting himself by translating books for various publishers and writing copy for advertising agencies. He was an older, solitary man who liked to spend his leisure time walking and talking with his compatriots. During such meetings the conversation centered around purely English problems; Savak was ubiquitous, even in London, and wise people avoided talking about the problems of their homeland.

Near the end of his sojourn he received several letters, through private channels, from his brother in Teheran. The brother wrote that interesting times were coming and urged him to return. Mahmud feared interesting times, but since his brother had always held the ascendancy in their family, he packed his luggage and returned to Teheran.

He couldn't recognize the city.

The onetime desert oasis had become a stunning overcrowded metropolis of five million people. A million cars strained in the narrow streets, immobile because a line going one way would meet a line going another way, while other lines of traffic were cutting across, slicing through from left and right, from northeast and southwest, forming giant smoking, roaring, stellar coils stuck in narrow cagelike lanes. Thousands of car horns blared from dawn to dusk, without purpose.

He noticed that the people, once quiet and courteous, now quarreled at the slightest provocation, burst out angrily for no reason at all, jumped down each other's throats, screamed and cursed. These people seemed like weird, surrealistic bifurcated monsters whose upper half would bow obsequiously before anyone important or endowed with authority, while at the same time their hind parts were trampling on anyone weaker. This apparently led to an inner equilibrium that, however mean and pitiable, made it possible for them to survive.

He found himself dreading the thought that, when he came face to face with such a monster, he would be unable to tell which of its functions, the bowing or the trampling, would come first. But he found soon enough that the trampling reflex predominated; it naturally presented itself and withdrew only under the extreme pressure of grave circumstances.

During his first days he went to the local park, sat down beside a man on a bench, and tried to start a conversation. But the man stood up without a word and walked briskly away. After a time, he approached another passer-by, who gave him a look of terror as if he had run into a lunatic. So he gave up and decided to return to his hotel.

The gruff, petulant man at the desk told him he had to report to the police. For the first time in eight years he felt true terror and realized instantly that such terror can never be outgrown: It was the same touch of ice against the bare back, the same heaviness in his feet that he remembered so well from years gone by.

The police occupied an obscure, foul-smelling building down the street from the hotel. Mahmud took his place in a long line of sullen, listless people. On the other side of the railing, the policemen were sitting reading newspapers. Total silence reigned in the big, crowded room: The police were reading, and no one in the line dared so much as whisper. Then, the station suddenly opened for business. The police scraped their chairs back and forth, rummaged through their desks, and began cursing their waiting clients with the choicest obscenities.

Where does this universal boorishness come from? wondered the frightened Mahmud. When his turn came, the police gave him a questionnaire and told him to fill it out immediately. He kept hesitating over each item and noticed that the whole room was watching him suspiciously. Terrified, he began writing nervously and awkwardly as if he were semi-illiterate. He felt sweat breaking out on his forehead, discovered he had forgotten his handkerchief, and began perspiring all the more.

After handing in the questionnaire he hurried out into the street and, walking along distractedly, ran into another pedestrian. The stranger started cursing him. Some passers-by stopped to gawk and in this way Mahmud committed a crime — his behavior had provoked a gathering. The law forbade all unauthorized assemblies. A policeman showed up and Mahmud had to explain that it was all an accident and that not a word had been spoken against the Shah during the whole contretemps. Nevertheless the policeman took down his name and address and pocketed a thousand rials.

Mahmud returned downcast to the hotel. The police had already written his name down — twice, in fact. He started thinking about what would happen if the two entries were brought together somehow. Then he consoled himself with the thought that it might all vanish in the bureaucracy's bottomless confusion.

His brother came by in the morning and Mahmud told him, as soon as they had greeted each other, that the police already had his name twice. Wouldn't it be wiser, he asked, to go back to London?

Mahmud's brother wanted to talk, but he pointed to the light fixture, telephone, electrical outlets, and night lamp: let's take a ride in the suburbs, he said. In the brother's old, beat-up car they headed for the mountains. When the road grew deserted they parked. It was March, with a keen wind and snow piled all around. They hid behind a tall boulder and stood there shivering.

("It was then that my brother told me I had to stay because the revolution had begun and I would be needed. 'What revolution? Are you mad?' I asked. All disturbances frightened me, and in general I can't stand politics. Every day I practice yoga, read poetry, and translate. What do I need politics for? But my brother told me I didn't understand anything and proceeded to explain. The starting point, he said, was Washington. That was where our fate would be decided. 'Right now, Jimmy Carter is talking about human rights. The Shah will have to pay attention. He has to stop using torture, release some prisoners, and create at least the appearance of democracy. That will be enough to get us started!' My brother was becoming excited, and I hushed him even though there was no one around. During this meeting he handed me a typescript of more than two hundred pages. It was a memorandum by the writer Ali Asqara Jawadi — an open letter to the Shah. In it, Jawadi wrote about the current crisis, about the subjugation of the country, and the scandals of the monarchy. My brother said that the document was circulating secretly and that people were making more copies of it. 'Now,' he added, 'we are waiting to see how the Shah responds. Whether Jawadi goes to jail or not. For the time being he is getting threatening telephone calls but nothing more. There is a café he comes to — you'll be able to talk to him.' I replied I was afraid to meet someone who was surely under surveillance.")

They went back to the city, where Mahmud locked himself in his room and spent the night reading the memorandum. Jawadi accused the Shah of destroying the moral foundations of the country. All thinking, he wrote, was being annihilated, and the most enlightened people were being silenced. Culture found itself behind bars or had to go underground. Jawadi warned that you could not measure progress by the number of tanks and machines. Man, with his sense of liberty and dignity, was the measure of progress. As he read, Mahmud listened for footsteps in the corridor.

The next day he worried about what to do with the typescript. Not wanting to leave it in his room, he took it with him. But as he walked down the street he realized that such a bundle of paper looked suspicious, so he bought a newspaper, which he folded around the typescript. Even so, he was in constant fear of being stopped and searched. It was the worst in the hotel lobby, where he was certain the package attracted attention. So he decided to limit his comings and goings, just to be on the safe side.

Mahmud tried gradually to find out what had happened to his old friends, his university classmates. Some, unfortunately, had died, many had emigrated, and a few were in jail. At last, though, he managed to track down several current addresses. At the university he called on Ali Kaidi, an old companion on mountain excursions. Kaidi had become a professor of botany, a specialist in sclerophyllous plants. Cautiously, Mahmud asked him about the situation in the country. Kaidi thought for a moment and said that for years he had devoted all his time to sclerophyllous plants. He went on to develop the topic, saying that sclerophyllous plants were to be found in areas with specific climatic conditions: rain in winter, summers hot and dry. In winter, it was ephemeral species like the therophytes and geophytes that flourished, while in summer it was the xerophytes, which had the ability to limit their transpiration. Mahmud, to whom these words meant nothing, asked his friend in a general way whether major events could be expected. Kaidi again fell to musing and began after a while to talk about the splendid crown of the Atlantic cedar (*Cedrus atlanticus*). "And yet," he added, warming to the subject, "I have examined the Himalayan cedar (*Cedrus deodora*), which grows in our country, and I must say that it is even more beautiful!"

Another day he came across an old friend with whom he had tried to write a play at school. Now this friend had become mayor of Karaj. The mayor invited Mahmud to dinner at a good restaurant, and near the end of the meal the latter asked about the mood of society. The mayor did not want to go beyond the affairs of his town. In Karaj, he said, they were asphalting the main roads. They had begun to build a sewer system, which even Teheran lacked. The crushing avalanche of numbers and jargon convinced Mahmud he had asked the wrong question. But he made up his mind to press on and inquired of his old schoolmate what was the most common subject of conversation in the city. "How should I know? Their own problems. These people don't think. Nothing matters to them. They are lazy, apolitical, and they can't see past the ends of their noses. The problems of Iran, indeed! What do they care?" And he went on talking about how they had built a new paraldehyde factory and were going to cover the country with their paraldehyde. Mahmud felt like an ignoramus, a relic, because he didn't even know what the word meant. "And, generally speaking," he asked his friend, "don't you have any bigger problems to worry about?" The other man replied, "And how!" He leaned over the table and whispered, "The output of these new factories is only fit to be thrown away. Trash and scrap. People don't want to work, and they don't give a damn about what they produce. Everywhere there's the same listlessness, some kind of vague, sullen resistance. The whole country is stuck on a sandbar." "But why?" Mahmud demanded. "I can't say," his friend answered, sitting up and beckoning to the waiter. "It's hard for me to say" — and Mahmud watched as the frank soul of the sometime schoolboy dramatist, having emerged for a moment to voice some unusual words, swiftly disappeared again behind a barricade of generators, conveyors, relays, and control keys.

("For these people the concrete has become an asylum, a hideout, salvation. Cedar — well, yes, that's something concrete; so is asphalt. You can speak out about the concrete, express yourself as freely as you like. The great thing about concrete is that it has its own clearly demarcated armed frontiers with warning bells along them. When a mind immersed in the concrete begins to approach that border, the bells warn that just beyond lies the field of treacherous general ideas, undesirable reflections, and syntheses. At the sound of this signal the cautious mind recoils and dives back into the concrete. We can see the whole process in the face of our interlocutor. He might be going along, talking in the most lively of ways, quoting numbers, percentages, names, and dates. We can see how firmly he's anchored in the concrete, like a rider in the saddle. Then we ask: 'That's all well and good, but why are people, in some way, shall we say, imperfectly satisfied?' At this point we can see how his face changes. The alarm bells have gone off: *Attention! You are about to cross the border of the concrete!* He grows silent and looks desperately for a way out — which is, of course, to retreat back into the concrete. Glad to have escaped the trap, panting with relief, he again starts talking with animation, haranguing and crushing us with the concrete in any form whatsoever: an object, an existence, a creature, or a phenomenon. It is a characteristic of disparate concretes that they cannot join together spontaneously to create general images. For example, two negative concretes can exist side by side, but they will not form a joint image until human thought welds them together. But the alarm bells prevent that synthesizing thought from ever occurring, so the negative concretes go on coexisting without forming any disturbing pattern. To succeed in making each person close himself within the borders of his concrete existence is to create an atomized society made up of *n*-number of concrete individuals unable to unite into a harmoniously acting comity.")

Mahmud, however, decided to tear himself away from mundane problems and sail into the realm of imagination and emotion. He traced another friend who, he learned, had become a respected poet. Hassan Rezvani received him in a luxurious modern villa. They sat at the edge of the swimming pool (the summer heat had set in) sipping gin and tonic from frosty glasses. Hassan complained of tiredness: He had just returned the day before from a trip to Montreal, Chicago, Paris, Geneva, and Athens. He had traveled around giving lectures on the Great Civilization, the Revolution of the Shah and the Nation. It had been hard work, he confessed, because noisy subversives had prevented him from speaking and had insulted him. Hassan showed Mahmud a new volume of his poems, dedicated to the Shah. The first poem bore the title "Where He Casts His Glance, Flowers Bloom." If, so the poem said, the Shah merely looked anywhere at all, a carnation or a tulip would blossom forth.

> And where longer his glance reposes,
> There blossom roses.

Another poem was titled "Where He Stands, a Spring Appears." In these verses the author assured his readers that wherever the monarch sets his foot, a spring of crystal-clear water will appear:

Let the Shah stop somewhere and stand
And a broad river flows across the land.

These verses were read on the radio and in schools. The monarch himself referred to them in flattering terms and endowed Hassan with a Pahlavi Foundation fellowship.

Walking down the street one day, Mahmud saw a man standing under a tree. Drawing nearer, with difficulty he recognized Mohsen Jalaver, with whom he had broken into print years before in a student magazine. Mahmud knew that Mohsen had been tortured and jailed for sheltering a mujahedeen friend in his apartment. Mahmud stopped and held out his hand in greeting. Mohsen looked at him blankly. Mahmud pronounced his own name as a reminder. Mohsen reacted only by saying, "I don't care." He just stood there, slumped over and staring at the ground. "Let's go somewhere," Mahmud said. "I'd like to talk with you." Still motionless, his head dropping, Mohsen replied, "I don't care." Mahmud felt a chill. "Look," he tried again, "why don't we make a date to talk soon?" Mohsen didn't reply, but only slumped lower. Finally, in a strangled whisper, he said, "Take the rats away."

Sometime later, Mahmud rented a small apartment in the center of town. He was still unpacking when three men came in, greeted him as a new resident of the district, and asked whether he belonged to Rastakhiz, the Shah's party. Mahmud said he did not belong, since he had only recently returned from spending some years in Europe. This raised their suspicions: Those who had a chance to leave seldom returned. They began asking why he had come back, and one of them wrote down Mahmud's answers in a notebook. With terror, Mahmud realized he was now going into the records for the third time. When the visitors handed him a membership application, Mahmud replied that he had been apolitical all his life and did not intend to join. They looked at him dumbfounded — the new tenant, they must have thought, could not know what he was saying. So they gave him a leaflet in which a statement of the Shah's was printed in capital letters: THOSE WHO WILL NOT JOIN THE RASTAKHIZ PARTY ARE EITHER TRAITORS WHO BELONG IN PRISON OR PEOPLE WHO DO NOT BELIEVE IN THE SHAH, THE NATION, AND THE HOMELAND AND THUS OUGHT NOT TO EXPECT TO BE TREATED IN THE SAME WAY AS OTHERS. Nevertheless, Mahmud had the backbone to ask to think it over for a day, saying that he wanted to discuss it with his brother.

"You have no choice," his brother said. "We all belong! The whole nation has to belong as if it were a single man." Mahmud went home, and when the activists returned the next day he declared his allegiance to the party. Thus he became a warrior of the Great Civilization.

Soon he received an invitation to the nearby Rastakhiz local headquarters. A meeting of party members in the creative arts was in progress, attended by all those who wanted to contribute their work to the thirty-seventh anniversary of the Shah's coronation. The whole life of the empire flowed from anniversary to anniversary in an unctuous, ornate, dignified rhythm with the solemn and resplendent celebration of each date connected to the Shah and his outstanding achievements: the White Revolution and the Great Civilization. Vast staffs of people kept watch, calendars in hand, to make sure the monarch's birthday, his last wedding, his coronation, and the births of the heir to the throne and the other happily begotten offspring would not be forgotten. New feasts swelled the list of traditional holidays. As soon as one celebration ended, the preparations for the next one began, fever and excitement charged the air, all work came to a halt, and everyone made ready for the next day that would pass amid sumptuous banqueting, showers of distinctions, and a sublime liturgy.

As Mahmud was leaving the meeting, the writer and translator Golam Qasemi came up to him. They had not seen each other for years; while Mahmud was staying in London, Golam had remained at home writing stories that glorified the Great Civilization. He lived a splendid life, with free access to the palace and his books published in leather bindings. Golam had something to tell Mahmud. He dragged him to an Armenian café, spread a weekly on the table, and said proudly, "Look what I've managed to get published!" It was his translation of a poem by Paul Eluard. Mahmud glanced at it and said, "Well, what's so remarkable about this? What are you so proud of?" "What?" Golam burst out. "Don't you understand anything? Read it carefully:

> Now is the time of sorrow, of darkest night
> When even the blind must not be sent outside."

As he read, he underlined every word with his fingernail. "All the effort, all the trouble it took me," he said excitedly, "to get this printed, to convince Savak that it could appear! In this country where everything is supposed to inspire optimism, blossoming, smiles — suddenly 'the time of sorrow'! Can you imagine?" Golam was wearing the face of the victor, elated at his own courage.

It was only at this moment, looking at Golam's cunning face, that Mahmud believed for the first time in the approaching revolution. It seemed to him that he suddenly understood everything. Golam can sense the coming catastrophe. He is beginning to manoeuver shrewdly, to shift his battle lines, to try to purge himself of blame, to pay tribute to the rumbling force that already resounds in his frightened and besieged heart. Golam has just sneaked a thumbtack onto the scarlet cushion the Shah sits on. This is hardly a bomb. It won't kill the Shah, but it makes Golam feel better — he has joined the opposition, however hermetically. Now he will show off the thumbtack, talk it up, seek the praise and recognition of his friends, and revel in the feeling of having shown his independence.

But Mahmud's old doubts come back in the evening. He and his brother were walking along streets that grew more and more empty, past faces deprived of any vitality. Exhausted pedestrians were trudging home or standing silently at bus stops. Some men were sitting against a wall, dozing, their faces on their knees. Mahmud pointed at them and asked, "Who is going to carry out this revolution of yours? They are all sleeping." His brother replied, "These very people will do it. One day they will sprout wings." But Mahmud could not imagine it.

("And yet early in the summer I myself began to feel something changing, something reviving in people, something in the air. The atmosphere was indefinable, a little like the first glimmer of consciousness after a tormenting dream. In the first place, the Americans forced the Shah to release some intellectuals from prison. The Shah cheated — he released some and locked up others. But the important thing was that he'd given in, and the first crack, the first little gap, appeared in the rigid system. Into that gap stepped people who wanted to resurrect the Iranian Writers' Organization, which the Shah had dissolved in '69. All organizations, even the most innocent, had been banned. Only Rastakhiz and the mosque remained. *Tertium non datur.* The government continued to say no to a writers' union. Accordingly, secret meetings began in private homes, most often in old country houses outside Teheran where it was easier to maintain secrecy. They called these meetings 'cultural evenings.' First there would be a poetry reading, and then the discussion of the current situation would begin. It was at one of these meetings that I first saw people who had been in prison. They were writers, scientists and students. I looked closely at their faces, trying to see what scars great fear and suffering made. I thought they were behaving normally. They acted hesitantly, as if the light and the presence of others made them dizzy. They kept a watchful distance from their surroundings, as if the approach of any other person could lead to a beating. One of them looked awful — he had burn scars on his face and hands, and he walked with a cane. He was a student in the law school, and fedayeen brochures had been found in a search of his home. I remember his telling how he was led by the Savak agents into a big room, one of whose walls was whitehot iron. There were rails on the floor, a metal chair on the rails; the Savak men strapped him into the chair. Then they pushed a button and the chair began moving toward the wall in a slow, jerky movement, an inch a minute. He calculated it would take two hours to reach the wall, but after an hour he could no longer stand the heat and began shouting that he would admit everything, even though there was nothing to admit — he'd found the brochures lying in the street. We all listened silently as the student cried. I'll always remember what he then said: 'God,' he said, 'why have you chastised me with such a terrible deformity as thinking? Why have you taught me to think, instead of teaching me the humility of cattle!' In the end he fainted, and we carried him into the next room. Other survivors of the dungeon, in contrast, usually remained silent.")

But Savak quickly tracked down the location of these meetings. One night, when they had left the house and were walking along the path by the road, Mahmud heard a sudden rustling in the bushes off to the side. After a moment of confusion he heard shouts. Then he felt a monstrous blow to the back of his head, and the darkness grew violently deeper. He staggered, fell face-first on the stone pathway, and lost consciousness. He came to in his brother's arms. In the darkness, his eyes swollen and covered with blood, he could barely make out his brother's gray, bruised face. He heard moans, someone cried out for help, and after a moment he recognized the voice of the student, who must have gone into shock. As if it came from deep in the earth, the voice kept repeating, "Why did you teach me to think? Why did you chastise me with this horrible deformity?" Now Mahmud could see that the arm of one of those standing near him was dangling, broken, and he saw another man kneeling by him with blood oozing from his mouth. Trying to keep close together, the group moved slowly toward the highway in deadly fear the beating would start again.

Next morning Mahmud stayed in bed with a swollen head and a stitched-up forehead. The housekeeper brought him a newspaper which had an account of the previous night's incident: "Last night in the vicinity of Kan, a group of recidivistic social outcasts organized a repugnant orgy at one of the local farmhouses. The patriotic inhabitants of the area complained several times about the impropriety and repulsiveness of their behavior. Nevertheless the riotous gang, instead of paying due attention to the local patriots, attacked them with stones and clubs. The people who were attacked had to defend themselves and restore order to the area." Mahmud groaned, feeling feverish, his head spinning.

"The Shah's days are numbered," Mahmud's brother was saying firmly a few days later. "No one can butcher a defenseless nation for years." "Numbered?" Mahmud asked in astonishment, lifting his bandaged head. "Have you lost your mind? Have you seen his army?" Of course his brother had seen it, the question was rhetorical. Mahmud had been constantly exposed to the imperial divisions at the movies and on television: parades, maneuvers, fighters, rockets, the barrels of heavy artillery aiming straight at his heart. He'd look with disgust at the rows of elderly generals who drew themselves laboriously to attention before the monarch. I wonder, he'd think, how they'd behave if a real bomb went off nearby. They'd all have heart attacks. Every month more and more tanks and mortars crowded the TV screen. Mahmud thought they constituted a terrible force that could grind any opposition into dust and blood.

The scorching summer months began. The desert that embraces Teheran from the south panted fire. Mahmud felt better now and decided to resume his habit of evening walks after a long hiatus. He strolled out. It was late. He was walking through dark little streets near some grim, gigantic construction site being rapidly completed — the new Rastakhiz headquarters. He thought he saw a figure moving in the darkness and heard someone coming out of the bushes. But there are no bushes here! He tried to calm down. Frightened, nevertheless, he turned into the next street. He was afraid, even though he knew the fear had no precise cause. He felt cold and decided to head home. He was walking downhill near the center of town. Suddenly he heard footsteps behind him. He was surprised, because he had been sure the street was empty, that there was no one around. He quickened his pace involuntarily, and whoever was behind him did the same. They walked in step for a while, rhythmically, like two honor guards. Mahmud decided to speed up even more. Now he was walking with short, sharp steps. The other one did the same, and came even closer. Mahmud, trying to think of a way out, slowed down. But fear conquered common sense, and he lengthened his stride again to escape. He was covered with goose pimples. He was terrified of provoking the other. He thought he was postponing the blow, but whoever was behind him drew closer and Mahmud could hear the other's breathing as their steps echoed together in the tunnel of the street. Finally Mahmud broke down and started to run. The other gave chase and Mahmud rushed onward, his jacket flapping like a black banner. Suddenly he realized others had joined the pursuit, dozens of footsteps were rumbling behind him with the clatter of an incipient avalanche. He kept running though he was out of breath. He was soaking wet, semiconscious, and felt he would collapse in a second. With the last of his strength he grabbed hold of a nearby gate, swung himself up onto the grating of a barred window, and hung there, suspended. He thought his heart would burst, and he felt an alien fist breaking through his ribs dealing painful, deathly blows ravaging his insides. Finally he brought himself under control and looked around. The only living soul in the street was a gray cat hurrying along the wall. Slowly, with his hand over his heart, he dragged himself home, broken, depressed, vanquished.

("It all began with that night attack when we were leaving the meeting. From then on I felt the fear. It would hit me at the most unexpected moments. I was ashamed, but I couldn't deal with it. It began to disturb me profoundly. I thought with horror that by carrying that fear inside I'd involuntarily become part of a system founded on fear. A terrible, yet indissoluble, relation, a sort of pathological symbiosis, had established itself between me and the dictator. Through my fear I was supporting a system I hated. The Shah could depend on me — on my fear, that is, on the fact that my fear would not let him down. If I could have gotten rid of my fear, I could have undermined the foundations of the throne just a little, but I was as yet unable to do that.")

Mahmud felt bad all summer. Apathetically he would receive news his brother brought him.

Everyone was living on top of a volcano in those days, and anything could set off the eruption. A horse ran mad and attacked people in Kermanshah — a peasant had ridden the animal into town and tethered it to a tree along the main street. It shied and reared up at some passing cars, broke free, and injured several people. Finally a soldier shot it. People crowded around the dead animal. The police arrived and began to disperse the crowd. Someone shouted, "And where were the police when the horse was trampling the people?" Then a fight broke out. The police opened fire. But the crowd kept growing. The crowd was boiling mad, and people began putting up barricades. Then the army came in and the town commander ordered a curfew. Mahmud's brother asked him, "Do you think it would have taken much more for an uprising to erupt there?" But Mahmud, as usual, thought his brother was exaggerating.

As Mahmud was walking along Reza Khan Boulevard one day early in September, he noticed a commotion in the street. He could see, in the distance, at the main entrance to the university, military trucks, helmets, guns, and soldiers in green fatigues. They were grabbing students and hauling them off to the trucks. Mahmud heard screams and saw young men running away down the street. Suddenly there was a wail of sirens, and the trucks full of students began moving up the street. The students stood squeezed onto the platforms, their hands bound with ropes, soldiers surrounding them. Apparently the roundup was over, and Mahmud decided to go tell his brother the army had raided the university. A young high school teacher named Ferejdun Ganji, whom Mahmud remembered meeting at the cultural evening before the police assault, was there. According to Mahmud's brother, when Ganji had gone to school the day after the night assault, the principal, who had already received a telephone call from Savak, fired him, shouting that he was a hooligan and a bully and that he, the principal, was ashamed to let innocent students see him. Ganji had now been unemployed for a long time, roaming around in search of work.

The brother decided they'd go to dinner at the bazaar. In the crowded stuffy back alleys, Mahmud noticed a lot of young people staggering around in an opium daze. Some of them were sitting on the sidewalk, staring ahead with glassy, unseeing eyes. Others were harassing passers-by, calling them names and making fists at them. "How can the police tolerate this?" he asked his brother. "Quite easily," the latter answered. "From time to time a crowd like this comes in handy. Today they'll be given clubs and a few pennies and sent to beat up the students. Later the press will write about the healthy, patriotic youth who answered the call of the party and taught a lesson to the good-for-nothing dregs of society nesting within the university's walls."

They entered a restaurant and took a table in the middle of the room. They were still waiting for service when Mahmud noticed two brawny men lounging at the next table. Savak! — the idea shot through his mind. "What do you say?" he asked his brother and Ganji. "Let's move closer to the door." They changed tables, and the waiter appeared at once. But while his brother was ordering, Mahmud's eyes fell on two handsome, coquettishly dressed men holding hands. Savak agents pretending to be homosexuals! he thought with terror. "I'd rather sit by the window," he suggested to his brother. "I want to see what's going on in the bazaar." They moved to the new table. Barely had they begun to eat, however, when three men came in and, without a word, as if they had planned it in advance, took a table at the same window from which Mahmud was observing the bazaar. "We're being watched," he whispered, and at the same instant he noticed that the waiters, who had been following their table hopping, were looking at them suspiciously. He realized that, to the waiters, they themselves must have looked like Savak agents moving around the room in search of prey. He lost his appetite and the food swelled in his mouth. Pushing his plate aside, he motioned with his head to leave.

They reached his brother's home and decided to drive to the mountains and get away from the wearying city and breathe some fresh air. They drove north through the nouveau-riche district of Shemiran, where the air still smelled of cement. They passed imposing mansions, ostentatious villas, luxurious restaurants and dress shops, spacious gardens, exclusive country clubs with swimming pools and tennis courts. Here every square foot of desert — the desert stretched away in all directions — cost hundreds if not thousands of dollars and even so was in great demand. This was the charmed circle of the court elite, another world, another planet.

In the next weeks, there were new demonstrations, new protest letters, and secret lectures and discussions. In November a committee for the defense of human rights and an underground students' union were established. At times Mahmud visited the nearby mosques and saw the crowds of people there, but the prevailing attitude of fervent piety remained alien to him, and he did not know how to make contact with that world. You have to ask yourself, he thought, where all these people are going. Most of them could not even read and write. They found themselves in an incomprehensible, hostile world that was cheating and exploiting them and held them in contempt. They wanted to find some sort of shelter for themselves, some relief and protection. But one thing they knew: In this unfriendly reality, only Allah remained the same as back in their villages, as always, as everywhere.

He was reading a lot now and translating London and Kipling. When he remembered his English years, he thought about the differences between Europe and Asia and repeated Kipling's formula to himself: "East is east, and West is west, and never . . ." Never, no, they will never meet, and they will never understand each other. Asia will reject every European transplant as a foreign body. The Europeans will be shocked and outraged, but they will be unable to change Asia. In Europe epochs succeed each other, the new drives out the old, the earth periodically cleanses itself of its past so that people of our century have trouble understanding our ancestors. Here it is different, here the past is as alive as the present, the unpredictable cruel Stone Age coexists with the calculating, cool age of electronics — the two eras live in the same man, who is as much the descendant of Genghis Khan as he is the student of Edison . . . if, that is, he ever comes into contact with Edison's world.

One night at the beginning of January Mahmud heard a banging on his door. He jumped out of bed.

("It was my brother. I could see he was extremely agitated. Out in the corridor, he said only one word — 'Massacre!' He didn't want to sit down, kept walking around the room, spoke chaotically. He said the police had opened fire on civilians in the streets of Qom. He mentioned five hundred dead. A lot of women and children had perished. It had all come about because of what seemed like a trivial matter. An article criticizing Khomeini had appeared in the newspaper *Etelat*. It had been written by someone from the palace or the government. When the paper reached Qom, Khomeini's city, people started gathering in the streets to talk about it. The police opened fire. A panic broke out in the square — people wanted to get away but there was nowhere to run because the police were blocking all the streets and kept on firing. I remember that all Teheran was agitated the following day. You could feel that dark and terrible times were approaching.")

THE DEAD FLAME

The revolution put an end to the Shah's rule. It destroyed the palace and buried the monarchy. It all began with an apparently small mistake on the part of the imperial authority. With that one false step, the monarchy signed its own death warrant.

The causes of a revolution are usually sought in objective conditions — general poverty, oppression, scandalous abuses. But this view, while correct, is one-sided. After all, such conditions exist in a hundred countries, but revolutions erupt rarely. What is needed is the consciousness of poverty and the consciousness of oppression, and the conviction that poverty and oppression are not the natural order of this world. It is curious that in this case, experience in and of itself, no matter how painful, does not suffice. The indispensable catalyst is the word, the explanatory idea. More than petards or stilettoes, therefore, words — uncontrolled words, circulating freely, underground, rebelliously, not gotten up in dress uniforms, uncertified — frighten tyrants. But sometimes it is the official, uniformed, certified words that bring about the revolution.

Revolution must be distinguished from revolt, *coup d'état*, palace takeover. A coup or a palace takeover may be planned, but a revolution — never. Its outbreak, the hour of that outbreak, takes everyone, even those who have been striving for it, unawares. They stand amazed at the spontaneity that appears suddenly and destroys everything in its path. It demolishes so ruthlessly that in the end it may annihilate the ideals that called it into being.

It is a mistaken assumption that nations wronged by history (and they are in the majority) live with the constant thought of revolution, that they see it as the simplest solution. Every revolution is a drama, and humanity instinctively avoids dramatic situations. Even if we find ourselves in such a situation we look feverishly for a way out, we seek calm and, most often, the commonplace. That is why revolutions never last long. They are a last resort, and if people turn to revolution it is only because long experience has taught them there is no other solution. All other attempts, all other means have failed.

Every revolution is preceded by a state of general exhaustion and takes place against a background of unleashed aggressiveness. Authority cannot put up with a nation that gets on its nerves; the nation cannot tolerate an authority it has come to hate. Authority has squandered all its credibility and has empty hands, the nation has lost the final scrap of patience and makes a fist. A climate of tension and increasing oppressiveness prevails. We start to fall into a psychosis of terror. The discharge is coming. We feel it.

As for the technique of the struggle, history knows two types of revolution. The first is revolution by assault, the second revolution by siege. All the future fortune, the success, of a revolution by assault is decided by the reach of the first blow. Strike and seize as much ground as possible! This is important because such a revolution, while the most violent, is also the most superficial. The adversary has been defeated, but in retreating he has preserved a part of his forces. He will counter-attack and force the victor to withdraw. Thus, the more far-reaching the first blow, the greater the area that can be saved in spite of later concessions. In a revolution by assault, the first phase is the most radical. The subsequent phases are a slow but incessant withdrawal to the point at which the two sides, the rebelling and the rebelled-against, reach the final compromise. A revolution by siege is different; here the first strike is usually weak and we can hardly surmise that it forebodes a cataclysm. But events soon gather speed and become dramatic. More and more people take part. The walls behind which authority has been sheltering crack and then burst. The success of a revolution by siege depends on the determination of the rebels, on their will power and endurance. One more day! One more push! In the end, the gates yield, the crowd breaks in and celebrates its triumph.

It is authority that provokes revolution. Certainly, it does not do so consciously. Yet its style of life and way of ruling finally become a provocation. This occurs when a feeling of impunity takes root among the elite: We are allowed anything, we can do anything. This is a delusion, but it rests on a certain rational foundation. For a while it does indeed look as if they can do whatever they want. Scandal after scandal and illegality after illegality go unpunished. The people remain silent, patient, wary. They are afraid and do not yet feel their own strength. At the same time, they keep a detailed account of the wrongs, which at one particular moment are to be added up. The choice of that moment is the greatest riddle known to history. Why did it happen on that day, and not on another? Why did this event, and not some other, bring it about? After all, the government was indulging in even worse excesses only yesterday, and there was no reaction at all. "What have I done?" asks the ruler, at a loss. "What has possessed them all of a sudden?" This is what he has done: He has abused the patience of the people. But where is the limit of that patience? How can it be defined? If the answer can be determined at all, it will be different in each case. The only certain thing is that rulers who know that such a limit exists and know how to respect it can count on holding power for a long time. But there are few such rulers.

How did the Shah violate this limit and pass sentence on himself? Through a newspaper article. Authority ought to know that a careless word can bring down the greatest empire. It seems to know this, seems to be vigilant, and yet at a certain moment the instinct for self-preservation fails and, self-assured and overweening, it commits the mistake of arrogance and perishes. On January 8, 1978, an article attacking Khomeini appeared in the government newspaper *Etelat*. At the time, Khomeini was fighting the Shah from abroad, where he lived as an émigré. Persecuted by the despot, expelled from the country, Khomeini was the idol and conscience of the people. To destroy the myth of Khomeini was to destroy something holy, to shatter the hopes of the wronged and the humiliated. Such exactly was the intention of the article.

What should one write to ruin an adversary? The best thing is to prove he is not one of us — the stranger, alien, foreigner. To this end we create the category of the true family. We here, you and I, the authorities and the nation, are a true family. We live in unity, among our own kind. We have the same roof over our heads, we sit at the same table, we know how to get along with each other, how to help each other out. Unfortunately, we are not alone. All around us are hordes of strangers, aliens, foreigners who want to destroy our peace and quiet and take over our home. What is a stranger? Above all, a stranger is someone worse than us — and dangerous at the same time. If only he were merely worse, and left well enough alone! Not a chance! He is going to muddy the waters, make trouble, destroy. He is going to set us at odds with each other, make fools of us, break us. The stranger lies in wait for you.

He is the cause of your misfortunes. And where does his power come from? From the fact that there are strange (foreign, alien) forces behind him. These forces may be identified or not, but one thing is certain: They are powerful. Or rather, they are powerful if we treat them lightly. If, on the other hand, we remain vigilant and keep fighting, then we will be stronger. Now look at Khomeini. There's a stranger for you. His grandfather came from India, so let's ask ourselves: Whose interest is this foreigner's grandson serving? That was the first part of the article. The second part had to do with health. What a great thing it is that we're healthy! For our true family is also a healthy family. Of sound body and mind. To whom do we owe this health? To our authorities, who have assured us a good, happy life and are therefore the best authorities under the sun. And who could oppose such authorities? Only someone devoid of common sense. Since ours are the best authorities, it would take a madman to fight against them. A sound community must identify such fools and send them away, into isolation. Thus, it's a good thing the Shah expelled him from the country. Otherwise, Khomeini would have had to be locked up in a lunatic asylum.

When this newspaper article reached Qom, it made the people indignant. They congregated in the streets and the squares. Those who could read read aloud to the others. The commotion drew people into larger and larger groups, shouting and debating — interminable debating is a passion with the Iranians, anywhere, at any time of day or night. The groups most agitated by this incessant talk were like magnets; they kept attracting new listeners, until in the end a massive crowd had assembled in the main square. And that is exactly the thing that the police most dislike. Who gave permission for this great mass? Nobody. No permission has been given. And who gave them permission to shout? To wave their hands around? The police know in advance that these were rhetorical questions and that it was time to get down to business.

Now the most important moment, the moment that will determine the fate of the country, the Shah, and the revolution, is the moment when one policeman walks from his post toward one man on the edge of the crowd, raises his voice, and orders the man to go home. The policeman and the man on the edge of the crowd are ordinary, anonymous people, but their meeting has historic significance. They are both adults, they have both lived through certain events, they have both had their individual experiences. The policeman's experience: If I shout at someone and raise my truncheon, he will first go numb with terror and then take to his heels. The experience of the man at the edge of the crowd: At the sight of an approaching policeman I am seized by fear and start running. On the basis of these experiences we can elaborate a scenario: The policeman shouts, the man runs, others take flight, the square empties. But this time everything turns out differently. The policeman shouts, but the man doesn't run. He just stands there, looking at the policeman. It's a cautious look, still tinged with fear, but at the same time tough and insolent. So that's the way it is! The man on the edge of the crowd is looking insolently at uniformed authority. He doesn't budge. He glances around and sees the same look on other faces. Like his, their faces are watchful, still a bit fearful, but already firm and unrelenting. Nobody runs though the policeman has gone on shouting; at last he stops. There is a moment of silence. We don't know whether the policeman and the man on the edge of the crowd already realize what has happened. The man has stopped being afraid — and this is precisely the beginning of the revolution. Here it starts. Until now, whenever these two men approached each other, a third figure instantly intervened between them. That third figure was fear. Fear was the policeman's ally and the man in the crowd's foe. Fear interposed its rules and decided everything. Now the two men find themselves alone, facing each other, and fear has disappeared into thin air. Until now their relationship was charged with emotion, a mixture of aggression, scorn, rage, terror. But now that fear has retreated, this perverse, hateful union has suddenly broken up; something has been extinguished. The two men have now grown mutually indifferent, useless to each other; they can go their own ways. Accordingly, the policeman turns around and begins to walk heavily back toward his post, while the man on the edge of the crowd stands there looking at his vanishing enemy.

Fear: a predatory, voracious animal living inside us. It does not let us forget it's there. It keeps eating at us and twisting our guts. It demands food all the time, and we see that it gets the choicest delicacies. Its preferred fare is dismal gossip, bad news, panicky thoughts, nightmare images. From a thousand pieces of gossip, portents, ideas, we always cull the worst ones — the ones that fear likes best. Anything to satisfy the monster and set it at ease. Here we see a man listening to someone talking, his face pale and his movements restless. What's going on? He is feeding his fear. And what if we have nothing to feed it with? We make something up, feverishly. And what if (seldom though this may occur) we can't make anything up? We rush to other people, look for them, ask questions, listen and gather portents, for as long as it takes to satiate our fear.

All books about all revolutions begin with a chapter that describes the decay of tottering authority or the misery and sufferings of the people. They should begin with a psychological chapter, one that shows how a harassed, terrified man suddenly breaks his terror, stops being afraid. This unusual process, sometimes accomplished in an instant like a shock or a lustration, demands illuminating. Man gets rid of fear and feels free. Without that there would be no revolution.

The policeman returns to his post and reports to the commander. The commander sends in the riflemen and orders them to take up positions on the roofs of the houses around the square. He himself drives to the center of town and uses loudspeakers to call on the crowd to disperse. But no one wants to listen. So he withdraws to a safe place and gives the order to open fire. Automatic weapons fire cascades onto the heads of the people. Panic breaks out, there is tumult, those who can, escape. Then the shooting stops. The dead remain on the square.

It is not known whether the Shah was shown the pictures of this square photographed by the police after the massacre. Let's say that he was. Let's say that he wasn't. The Shah worked a great deal, and he may not have had time. His working day began at seven in the morning and ended at midnight. He actually rested only in winter, when he went to St. Moritz to ski. Even there he allowed himself only two or three runs before returning to his residence and going back to work. Recalling these occasions, Madame L. states that the Empress behaved very democratically at St. Moritz. As evidence she produces a photograph showing the Empress waiting in line for the ski lift. Yes, just like that — standing there, leaning on her skis, a smart, pleasant woman. And yet, says Madame L., they had so much money that she could have ordered a ski lift built just for herself!

The dead are wrapped in white sheets and laid on wooden biers here. The pallbearers walk briskly, breaking into a trot at times, creating an impression of great haste. The whole procession hurries, there are cries and lamentations, the mourners are restless and uneasy. It is as if the dead man's very presence exasperates them, as if they want to commit him to the earth immediately. Afterwards they lay out food on the grave and the funeral banquet takes place. Whoever passes by is invited to join in and given food. Those who are not hungry get only some fruit, an apple or an orange, but everyone must eat something.

On the following day, the period of commemoration begins. People ponder the dead man's life, his kind heart and upright character. This period lasts forty days. On the fortieth day, family, friends, and acquaintances gather in the home of the deceased. Neighbors collect around the house — the whole street, the whole village, a crowd of people. It is a crowd of commemoration, a lamenting crowd. Pain and grief reach their piercing apogee, their mourning, desperate crescendo. If the death was natural, congruent with the usual human lot, this gathering — which can go on round the clock — consists of some hours of ecstatic, pathetic discharge, followed by a mood of dulled and humble resignation. But if the death was a violent one, inflicted by somebody, a spirit of retaliation and a thirst for revenge seize the people. In an atmosphere of unfettered wrath and aggravated hatred, they pronounce the name of the killer, the author of their sorrow. And it is believed that, even if he is far away, he will shudder at that moment: Yes, his days are numbered.

A nation trampled by despotism, degraded, forced into the role of an object, seeks shelter, seeks a place where it can dig itself in, wall itself off, be itself. This is indispensable if it is to preserve its individuality, its identity even its ordinariness. But a whole nation cannot emigrate, so it undertakes a migration in time rather than in space. In the face of the encircling afflictions and threats of reality, it goes back to a past that seems a lost paradise. It regains its security in customs so old and therefore so sacred that authority fears to combat them. This is why a gradual rebirth of old customs, beliefs, and symbols occurs under the lid of every dictatorship — in opposition to, against the will of the dictatorship. The old acquires a new sense, a new and provocative meaning. This happens hesitantly and often secretly at first, but as the dictatorship grows increasingly unbearable and oppressive, the strength and scope of the return to the old increase. Some voices call this a regressive return to the middle ages. So it may be. But more often, this is the way the people vent their opposition. Since authority claims to represent progress and modernity, we will show that our values are different. This is more a matter of political spite than a desire to recapture the forgotten world of the ancestors. Only let life get better and the old customs lose their emotional coloration to become again what they were — a ritual form.

Such a ritual, suddenly transformed into a political act under the influence of the growing opposition spirit, was the commemoration of the dead forty days after their death. What had been a ceremony of family and neighbors turned into a protest meeting. Forty days after the Qom events, people gathered in the mosques of many Iranian towns to commemorate the victims of the massacre. In Tabriz, the tension grew so high that an insurrection broke out. A crowd marched through the street shouting "Death to the Shah." The army rolled in and drowned the city in blood. Hundreds were killed, thousands were wounded. After forty days, the towns went into mourning — it was time to commemorate the Tabriz massacre. In one town — Isfahan — a despairing, angry crowd welled into the streets. The army surrounded the demonstrators and opened fire; more people died. Another forty days pass and mourning crowds now assemble in dozens of towns to commemorate those who fell in Isfahan. There are more demonstrations and massacres. Forty days later, the same thing repeats itself in Meshed. Next it happens in Teheran, and then in Teheran again. In the end it is happening in nearly every city and town.

Thus the Iranian revolution develops in a rhythm of explosions succeeding each other at forty-day intervals. Every forty days there is an explosion of despair, anger, blood. Each time the explosion is more horrible — bigger and bigger crowds, more and more victims. The mechanism of terror begins to run in reverse. Terror is used in order to terrify. But now, the terror that the authorities apply serves to excite the nation to new struggles and new assaults.

The Shah's reflex was typical of all despots: Strike first and suppress, then think it over: What next? First display muscle, make a show of strength, and later perhaps demonstrate you also have a brain. Despotic authority attaches great importance to being considered strong, and much less to being admired for its wisdom. Besides, what does wisdom mean to a despot? It means skill in the use of power. The wise despot knows when and how to strike. This continual display of power is necessary because, at root, any dictatorship appeals to the lowest instincts of the governed: fear, aggressiveness toward one's neighbors, bootlicking. Terror most effectively excites such instincts, and fear of strength is the wellspring of terror.

A despot believes that man is an abject creature. Abject people fill his court and populate his environment. A terrorized society will behave like an unthinking, submissive mob for a long time. Feeding it is enough to make it obey. Provided with amusements, it's happy. The rather small arsenal of political tricks has not changed in millennia. Thus, we have all the amateurs in politics, all the ones convinced they would know how to govern if only they had the authority. Yet surprising things can also happen. Here is a well-fed and well-entertained crowd that stops obeying. It begins to demand something more than entertainment. It wants freedom, it demands justice. The despot is stunned. He doesn't know how to see a man in all his fullness and glory. In the end such a man threatens dictatorship, he is its enemy. So it gathers its strength to destroy him.

Although dictatorship despises the people, it takes pains to win their recognition. In spite of being lawless — or rather, because it is lawless — it strives for the appearance of legality. On this point it is exceedingly touchy, morbidly oversensitive. Moreover, it suffers from a feeling (however deeply hidden) of inferiority. So it spares no pains to demonstrate to itself and others the popular approval it enjoys. Even if this support is a mere charade, it feels satisfying. So what if it's only an appearance? The world of dictatorship is full of appearances.

The Shah, too, felt the need of approval. Accordingly, when the last victims of the Tabriz massacre had been buried, a demonstration of support for the monarchy was organized in that city. Activists of the Shah's party, Rastakhiz, were assembled on the great town commons. They carried portraits of their leader with suns painted above his monarchical head. The whole government appeared on the reviewing stand. Prime Minister Jamshid Amuzegar addressed the gathering. The speaker wondered how a few anarchists and nihilists could destroy the nation's unity and upset its tranquility. "They are so few that it is even hard to speak of a group. This is a handful of people." Fortunately, he said, words of condemnation were flowing in from all over the country against those who want to ruin our homes and our well-being — after which a resolution of support for the Shah was passed. When the demonstration ended, the participants sneaked home. Most were carried by buses to the nearby towns from which they'd been imported to Tabriz for the occasion.

After this demonstration, the Shah felt better. He seemed to be getting back on his feet. Until then he had been playing with cards marked with blood. Now he made up his mind to play with a clean deck. To gain popular sympathy, he dismissed a few of the officers who had been in charge of the units that opened fire on the inhabitants of Tabriz. Among the generals, this move caused murmurs of discontent. To appease the generals, he ordered that the inhabitants of Isfahan be fired on. The people responded with an outburst of anger and hatred. He wanted to appease the people, so he dismissed the head of Savak. Savak was appalled. To appease Savak, the Shah allowed them to arrest whomever they wished. And so by reversals, detours, meanderings, and zigzags, step by step, he drew nearer to the precipice.

The Shah was reproached for being irresolute. Politicians, they say, ought to be resolute. But resolute about what? The Shah was resolute about retaining his throne, and to this end he explored every possibility. He tried shooting and he tried democratizing, he locked people up and he released them, he fired some and promoted others, he threatened and then he commended. All in vain. People simply did not want a Shah anymore; they did not want that kind of authority.

The Shah's vanity did him in. He thought of himself as the father of his country, but the country rose against him. He took it to heart and felt it keenly. At any price (unfortunately, even blood) he wanted to restore the former image, cherished for years, of a happy people prostrate in gratitude before their benefactor. But he forgot that we are living in times when people demand rights, not grace.

He also may have perished because he took himself too literally, too seriously. He certainly believed that the people worshipped him and thought of him as the best and worthiest part of themselves, the highest good. The sight of their revolt was inconceivable, shocking, too much for his nerves. He reckoned he had to react immediately. This led him to violent, hysterical, mad decisions. He lacked a certain dose of cynicism. He could have said: "They're demonstrating? So let them demonstrate. Half a year? A year? I can wait it out. In any case, I won't budge from the palace." And the people, disenchanted and embittered, willy-nilly, would have gone home in the end because it's unreasonable to expect people to spend their whole lives marching in demonstrations. But the Shah didn't want to wait. And in politics you have to know how to wait.

He also perished because he did not know his own country. He spent his whole life in the palace. When he would leave the palace, he would do it like someone sticking his head out the door of a warm room into the freezing cold. Look around a minute and duck back in! Yet the same structure of destructive and deforming laws operates in the life of all palaces. So it has been from time immemorial, so it is and shall be. You can build ten new palaces, but as soon as they are finished they become subject to the same laws that existed in the palaces built five thousand years ago. The only solution is to treat the palace as a temporary abode, the same way you treat a streetcar or a bus. You get on, ride a while, and then get off.

And it's very good to remember to get off at the right stop and not ride too far.

The most difficult thing to do while living in a palace is to imagine a different life — for instance, your own life, but outside of and minus the palace. Toward the end, the ruler finds people willing to help him out. Many lives, regrettably, can be lost at such moments. The problem of honor in politics. Take de Gaulle — a man of honor. He lost a referendum, tidied up his desk, and left the palace, never to return. He wanted to govern only under the condition that the majority accept him. The moment the majority refused him their trust, he left. But how many are like him? The others will cry, but they won't move; they'll torment the nation, but they won't budge. Thrown out one door, they sneak in through another; kicked down the stairs, they begin to crawl back up. They will excuse themselves, bow and scrape, lie and simper, provided they can stay — or provided they can return. They will hold out their hands — Look, no blood on them. But the very fact of having to show those hands covers them with the deepest shame. They will turn their pockets inside out — Look, there's not much there. But the very fact of exposing their pockets — how humiliating! The Shah, when he left the palace, was crying. At the airport he was crying again. Later he explained in interviews how much money he had, and that it was less than people thought.

I spent whole days roaming around Teheran with no purpose or end in mind. I was escaping from the wearisome emptiness of my room and from my aggressive, slanderous hag of a cleaning woman. She was always asking for money. She took my clean, pressed shirts when they came back from the laundry, dunked them in water, strung them on a line — and demanded payment. For what? For ruining my shirts? Her scrawny claw was always thrust out from beneath her chador. I knew she had no money. But neither had I. This was something she couldn't understand. A man from the outside world is by definition rich. The hotel owner shrugged her shoulders — "I can't do anything about it. As a result of the revolution, my dear sir, that woman now has power." The hotel owner treated me as a natural ally, a counterrevolutionary. She assumed that my views were liberal; liberals, as people of the center, were at that time under the sharpest attack. Choose between God and Satan! Official propaganda expected a clear declaration from everyone; the time of the purges and of what they called "examining each other's hands" had begun.

I spent December wandering around the city. New Year's Eve, 1979, was approaching. A friend phoned with news that he was planning a party, a genuine, discreetly camouflaged evening of fun, and wanted me to come. I refused, saying I had other plans. What plans? He was astounded, for in fact what could you do in Teheran on such an evening? Strange plans, I replied, which was as close to the truth as I could come. I'd made up my mind to go to the US Embassy on New Year's Eve. I wanted to see what this place the whole world was talking about would look like that night. I left the hotel at eleven. I didn't have far to walk — a mile and a half, perhaps, easy going because it was downhill. The cold was penetrating, the wind dry and frigid; there must have been a snowstorm raging in the mountains. I walked through streets empty of pedestrians and patrols, empty of everyone but a peanut vendor sitting in his booth in Valiahd Square, all wrapped and muffled against the cold in warm scarves like the autumnal vendors on Polna Street in Warsaw. I bought a bag of peanuts and gave him a handful of rials — too many; it was my Christmas present. He didn't understand. He counted out what I owed him and handed back the change with a serious, dignified expression. Thus was rejected the gesture I'd hoped would bring me at least a momentary closeness with the only other person I'd encountered in the dead, frozen city. I walked on, looking at the decaying shop windows, turned into Takhte-Jamshid, passed a burned-out bank, a fire-scarred cinema, an empty hotel, an unlit airline office. Finally I reached the Embassy. In the daytime, the place is like a big marketplace, a busy encampment, a noisy political amusement park where you come to scream and let off steam. You can come here, abuse the mighty of the world, and not face any consequences at all. There's no lack of volunteers; the place is thronged. But just now, with midnight approaching, there was no one. I walked around what could have been a vast stage long abandoned by the last actors. There remained only pieces of unattended scenery and the disconcerting atmosphere of a ghost town. The wind fluttered the tatters of banners and rippled a big painting of a band of devils warming themselves over the inferno. Further along, Carter in a star-spangled top hat was shaking a bag of gold while the inspired Imam Ali prepared for a martyr's death. A microphone and batteries of speakers still stood on the platform from which excited orators stirred the crowds to wrath and indignation. The sight of those unspeaking loudspeakers deepened the impression of lifelessness, the void. I walked up to the main entrance. As usual, it was closed with a chain and padlock, since no one had repaired the lock in the gate that the crowd broke when it stormed the Embassy. Near the gate, two young guards crouched in the cold as they leaned against the high brick wall, automatic rifles slung over their shoulders — students of the Imam's line. I had the impression they were dozing. In the background, among the trees, stood the lighted building where the hostages were held. But much as I scrutinized the windows, I saw no one, neither figure nor shadow. I looked at my watch. It was midnight, at least in Teheran, and the New Year was beginning. Somewhere in the world clocks were striking, champagne was bubbling, elaborate fêtes were going on amid joy and elation in glittering, colorful halls. That might have been happening on a different planet from this one where there wasn't even the faintest sound or glimmer of light. Standing there freezing, I suddenly began wondering why I had left that other world and come here to this supremely desolate, extremely depressing place. I didn't know. It simply crossed my mind this evening that I ought to be here. I didn't know any of them, those fifty-two Americans and those two Iranians, and I couldn't even communicate with them. Perhaps I had thought something would happen here. But nothing happened.

The anniversary of the Shah's departure and the fall of the monarchy was approaching. To mark the occasion, the television showed dozens of films about the revolution. In many ways they were all alike. The same pictures and situations recurred. Scenes of an enormous procession always made up Act One. It's difficult to convey the dimensions of such a procession. It is a human river, broad and boiling, flowing endlessly, rolling through the main street from dawn till dusk. A flood, a violent flood that in a moment will engulf and drown everything. A forest of upraised, rhythmically menacing fists, portentous forest. A clamoring throng chanting, Death to the Shah! Very few close-ups of faces. The cameramen were fascinated by the sight of this incipient avalanche; they are stricken by the dimensions of what they see, as if they found themselves at the foot of Everest. Over the last months of the revolution these surging millions marched through the streets of every city. They carried no weapons; their strength lay in their numbers and their ardent, unshakable determination.

Act Two is the most dramatic. The cameramen stand on the roofs of buildings, filming the unfolding scene from above, a bird's-eye view. First they show us what's happening in the street. Two tanks and two armored cars are parked there. Soldiers in helmets and bulletproof vests have already taken up firing positions on the sidewalks and road. They wait. Now the cameramen show the approaching demonstration. First it appears in the distant perspective of the street, but soon we'll see it close up. Yes, there's the head of the procession. Men are marching, and women and children, too. They're wearing white, symbolizing readiness to die. The cameramen show us their faces, still alive. Their eyes. The children, already tired but calm, want to see what's going to happen. The crowd, marching directly toward the tanks, never slowing down or stopping — a hypnotized crowd? spellbound? moonstruck? — marches as if it sees nothing, as if wandering across an uninhabited earth, a crowd that at this moment has already begun to enter heaven. Now the picture trembles because the hands of the cameraman are trembling. A thump, shooting, the whizz of bullets, screams coming from the television. Close-ups of soldiers changing clips. Close-up of a tank turret pivoting from left to right. Close-up of an officer, comic relief, his helmet has fallen over his eyes. Close-up of the pavement, and then the image flies violently up the wall of the house across the street, over the roof and the chimney into blank space with only the edge of a cloud visible, and then an empty frame and blackness. The inscription on the screen says this was the last footage shot by the cameraman, but others survived to retrieve and preserve the testimony.

The last act is the postmortem. The dead are lying here and there, a wounded man is dragging himself toward a gate, ambulances speed past, people are running, a woman is crying, holding out her hands, a thickset, sweaty man is trying to lift someone's body. The crowd has retreated, dispersed, ebbed in chaos, down small side streets. A helicopter skims low over the roofs. The usual traffic has already begun a few blocks away, the everyday life of the city.

I remember one such scene: Demonstrators are marching. As they pass a hospital, they fall silent. The marchers do not want to disturb the patients. Or another sight: Boys trail at the end of the procession, picking up litter and throwing it into trash-cans. The road that the demonstrators have walked on must be clean. A fragment of a film: Children are returning home from school. They hear shooting and run toward the bullets, to where soldiers are firing on demonstrators. The children tear sheets from their notebooks and dip them in the fresh blood on the sidewalks and then, holding the bloody pages aloft, run through the streets displaying them to passers-by, as a warning — Watch out! There's shooting over there! The film from Isfahan was shown several times. A demonstration, a sea of heads, is crossing a vast square. Suddenly the army opens fire from all sides. The crowd rushes to escape amid cries, tumult, disorderly flight, and in the end the square empties. Just at the moment when the last survivors flee out of sight, revealing the naked surface of the enormous square, we notice that a legless invalid in a wheelchair has been left at the very center. He too wants to get away, but one wheel is stuck (the film does not show why). He instinctively hides his head between his arms as bullets are flying all around. Then he desperately works the wheels, but instead of moving, he turns around and around in one spot. It's such a shocking spectacle, the soldiers stop firing for a moment, as if awaiting special orders. Silence. We see a broad, empty vista, deep in the center of which, barely perceptible from this distance, looking like a maimed, dying insect, the crooked figure of a solitary human being is still struggling, as the net tightens and closes. They shoot again, with only one target left. Soon motionless for good, he remained (according to the film's narrator) at the center of the square for an hour or two, like a public monument.

The cameramen overuse the long shot. As a result, they lose sight of details. And yet it is through details that everything can be shown. The universe in the raindrop. I miss close-ups of the people who march in the demonstrations. I miss the conversations. That man marching in the demonstration, how full of hopes he is! He is marching because he is counting on something. He is marching because he believes he can get something done. He is sure that he will be better off. He is marching, thinking: So, if we win, nobody's going to treat me like a dog anymore. He's thinking of shoes. He'll buy decent shoes for the whole family. He's thinking of a home. If we win, I'll start living like a human being. A new world: He, an ordinary man, is going to know a minister personally and get everything taken care of. But why a minister! We'll form a committee ourselves to run things! He has other ideas and plans, none too precise or distinct, but they're all good, they're all the kind that cheer you up, because they possess the best of attributes: They'll be carried out. He feels high, he feels the power mounting in him, for as he marches he is also participating, taking his destiny into his hands for the first time, taking part for the first time, exerting influence, deciding about something — he *is*.

I once saw a spontaneous march come about. A man was walking down the street leading to the airport; he was singing. It was a song about Allah — Allah Akbar! He had a fine, carrying voice of splendid, moving tone. He was paying attention to nothing and nobody as he walked. I followed him because I wanted to hear him singing. In a moment a handful of children playing in the street joined him and began to sing.

Then there was a group of men and, emerging bashfully from the sides, some women. When there were about a hundred marchers, the crowd began to multiply quickly, at a geometric rate, in fact. A crowd draws a crowd, as Canetti remarked. Here they like to be in a crowd, a crowd strengthens them and adds to their importance. They express themselves through the crowd, they seek the crowd, and in a crowd they obviously get rid of something they carry inside themselves when they are alone, something that makes them feel bad.

On that same street (formerly called Shah Reza and now Engelob) an old Armenian sells spices and dried fruit. Because the inside of the shop is cramped and cluttered, he displays his goods on the sidewalk — bags, baskets, and jars of raisins, almonds, dates, nuts, olives, ginger, pomegranates, plums, pepper, millet, and dozens of other delicacies with names and uses unknown to me. Seen from a distance, against the background of crumbling gray plaster, they look like a rich and colorful palette, like a painting of tasteful and imaginative composition. Moreover, the shopkeeper changes the layout of the colors from day to day: Brown dates lie beside pastel pistachios and green olives — and the next day white almonds have taken the place of the fleshy dates and a pile of pepper pods is burning scarlet where there had been golden millet. Not only for the sake of the sensation do I visit this coloristic design. The daily fate of the exhibition is also a source of information about what's going to happen in politics, for Engelob is the boulevard of demonstrations. If there is no sidewalk display in the morning, then the Armenian is getting ready for a hot day — there will be a demonstration. He would rather hide his fruits and spices than leave them out to be trampled by the crowd. This also means that I have to get down to work and establish who is going to demonstrate, and for what. If, on the other hand, I can see the Armenian's variegated glowing palette from far down Engelob Street, then I know it's going to be an ordinary, peaceful, uneventful day and I can go with easy conscience to Leon's for a glass of whisky.

Further down Engelob Street is a baker's that sells fresh, hot bread. Iranian bread is shaped like a big, flat cake. The oven in which these cakes are baked is a hole dug into the ground, ten feet deep, with walls of inlaid clay. A fire burns at the bottom. If a woman betrays her husband, she is thrown into such a well of fire. Razak Naderi, a boy of twelve, works at this bakery. Somebody ought to make a film about Razak. At the age of nine he came to Teheran looking for work, leaving his mother, two younger sisters, and three younger brothers behind in his village near Zanjan, six hundred miles from the capital. From that time on he has had to support his family. He gets up at four and kneels by the oven door. The fire is roaring, and frightful heat pours out of the oven. With a long rod, Razak sticks the loaves on the clay walls and sees they are taken out when they are done. He works this way until nine in the evening. What he makes, he sends to his mother. His possessions consist of a suitcase and the blanket in which he wraps himself at night. Razak continually changes jobs and is often unemployed. He knows that he can blame only himself. After three or four months he simply begins to long for his mother. He struggles against the feeling for a while, but he ends up getting on the bus and returning to his village. He would like to stay with his mother as long as possible, but he knows he cannot — he is the sole support of the family, and he has to work. He goes back to Teheran and finds that someone else has taken his job. So Razak goes to Gomruk Square, the gathering place of the unemployed. This is the cheap labor market, and whoever comes here sells himself for the lowest wages. Yet Razak has to wait a week or two before someone hires him. He stands on the square all day, freezing, soaked, hungry. Finally a man turns up and notices him. Razak is happy; he is working again. But the joy wears off quickly, the sharp longing soon returns, so he returns again to see his mother and returns again to Gomruk Square. Right next to Razak there is the great world of the Shah, the revolution, Khomeini and the hostages. Everybody is talking about it. Yet Razak's world is even bigger. It is so big that Razak roams around it and can't find a way out.

Engelob Street in autumn and winter, 1978 — endless protest demonstrations pass here. The same thing is happening in all the big cities. The revolt is sweeping the country. Strikes begin. Everybody goes on strike; industry and transport stop dead. Despite the tens of thousands of victims, the pressure keeps growing. Yet the Shah stays on the throne, and the palace is not giving in.

In every revolution, a movement grapples with a structure. The movement attacks the structure, trying to destroy it, while the structure defends itself and tries to extinguish the movement. The two forces, equally powerful, have different properties. The properties of a movement are spontaneity, impulsiveness, dynamic expansiveness — and a short life. The properties of a structure are inertia, resilience, and an amazing, almost instinctive ability to survive. A structure is rather easy to create, and incomparably more difficult to destroy. It can long outlast all the reasons that justified its establishment. Many weak or even fictitious states have been called into being. But states, after all, are structures, and none of them will be crossed off the map. There exists a sort of world of structures, all holding one another up. Threaten one and the others, its kindred, rush to its assistance. The elasticity that helps it to survive is another trait of a structure. Backed into a corner, under pressure, it can suck in its belly, contract, and wait for the moment when it can start expanding again. Interestingly, such renewed expansion always takes place exactly where there had been a contraction. Structures tend toward a return to the status quo, which they regard as the best of states, the ideal. This trait belies the inertia of the structure. The structure is capable of reacting only according to the first program fed into it. Enter a new program — nothing happens, it doesn't react. It will wait for the previous program. A structure can also act like a roly-poly toy: Just when it seems to have been knocked over, it pops back up. A movement unaware of this property of the structure will wrestle with it for a long time, then grow weak, and in the end suffer defeat.

The theater of the Shah: The Shah was a director who wanted to create a theater on the highest, international level. He liked the audience, he wanted to please. Yet he never knew the true nature of art, never had the imagination and wisdom a director needs, and thought that money and a title were enough. He created an enormous stage on which action could unfold in many places simultaneously. On that stage he decided to mount a play titled *The Great Civilization*. He imported scenery from abroad for vast sums. There were all sorts of devices, machines, equipment — whole mountains of concrete, cable, and plastic. Many of the props were actual armaments: tanks, planes, rockets. Elated, proud, the Shah strutted across the stage, listening to the paeans and speeches of approval that flowed from a multitude of loudspeakers. The spotlights played across the scenery, and then converged on the figure of the Shah. He stood or walked in their beams. It was a one-character play, and the actor was also the director. Everyone else was an extra. Generals, ministers, distinguished ladies, lackeys — the great court — moved across the upper level of the stage. Below came the intermediate levels, and at the very bottom the extras of the lowest category. These were the most numerous. Enticed by high wages — the Shah had promised them mountains of gold — they flocked into the cities from the poor villages. The Shah was always on stage, monitoring the action and directing the extras. If he made a gesture, the generals would stand at attention, the ministers would kiss his hand, and the ladies would curtsey. When he walked down to one of the lower levels and nodded his head, officials would rush to his presence in the expectation of prizes and promotions. Only rarely and briefly would he appear on the ground floor of the stage. The extras there behaved apathetically. They were lost, oppressed by the city, uncertain of themselves, cheated and exploited. They felt like foreigners amid the unfamiliar scenery, in the hostile aggressive world surrounding them. The only point of reference in the alien landscape was the mosque, for there had also been a mosque in the village. So they went to the mosque.

The play takes place on several levels at the same time; many things are happening on stage. The scenery begins to move and light up, wheels turn, chimneys smoke, tanks roll back and forth, ministers kiss the Shah, officials hurry after rewards, policemen frown, mullahs talk and talk, extras keep their mouths shut and work. There is more and more crowding and bustle. The Shah walks, beckoning here and pointing a finger there, always in the spotlight. Suddenly confusion breaks out on stage as if everyone had forgotten his part. Yes, they're throwing away the script and making up lines on their own. Revolt in the theater! The spectacle turns into something else, it becomes a violent, rapacious spectacle. The extras from the ground floor, long disenchanted, ill-paid, despised, begin storming the upper levels. Those on the intermediate levels now become rebellious as well and join the ones from the bottom. The black flags of the Shiites appear on stage and the war song of the demonstrators pours from the loudspeakers. Allah Akbar! Tanks roll back and fourth, the police open fire. The prolonged cry of the muezzin resounds from the minaret. On the highest level, there is unprecedented confusion. Ministers stuff bags full of banknotes and take flight, ladies grab jewelry boxes and vanish, butlers wander around as though lost. Green-jacketed fedayeens and mujahedeens appear, armed to the teeth. They've taken over the arsenals. The soldiers who used to fire on the crowds now fraternize with the people and stick red carnations in the barrels of their rifles. Candy is strewn over the stage; in the universal joy, shop-keepers are throwing basketfuls of sweets to the crowds. Even though it is noon, all the cars have their headlights on. A big assembly is taking place in the cemetery. Everybody is there, weeping for those killed. A mother says that her son, a soldier, committed suicide rather than fire on his brethren, the demonstrators. The gray-haired Ayatollah Teleghani makes a speech. One by one, the spotlights go out. In the last scene the gem-encrusted peacock throne — the throne of the Shahs — comes down from the top floor to the ground floor in dazzling, many-colored radiance. On the throne sits an extraordinary, outsized figure of majestic sublimity, radiating a stunning brilliance of its own. Its hands and feet, its head and its body, are connected to wires and cables. The sight of this figure overpowers us, we dread it, we feel a reflex that would bring us to our knees. But a group of electricians comes on stage, unplugging the cables and cutting the wires. The brilliance begins to fade, and the figure itself grows smaller and more ordinary. Finally the electricians step aside and an elderly, slim man, indeed the kind of gentleman we might encounter at a movie, in a café, or in a line, rises from the throne, brushes his suit, straightens his tie, and walks off stage on his way to the airport.

The picture was clipped from a newspaper so carelessly the caption is missing. It shows a monument of a man on a horse, atop a tall granite pedestal. The rider, a figure of herculean build, is seated comfortably in the saddle, in his left hand resting on its horn, his right pointing to something ahead (probably the future). A rope is tied around the neck of the rider, and a similar rope around that of his mount. In the square at the base of the monument stand groups of men pulling on the two lines. All this is taking place in a thronged plaza, with the crowd watching as the men tugging on the ropes strain against the resistance of the massive bronze statue. The photograph captures the very moment when the ropes are stretched tight as piano wires and the rider and his mount are just tilting to the side — an instant before they crash to earth. We can't help wondering if these men pulling ropes with so much effort and self-denial will be able to jump out of the way, especially since the gawkers crowded into the plaza have left them little room. This photograph shows the pulling down of a monument to one of the Shahs (father or son) in Teheran or some other Iranian city. It is hard to be sure about the year the photograph was taken, since the monuments of both Pahlavis were pulled down several times, whenever the occasion presented itself to the people.

A reporter from the Teheran newspaper *Kayhan* interviewed a man who wrecks monuments to the Shah:

— You've won a certain popularity in your neighborhood, Golam, as a man who pulls down monuments. You're even regarded as a sort of veteran in the field.

— That's right. I first pulled down monuments in the time of the old Shah, that is the father of Mohammed Reza, when he abdicated in '41. I remember what great joy there was in the city when news got around the old Shah had stepped down. Everybody rushed out to smash his monuments. I was just a young boy then, but I helped my father and the neighbors pull down the monument that Reza Khan had set up to himself in our neighborhood. I could say that that was my baptism of fire.

— Were you persecuted for it?

— Not on that occasion.

— Do you remember '53?

— Of course I remember. Wasn't that the most important year, when democracy ended and the regime began? In any case, I recall the radio saying that the Shah had escaped to Europe. When the people heard that, they went out into the street and started pulling down the monuments. And I have to say that the young Shah had been putting up monuments to himself and his father from the beginning, so over the years a lot accumulated that needed pulling down. My father was no longer alive then, but I was grown up and for the first time I brought them down on my own.

— So did you destroy all his monuments?

— Yes, every last one. By the time the Shah came back, there wasn't a Pahlavi monument left. But he started right back in, putting up monuments to himself and his father.

— Does that mean that you would pull down, he would set up, then you would pull down what he had set up, and it kept going on like this?

— That's right. Many times we nearly threw in the towel. If we pulled one down, he set up three. If we pulled down three, he set up ten. There was no end in sight.

— And when was the next time, after '53, that you wrecked them again?

— We intended to go to work in '63, when the rebellion broke out after the Shah imprisoned Khomeini. But instead the Shah began such a massacre that, far from pulling down monuments, we had to hide our hawsers.

— Am I to understand you had special hawsers for the job?

— Yes indeed! We hid our stout sisal rope with a ropeseller at the bazaar. It was no joke. If the police had picked up our trail, we would have gone to the wall. We had everything prepared for the right moment, all thought out and practiced. During the last revolution, I mean in '79, all those disasters happened because a lot of amateurs were knocking down monuments, and there were accidents when they pulled the statues onto their own heads. It's not easy to pull down monuments. It takes experience, expertise. You have to know what they're made of, how much they weigh, how high they are, whether they're welded together or sunk in cement, where to hook the line on, which way to pull, and how to smash them once they're down. We were already working at pulling it down each time they set up a new monument to the Shah. That was the best chance to get a good look and see how it was built, whether the figure was hollow or solid, and, most important, how it was attached to the pedestal and how it was reinforced.

— It must have taken up a lot of your time.

— Right! More and more monuments were going up in the last few years. Everywhere — in the squares, in the streets, in the stations, by the road. And besides, there were others setting up monuments as well. Whoever wanted to get a jump on the competition for a good contract hurried to be the first one to put up a monument. That's why a lot of them were built cheaply and, when the time came, they were easy to bring down. But, I have to admit, there were times when I doubted we'd get them all. There were hundreds of them. But we weren't afraid to work up a sweat. My hands were all blisters from the ropes.

— So, Golam, you've had an interesting line of work.

— It wasn't work. It was duty. I'm very proud to have been a wrecker of the Shah's monuments. I think that everyone who took part is proud to have done so. What we did is plain for all to see. All the pedestals are empty, and the figures of the Shahs have either been smashed or are lying in backyards somewhere.

The Shah had created a system capable only of defending itself, but incapable of satisfying the people. This was its greatest weakness and the true cause of its ultimate defeat. The psychological foundation of such a system is the ruler's scorn for his people and his conviction that the ignorant nation can always be deceived by continual promises. But there is an Iranian proverb that says: Promises have value only for those who believe in them.

Khomeini returned from exile and stayed briefly in Teheran before leaving for Qom. Everyone wanted to see him, several million people were waiting to shake his hand. Crowds besieged the school building where he was staying. Everyone felt entitled to a meeting with the ayatollah. After all, they had fought for his return. They had shed their blood. Elation and euphoria were in the air. People walked around slapping each other on the back, as if to say to each other — See! We can do anything!

Seldom does a people live through such moments! But just then the sense of victory seemed natural and justified. The Shah's Great Civilization lay in ruins. What had it been in essence? A rejected transplant. It had been an attempt to impose a certain model of life on a community attached to entirely different traditions and values. It was forced, an operation that had more to do with surgical success in itself than with the question of whether the patient remained alive or — equally important — remained himself.

The rejection of a transplant — once it begins, the process is irreversible. All it takes is for society to accept the conviction that the imposed form of existence does more harm than good. Soon the discontent becomes manifest, at first covertly and passively, then more and more overtly and assertively. There will be no peace until the imposed, alien body is purged. The organism grows deaf to persuasion and argument. It remains feverish, unable to reflect. And yet there were noble intentions and lofty ideals behind the Great Civilization. But the people saw them only as caricatures, that is, in the guise that ideals are given when translated into practice. In this way even sublime ideals become subject to doubt.

And afterward? What happened afterward? What should I write about now? About the way that a great experience comes to an end? A melancholy topic, for a revolt is a great experience, an adventure of the heart. Look at the people who are taking part in a revolt. They are stimulated, excited, ready to make sacrifices. At that moment they are living in a monothematic world limited to one thought: to attain the goal they are fighting for. Everything will be subjugated to that goal; every inconvenience becomes bearable; no sacrifice is too great. A revolt frees us from our own ego, from that everyday ego that now strikes us as small, nondescript — alien. Astounded, we discover in ourselves unknown energies and are capable of such noble behavior that we ourselves look on with admiration. And how much pride we feel at being able to rise so high! What satisfaction at being able to give so much of ourselves! But there comes a moment when the mood burns out and everything ends. As a matter of reflex, out of custom, we go on repeating the gestures and the words and want everything to be the way it was yesterday, but we know already — and the discovery appalls us — that this yesterday will never again return. We look around and make another discovery: those who were with us have also changed — something has burned out in them, as well, something has been extinguished. Our community falls suddenly to pieces and everyone returns to his everyday I, which pinches at first like ill-fitting shoes — but we know that they are our shoes and we are not going to get any others. We look uncomfortably into each other's eyes, we shy away from conversation, we stop being any use to one another.

This fall in temperature, this change of climate, belongs among the most unsettling and depressing of experiences. A day begins in which something should happen. And nothing happens. Nobody comes to call, nobody is waiting for us, we are superfluous. We begin to feel a great fatigue, apathy gradually engulfs us. We tell ourselves: I have to rest up, get in shape, build up my strength. We have to get some fresh air. We have to do something mundane — straighten up the apartment, fix the window. These are all defensive actions aimed at dodging the imminent depression. So we pull ourselves together and fix the window. But everything is not in order, we are not joyful, because the pebble stuck inside us keeps nagging.

I too shared that feeling that comes over us when we sit before a dying fire. I walked around a Teheran from which the traces of yesterday's experiences were vanishing. They were vanishing suddenly, and you could get the impression that nothing had happened here. A few burned cinemas, a few demolished banks — the symbols of foreign influence. Revolution attaches great importance to symbols, destroying some monuments and setting up others to replace them in the hope that through metaphor it can survive. And what of the people? Once again they had become pedestrian citizens, going somewhere, standing around street fires warming their hands, part of the dull landscape of a grey town. Once again each was alone, each for himself, closed and taciturn. Could they still have been waiting for something to happen, for some extraordinary event? I don't know, I can't say.

Everything that makes up the outward, visible part of a revolution vanishes quickly. A person, an individual being, has a thousand ways of conveying his feelings and thoughts. He is riches without end, he is a world in which we can always discover something new. A crowd, on the other hand, reduces the individuality of the person; a man in a crowd limits himself to a few forms of elementary behavior. The forms through which a crowd can express its yearnings are extraordinarily meager and continually repeat themselves: the demonstration, the strike, the rally, the barricades. That is why you can write a novel about a man, but about a crowd — never. If the crowd disperses, goes home, does not reassemble, we say that the revolution is over.

Now I visited the committee headquarters. Committee — that's what they called the organs of the new power. Unshaven men were sitting around tables in cramped, littered rooms. For the first time, I saw their faces. On my way here I had filed in my memory the names of people who had actively opposed the Shah or supported the rebels from the sidelines. Just such people, I assumed logically, ought to be running things now. I asked where I could find them. The members of the committee did not know. In any case, they weren't here. The whole durable structure in which one man held power, a second opposed him, a third made money, and a fourth criticized, the whole complex setup that had lasted for years, had been blown away like a house of cards. The names I asked about meant nothing to these bearded, barely literate oafs. What did they care that a couple of years ago Hafez Farman had criticized the Shah and paid for it with his job, while Kulsum Kitab was kissing ass and making a career for himself? That was the past. That world no longer existed. The revolution had transferred power to utterly new, anonymous people no one had heard of only yesterday. Now the bearded ones sat and deliberated full time. About what? About what was to be done. Yes, because the committee should do something. One after the other, they spoke. Each wanted to have his say, to make his speech. Watching, you could feel that this was essential to them, that they attached great weight to it. Each of them could go home afterward and tell his neighbors, I made a speech. People could ask each other, Did you hear about his speech? When he walked down the street, they could buttonhole him to say respectfully, You made an interesting speech! An informal hierarchy gradually shaped itself: At the top stood those who inevitably made impressive public appearances, while the bottom consisted of introverts, people with speech defects, whole hosts of those who could not overcome their stagefright, and finally those who could not see the point of endless blabbing. The next day the talkers would start from scratch, as though nothing had happened the day before, as if they had to begin all over again.

Iran — it was the twenty-seventh revolution I have seen in the Third World. Amid the smoke and the roar, rulers would change, governments fall, new people take their seat. But one thing was invariable, indestructible, and — I dread saying it — eternal: the helplessness. These chambers of the Iranian committees reminded me of what I had seen in Bolivia, Mozambique, the Sudan, Benin. What should we do? Do you know what to do? Me? Not me. Maybe you know. Are you talking to me? I'd go whole hog. But how? How do you go whole hog? Ah, yes, that's the problem. Everyone agrees: That is indeed a problem worth discussing. Cigarette smoke clouds the stuffy rooms. There are some good speeches, some not-so-good, a few downright brilliant. After a truly good speech, everyone feels satisfied; they have taken part in something that was a genuine success.

The whole thing began to intrigue me, so I sat down in one of the committee headquarters (pretending to wait for someone who was not there) and watched how they settled the simplest of problems. After all, life consists of settling problems, progress of settling them deftly and to the general satisfaction. After a while a woman came in to ask for a certificate. The man who could issue it was tied up in a discussion at the moment. The woman waited. People here have a fantastic talent for waiting — they can turn to stone and remain motionless forever. Eventually the man turned up, and they began talking. The woman spoke, he asked a question, the woman asked a question, he said something. After some haggling, they agreed. They began looking for a piece of paper. Various pieces of paper lay on the table, but none of them looked right. The man disappeared — he must have gone to look for paper, but he might just as well have gone across the street to drink some tea (it was a hot day). The woman waited in silence. The man returned, wiping his mouth in satisfaction (so he'd gone for tea after all), but he also had paper. Now began the most dramatic part of all — the search for a pencil. Nowhere was there a pencil, not on the table, nor in the drawer, nor on the floor. I lent him my pen. He smiled, and the woman sighed with relief. Then he sat down to write. As he began writing, he realized he was not quite sure what he was supposed to be certifying. They began talking, and the man nodded. Finally, the document was ready. Now it had to be signed by someone higher up. But the higher-up was unavailable. He was debating in another committee, and there was no way to get in touch with him because the telephone was not answering. Wait. The woman turned back into stone, the man disappeared, and I left to have some tea.

Later, that man will learn how to write certificates and will know how to do many other things. But after a few years, there will be another upheaval, the man we already know will be gone, and his place will fall to someone new who will start fumbling around for a piece of paper and a pencil. The same woman or another one will turn herself to stone and wait. Somebody will lend his pen. The higher-up will be busy debating. All of them, like their predecessors, will begin to move in the spellbound circle of helplessness. Who created that circle? In Iran, it was the Shah. The Shah thought that urbanization and industrialization are the keys to modernity, but this is a mistaken idea. The key to modernity is the village. The Shah got drunk on visions of atomic power plants, computerized production lines, and large-scale petrochemical complexes. But in an underdeveloped country, these are mere mirages of modernity. In that kind of country, most of the people live in poor villages from which they flee to the city. They form a young, energetic workforce that knows little (they are often illiterate) but possesses great ambition and is ready to fight for everything. In the city they find an entrenched establishment linked in one way or another with the prevailing authorities. So they first learn the ropes, settle in a bit, occupy starting positions, and go on the attack. In the struggle they make use of whatever ideology they have brought from the village — usually this is religion. Since they are the ones who are truly determined to get ahead, they often succeed. Then authority passes into their hands. But what are they to do with it? They begin to debate, and they enter the spellbound circle of helplessness. The nation stays alive somehow, as it must, and in the meantime they live better and better. For a while they are satisfied. Their successors are now roaming the vast plains, grazing camels, tending sheep, but they too will grow up, move to the city, and start struggling. What is the rule in all of this? That the newcomers invariably have more ambition than skill. As a result, with each upheaval, the country goes back to the starting point because the victorious new generation has to learn all over again what it cost the defeated generation so much toil to master. And does this mean that the defeated ones were efficient and wise? Not at all — the preceding generation sprang from the same roots as those who took its place. How can the spellbound circle of helplessness be broken? Only by developing the villages. As long as the villages are backward, the country will be backward — even if it contains five thousand factories. As long as the son who has moved to the city visits his native village a few years later as if it were some exotic land, the nation to which he belongs will never be modern.

When the committees discussed what to do next, everyone agreed on one point: Revenge came first. So the executions began. They found some sort of satisfaction in this activity. The newspapers carried front-page photographs of blindfolded people and the boys who were taking aim at them. The papers described these events at length and in detail. What the condemned said before death, how he behaved, what he wrote in his last letter. These executions evoked great indignation in Europe, but few people here understood such complaints. For them the principle of revenge was older than history. A Shah ruled, and then he was beheaded; a new one came along and he was beheaded. How else could you get rid of a Shah? He's not going to resign on his own, is he? Leave him and his supporters alive? The first thing you know, he'll organize an army and make a comeback. Put them in prison? They'll bribe the guards, make an escape, and start massacring whoever toppled them. In such a situation, killing is some sort of elementary reflex of self-preservation. This is a world in which the law is not understood as an instrument to protect man, but as a tool to destroy the adversary. Yes, it sounds cruel; there is a ghastly, implacable ruthlessness about it. Ayatollah Khalkali told us, a group of journalists, that after passing a sentence of death on former Prime Minister Hoveyda he suddenly became suspicious of the firing squad that was to carry out the sentence. He was afraid that they might let Hoveyda get away. So he took Hoveyda into his car. It was night, and, according to Khalkali, they sat talking in the car. About what, he did not say. Wasn't he afraid the condemned man would escape? No, no such thought occurred to him. Time passed. Khalkali was trying to think of someone he could entrust Hoveyda to. Finally he remembered some members of a particular committee near the bazaar. He took Hoveyda to them and left him there.

I am trying to understand them, but over and over again I stumble into a dark region and lose my way. They have a different attitude to life and death. They react differently to the sight of blood. At the sight of blood they become tense, fascinated, they fall into some sort of mystical trance; I can see their animated gestures and hear their cries. The owner of a nearby restaurant pulled up in front of my hotel in his new car. It was a brand-new Pontiac, gold, straight from the dealer. There was some commotion and I could hear chickens being slaughtered in the courtyard. First the people sprinkled the chicken blood over themselves, and then they smeared it on the body of the car. In a moment the automobile was red and dripping blood. This was the baptism of the Pontiac. Wherever there is blood, they crowd around to dip their hands in it. They could not explain to me why this is necessary.

For a few hours a week they manage to attain fantastic discipline. This happens on Friday, at the time of common prayer. That morning the first, most fervent Muslim walks into the vast square, spreads his rug, and kneels on its fringe. Then the next one comes and spreads his rug beside the first one's, even though the whole rest of the square is empty. Then comes the next believer, and the next. Later there are a thousand more, and then a million. They spread their rugs and kneel. They kneel in even, orderly rows, in silence, facing Mecca. Around noon the leader of the Friday prayer begins the ritual. They all stand, bow seven times, straighten up, squat on their haunches, fall to their knees, prostrate themselves, sit on their heels, and prostrate themselves once again. The perfect, undisturbed rhythm of a million bodies is a sight difficult to describe and — for me — rather an ominous one. When the prayers end, fortunately, the ranks break up at once, everyone starts gabbing, and pleasant, free-and-easy confusion dispels the tension.

Dissent soon broke out in the revolutionary camp. Everyone had opposed the Shah and wanted to remove him, but everyone had imagined the future differently. Some thought that the country would become the sort of democracy they knew from their stays in France and Switzerland. But these were exactly the people who lost first in the battle that began once the Shah was gone. They were intelligent people, even wise, but weak. They found themselves at once in a paradoxical situation: A democracy cannot be imposed by force, the majority must favor it, yet the majority wanted what Khomeini wanted — an Islamic republic. When the liberals were gone, the proponents of the republic remained. But they began fighting among themselves as well. In this struggle the conservative hardliners gradually gained the upper hand over the enlightened and open ones. I knew people from both camps, and whenever I thought about the people I sympathized with, pessimism swept over me. The leader of the enlightened ones was Bani Sadr. Slim, slightly stooping, always wearing a polo shirt, he would walk around, persuade, constantly enter into discussions. He had a thousand ideas, he talked a lot — too much — he dreamed incessantly of new solutions, he wrote books in a difficult, obscure style. In these countries an intellectual in politics is always out of place. An intellectual has too much imagination, he tends to hesitate, he is liable to go off in all directions at once. What good is a leader who does not know himself what he ought to stand up for? Beheshti, the hardliner, never behaved in this way. He would summon his staff and dictate instructions, and they were all grateful to him because now they knew how to act and what to do. Beheshti held the reins of the Shiite leadership, Bani Sadr commanded his friends and followers. Bani Sadr's power base lay among the intelligentsia, the students, and the mujahedeen. Beheshti's base was a crowd waiting for the call of the mullahs. It was clear that Bani Sadr had to lose. But Beheshti too would fall before the hand of the Charitable and Merciful One.

Combat squads appeared on the streets. These were groups of strong young people with knives sticking out of their hip pockets. They attacked students, and ambulances carried injured girls out of the university. Demonstrations began, the crowds shook their fists. But against whom this time? Against the man who wrote books in a difficult, obscure style. Millions of people were out of work, the peasants were still living in miserable mud huts, but what did that matter? Beheshti's men were engaged elsewhere — fighting the counterrevolution. Yes, they knew at last what to do and what to say. You don't have anything to eat? You have nowhere to live? We will show you who is to blame. It's that counterrevolutionary. Destroy him, and you can start living like a human being. But what sort of a counterrevolutionary is he — weren't we fighting together only yesterday against the Shah? That was yesterday, and today he's your enemy. Having heard this, the feverish crowd attacked without pausing to think whether the enemy was a real enemy, but you can't blame the people in the crowd. They want a better life and have wanted it for a long time without knowing, without understanding how it is that, despite continuous effort, sacrifice, and self-denial, that better life is still beyond the horizon.

Depression reigned among my friends. They predicted an imminent cataclysm. As always when hard times are coming, they, the intelligent ones, were losing their strength and their faith. They were filled with fear and frustration. They, who once would not have missed a demonstration for anything, now began to fear crowds. As I talked with them, I thought of the Shah. The Shah was traveling around the world and his face would appear in the papers occasionally, each time more wasted. Until the end he thought he would return to his country. He never did, but much of what he had done remained. A despot may go away, but no dictatorship comes to a complete end with his departure. A dictatorship depends for its existence on the ignorance of the mob; that's why all dictators take such pains to cultivate that ignorance. It requires generations to change such a state of affairs, to let some light in. Before this can happen, however, those who have brought down a dictator often act, in spite of themselves, like his heirs, perpetuating the attitudes and thought patterns of the epoch they themselves have destroyed. This happens so involuntarily and subconsciously that they burst into righteous ire if anyone points it out to them. But can all this be blamed on the Shah? The Shah inherited an existing tradition, he moved within the bounds of a set of customs that had prevailed for centuries. It is one of the most difficult things in the world to cross such boundaries, to change the past.

When I want to cheer myself up, I head for Ferdousi Street, where Mr. Ferdousi sells Persian carpets. Mr. Ferdousi, who has passed all his life in the familiar intercourse of art and beauty, looks upon the surrounding reality as if it were a B-film in a cheap, unswept cinema. It is all a question of taste, he tells me: The most important thing, sir, is to have taste. The world would look far different if a few more people had a drop more taste. In all horrors (for he does call them horrors), like lying, treachery, theft, and informing, he distinguishes a common denominator — such things are done by people with no taste. He believes that the nation will survive everything and that beauty is indestructible. You must remember, he tells me as he unfolds another carpet (he knows I am not going to buy it, but he would like me to enjoy the sight of it), that what has made it possible for the Persians to remain themselves over two and a half millennia, what has made it possible for us to remain ourselves in spite of so many wars, invasions, and occupations, is our spiritual, not our material, strength — our poetry, and not our technology; our religion, and not our factories. What have we given the world? We have given poetry, the miniature, and carpets. As you can see, these are all useless things from the productive viewpoint. But it is through such things that we have expressed our true selves. We have given the world this miraculous, unique uselessness. What we have given the world has not made life any easier, only adorned it — if such a distinction makes any sense. To us a carpet, for example, is a vital necessity. You spread a carpet on a wretched, parched desert, lie down on it, and feel you are lying in a green meadow. Yes, our carpets remind us of meadows in flower. You see before you flowers, you see a garden, a pool, a fountain. Peacocks are sauntering among the shrubs. And carpets are things that last — a good carpet will retain its color for centuries. In this way, living in a bare, monotonous desert, you seem to be living in an eternal garden from which neither color nor freshness ever fades. Then you can continue imagining the fragrance of the garden, you can listen to the murmur of the stream and the song of the birds. And then you feel whole, you feel eminent, you are near paradise, you are a poet.